A Critical Handbook of Children's Literature

Second Edition

F.G.Hall 1907

Rebecca J. Lukens

Miami University
Oxford, Ohio

Scott, Foresman and Company
Glenview, Illinois
Dallas, Texas   Oakland, New Jersey   Palo Alto, California
Tucker, Georgia   London, England

Library of Congress Cataloging in Publication Data

Lukens, Rebecca J., 1922–
  A critical handbook of children's literature.

  Includes bibliographies and index.
  1. Children's literature—History and criticism.
I. Title.
PN1009.A1L84   1981   809'.89282   81–18355
ISBN 0–673–15504–1   AACR2

  2 3 4 5 6—KPF—86 85 84 83 82

ACKNOWLEDGMENTS

Anonymous. "The Frog" from *What a Wonderful Bird the Frog Are,* edited by Myra Cohn Livingston. New York: Harcourt Brace Jovanovich, Inc., 1973, p. 21.

William H. Armstrong. *Sounder.* New York: Harper & Row, Publishers, 1969, p. 31.

Natalie Babbitt. *The Eyes of the Amaryllis.* New York: Farrar, Straus and Giroux, 1977, p. 105.

Karle Wilson Baker. "Days" from *Blue Smoke* by Karle Wilson Baker. Copyright 1919 by Yale University Press and reprinted with their permission.

Judy Blume. *Then Again, Maybe I Won't.* New York: Dell Publishing Co., Inc., 1971, pp. 154–155.

Clyde Robert Bulla. *Mika's Apple Tree: A Story of Finland.* New York: Thomas Y. Crowell Company, 1968, p. 19.

Sheila Burnford. Excerpts from *The Incredible Journey* by Sheila Burnford, by permission of Little, Brown and Co. in association with The Atlantic Monthly Press and Harold Ober Associates, Inc. Copyright © 1960, 1961 by Sheila Burnford.

Betsy Byars. *The Summer of the Swans.* New York: The Viking Press, 1970, pp. 35, 55.

Alice Childress. *A Hero Ain't Nothin' but a Sandwich.* New York: Coward, McCann & Geoghegan, Inc., 1973, pp. 9, 29, 41, 50, 59.

Beverly Cleary. *Ramona and Her Father.* New York: William Morrow and Company, 1977, pp. 59, 61.

Vera and William J. Cleaver. *Where the Lilies Bloom.* New York: J. P. Lippincott Co., 1969, p. 93.

Elizabeth Coatsworth. "Tracks in the Snow" by Elizabeth Coatsworth. Reprinted with permission of Macmillan Publishing Co., Inc. from *Away Goes Sally* by Elizabeth Coatsworth. Copyright 1934 by Macmillan Publishing Co., Inc., renewed 1962 by Elizabeth Coatsworth Beston.

Acknowledgments continued on Page 256.

Preface

A Critical Handbook of Children's Literature has grown out of my conviction that literature for children differs from literature for adults in degree, not in kind, and that writing for children should be judged by the same standards as writing for adults. Children, like adults, read to explore the world, to escape the confining present, to discover themselves, to become someone else. Since children are helped in choosing books by adults—in the roles of teachers, librarians, or parents—we hope to put into their hands the best literature for these purposes. As Walter de la Mare, who wrote for children, said, "Only the very rarest kind of best in anything can be good enough for the young."

How can we choose the rarest kind of best from the approximate 2500 children's books published each year as well as from the many books that remain in print year after year? What are the standards we can confidently apply in evaluating writing for children? We may have felt amused and touched when we read *Charlotte's Web* by E. B. White, but how do we discuss or decide its literary worth beyond these vague emotional feelings?

When we say a hearty "I like it!" we may be responding to believable and interesting characters, or to something we know is true about people. When we are disappointed in a book—"I don't like it!" —we may be rejecting the story's action as too coincidental, or its dialogue as too stilted. Learning to recognize such literary elements as character and plot and setting helps us to understand the effects a writer achieves and to appreciate the reasons for his or her choices. After all, Peter Rabbit and Rabbit in *Winnie-the-Pooh* are not the same, nor does the setting for *Wind in the Willows* have the same effect upon us as the setting in *Island of the Blue Dolphins.* We could say fairly easily *how* they are different, but we need to go beyond that and say *why* they are different. Why did the authors make the choices they made and what are the effects of those choices upon us as readers? This knowledge helps us to discover the reasons for our emotional responses. It sharpens our perceptions and increases our enjoyment of reading. To use a familiar analogy, do we go to the football game merely to find out who won? Or also to enjoy the plays and ploys that put the winning score on the scoreboard? In the same way, do we read only to find out how the story comes out? Or do we also take delight in the people, in the shifts and turns of events along the way, in the words that tingle our spines or quicken our pulses?

This revision includes a new chapter on the major genres of fiction. The chapter delineates the common elements of all fiction, and demonstrates how each genre may emphasize one element more than the others. Main points are provided in a chart to help readers more easily spot possible shortcomings of a story and pinpoint particularly significant elements.

Other revised chapters focus on the elements common to all imaginative literature—character, plot, setting, point of view, style, tone, and theme. These terms are explained simply and clearly and are illustrated with new or lasting examples from all genres of children's literature. Although these terms are the critical tools and basic vocabulary we use to discuss and evaluate any piece of imaginative literature, writing for children presents some special concerns and problems; each chapter concludes with a discussion of such matters.

Chapter study questions highlight the relationship of the element being considered to each of the genres. Also following each chapter is a list of recommended books cited in that chapter. The glossary and the index reflect new terms and new titles and authors of this revised edition, and an Appendix, listing the major prize-winning books over the years, has been added.

To fail to apply critical standards to children's literature is to say in effect that children's literature is inferior to adult literature, that children will not presumably benefit from good literature or be harmed by poor writing. This handbook takes the opposite view: children's literature *should* be judged by the same standards as adult literature, with some small differences, and children *can* benefit enormously now and for a lifetime by exposure to writing of high quality. The approach to children's literature offered in this handbook, along with wide reading in children's books and serious practice of the evaluative skills discussed here, will develop critical thinking and increase understanding of and pleasure in literature. This knowledge provides a firm basis for discriminating among the good and the poor in children's books. This handbook will help to identify the rarest of the best—and to pass it on to a new generation of readers.

For early and continuous support, I am grateful to JoAnn Johnson, my editor. For concrete suggestions regarding the new edition, I thank Helen Hill and Agnes Perkins, Eastern Michigan University. For reviews and suggestions regarding the new chapter and textual revisions, I am grateful to Norma Bagnall, Texas A.&M. University; Chandler Barbour, Towson State University; Edwyna Gilbert, University of Kansas; Wilma Jean Hardgrave, New Mexico State University; Tony Manna, University of Maine; Alleen Pace Nilsen, Arizona State University; John A. Rutherford, Radford University; and Robert Wiggins, University of California, Davis. For their suggestions and frequent letters of support I am also grateful to my many friends who have used the first edition.

REBECCA J. LUKENS

Contents

A Critical Handbook of
Children's Literature

1 Literature: What is it?

We pick up *McCalls* magazine at the drug store, *TV Guide* in the supermarket, *National Geographic* in the doctor's office, and pore over *Europe on $15 a Day* to give us information and vicarious experience, but they are not literature. Literature *may* give us information and vicarious experience, but it also gives us much more. What sets a chapter in *Wind in the Willows* apart from a *National Geographic* article on the plant and animal life of the English countryside? Many things, and they are at the heart of our definition of literature.

Why do we adults pick up and read a novel or a collection of poetry? For pleasure—not to find a lesson in ecology or history, not to be taught about the natural habitat of the bull snake, or about frontier dress during the French and Indian Wars. We choose literature that promises entertainment and, sometimes, escape. If other discoveries come to us too, we are pleased and doubly rewarded. However, our first motive for reading a novel or a poem is *pleasure.* We may lay the book aside with mixed feelings, but if there is no pleasure, we reject it completely or leave it unfinished. For adults who have had a variety of experiences, who have known success and failure, who have had to decide what is "good" and what is "bad," who have had to face their own shaky standards of morality, the nature of pleasure in literature may be modified from that for children. But some kind of pleasure is essential whether the reader is nine or thirty-nine years old.

Literature provides a second reward: *understanding.* This understanding comes from the exploration of the "human condition," the revelation of human nature, the discovery of humankind. It is not explicitly the function of literature, either for children or for adults, to try to reform human beings, or to set up guidelines for behavior; however, it is the province of literature to observe and to comment, to open individuals and their society for our observation and our understanding. If there is any question about what we are to understand, notice that our terms are "human" and "humankind," synonyms for "people."

As for information, it may or may not contribute to understanding. We may know a person's height, weight, hair color, ethnic background, and occupation. This is information. But until we are aware of temperament, anxieties, joys, and ambitions, we do not *know* that person. Information is not a person; spirit is.

When information is part of the story, we expect it to be accurate, of course, and relevant. The following passage from Johanna Spyri's *Heidi,* for example, contains much information, both summarized and detailed:

> Heidi began to tell her about life up on the mountain, and about the days spent in the pasture, and the winter life indoors. She told how her grandfather could make anything out of wood—three-legged stools, benches and chairs, and mangers into which hay could be put for Schwanli and Bärli. He had just finished a big new tub for summer bathing, and a new porringer and some spoons. Heidi became quite excited as she recounted the wonderful things his skillful hands fashioned from the wood.

The purpose of this passage, however, is not to supply information about Swiss handicrafts. Here are simplicity of life, skill in handiwork, and pride in creation—the spirit of a people and a way of life. Information alone without its contributing to understanding is not literature.

Then perhaps a narrative of people acting in a way we can understand is all that is necessary. No, that is not the case. We may have a short account with understandable action called "Stevie Visits the A&P," and yet it may not qualify as literature. While Stevie's visit might conceivably tell us something about the nature of childhood, it just as easily might not. The grocery store situation provides vivid details about prices and cuts of meat and varieties of vegetables, and the action may be credible because Mother chooses a ripe cantaloupe and pays at the checkout counter. However, the significance of the experience in terms of the characters' lives may be lacking—significance that helps us, whatever our age, to understand a little more about ourselves and others. In the most general terms, then, literature is reading that provides pleasure and understanding.

To return to the comparison of the *National Geographic* article and *Wind in the Willows:* We can feel fairly certain that we read the *National Geographic* article primarily for information, and we can also be reasonably sure that we read *The Wind in the Willows* primarily for pleasure; our second reward is understanding.

Literature has many other more specific appeals for us as readers.

Literature **shows human motives** for what they are, inviting the reader to identify with or to react to a fictional character. We see into the mind of the character, or into the subconscious that even the character does not know. Through the writer's careful choice of details from the past, the current environment, and the imaginary world of the character, we come to see clearly the character's motivation for action. If in these chosen details we see some similarity to our own lives, we nod our heads and identify with the character, feeling that we understand the motives and can justify the deeds. Or seeing the error in judgment that the character fails to see, we understand. Seeing motives we disapprove of, we condemn, or seeing a reflection of our own mistakes, we are compassionate.

Our *touchstone*[1] book, E. B. White's *Charlotte's Web,* the story that will serve us as a critical standard and a frequent example, shows one character, Wilbur, at one moment crying out: "I don't want to die! Save me, somebody! Save me!" However, months later his motive for action is selfless concern:

> "Templeton . . . I will make you a solemn promise. Get Charlotte's egg sac for me, and from now on I will let you eat first, when Lurvy slops me. I will let you have your choice of everything in the trough and I won't touch a thing until you're through."

Charlotte's motives are born of pure sympathy and a desire to help Wilbur the suffering child. She says briskly that Wilbur will not die, and weaves words into her web until late at night. Our identification with each response to Wilbur's life-and-death crises varies as our experience varies.

Literature also **provides form for experience.** When we look back on our lives, we notice the high spots: "the first time we met," or even "the day we sold the old refrigerator." What once seemed trivial, now, with the perspective given by distance in time, seems important. When we look back, we do not look at sequence, since chronology is merely the random succession of life's disordered events. Literature, by placing the relevant episodes—"and the next time we met"—into coherent sequence, gives order and form to experience, and shows life's unity or meaning.

In *Charlotte's Web* White selects events which, among other things, demonstrate the purpose in Charlotte's life. When she says, "By helping you, perhaps I was trying to lift up my life a trifle," we see more clearly the pattern of Charlotte's behavior. While she accepts the inevitability of death, she does not accept the prospect of passive waiting. Charlotte chooses instead to fill her days with order and purpose. As White directs our thoughts and alters our feelings into a chosen course, he gives form to the experience of the ongoing cycle of life.

Literature also ***reveals life's fragmentation.*** Not a day goes by without our being pulled in one direction after another by the demands of friendship—"Please help." Of obligation—"I promised I would." Of pressure—"It's due tomorrow." And of money—"I wish I could afford it." Life is fragmented, and daily experience proves it. However, literature, while it may remind us of our own and society's fragmentation, does not leave us there. Literature sorts the world out into segments we can identify and examine: friendship, greed, family, sacrifice, childhood, love, advice, old age, treasures, snobbery, and compassion are set before us for close observation. Little, if anything, is outside the province of literature.

Literature ***helps us to focus on essentials;*** it permits us to experience with different intensity but with new understanding the parts of life that we have known: We exclaim, "That's how it happened to me, too!" Or parts we have yet to meet: "Do you suppose I'll ever get my diploma?" Or experiences we may never have: "What must it be like to live on a reservation?" In the process of giving order to life and of providing vicarious experience, the writer sorts out the essential details from the nonessential. Undistracted by irrelevant experiences or minor anxieties, the reader focuses upon the essentials of action, people, events, and stresses. In retrospect, we see that life does not distribute events in order of their mounting intensity or their accumulative effects upon us. Literature, however, because it ignores the irrelevant and focuses on the essentials, makes significance clear. As we read, our detachment helps us to see events and their possible influences. We can know the challenge of making choices, feel the excitement of suspense, and glow with the warmth of accomplishment.

Literature can ***reveal the institutions of society.*** Every week we become aware of a new regulation on our personal lives—a higher tax on gasoline, a no-left-turn sign where we have always turned left, or the disappearance of our favorite Tuesday night TV show. A group of people called an institution, something bigger than we are, makes a judgment, and a form of institutional control determines for us something we would like to determine for ourselves. The institutions of society—like government, family, church, school, as well as forces that shape our jobs—urge and coerce us to conform to standards. Institutions occasionally seem so threatening, in fact, that we fear they will close in on our lives, restricting us completely. Yet we know that some restrictions establish the order needed for a group to survive. In this way necessary institutions are born and grow. Literature clarifies our reactions to institutions by showing appropriate circumstances where people give in to or struggle against them.

In the institution called farming, for example, it is unprofitable to keep a runt pig, because fattening him will not pay a good return on the dollar. In *Charlotte's Web,* within Wilbur's conflict with an institution, we see what a life-and-death struggle does to an immature innocent. We may not literally identify with Wilbur—since it is highly unlikely we will ever be commodities on an exchange market—but his struggle for life is nonetheless somewhat similar to our own. Wilbur soon discovers who his friends are, how resourceful they can be, how hard they will work for another's safety, and even, in Templeton's case, what a person's price may be. Through Wilbur's struggle with profitable farming we discover in a small way the impersonal nature of society. In other stories we may discover that racism has become institutionalized, or that although we individually hate war, it is ordered by a body larger than we are. The variety of such conflicts is seemingly infinite.

Not only do institutions affect our lives, but nature does, too. Literature **reveals nature as a force** that influences us. Tornadoes on the summer plains, avalanches in the springtime Rockies, hurricanes in the tropical Caribbean, blizzards on the Dakota prairies—we read of them each year, season by season, region by region. Nature constantly reminds us of its effects upon our lives. People's natural environment influences them, whether it be the stress of wind that wearies nerves, intense heat that produces boredom, or extreme cold and sunlessness that depress spirits. Literature by presenting human beings involved in conflict with such forces makes us see their effects upon human life.

In *Island of the Blue Dolphins* Scott O'Dell shows tenacious Karana clinging to the cliff as she clings to life, battling nature as it sends a tidal wave upon the island:

> The wave struck the cliff. It sent long tongues streaming around me so that I could neither see nor hear. The tongues of water licked into all the crevices, dragged at my hand and at my bare feet gripping the ledge. They rose high above me. . . .

Nature is a force affecting human beings, sometimes demanding that they exert all their powers against it. Although the struggling cannot conquer nature, human beings may struggle heroically and yet not be conquered. In such a conflict, the reader can applaud the human will.

Finally, literature forces us, leads us, entices, or woos us into **meeting a writer-creator** whose medium, words, we know; whose subject, human nature, we live with; whose vision, life's meaning, we hope to understand. We are the student-novice before the artist. In the hands of a gifted writer, we turn from passive followers into passionate advocates calling new followers. The writer's skill with words gives us a pleasure we want to share, and an understanding we have an urge to spread.

LITERATURE FOR CHILDREN

We sometimes forget that literature for children differs from literature for adults in degree, but not in kind. Literature for children can and should do the same things for young readers as literature does for adults. Children themselves are different from adults—once again, in degree but not in kind. They seek pleasure in a story or a poem, but the sources of their pleasure are more limited. Since their experiences are more limited than those of adults, children may not understand the same complexity of ideas. Since their understanding is more limited, the expression of ideas must be simpler—both in language and in form. Related to the necessity for simplicity in the expression of ideas are vocabulary and attention span. Stories are more directly told, with fewer digressions and more obvious relationships between characters and actions, or between characters themselves. Children are both more and less literal than adults. They may find discrepancies between two descriptions of a setting and hold the writer accountable for error. On the other hand, children may accept the fantastic more readily than many adults. As long as the world itself is so remarkably complex and incomprehensible, one more fantastic experience in story form presents no impossible hurdle. Often, for example, the personified animals and toys of the child's world, by behaving like human beings, may show what human beings are like. Children are frequently more open to experimenting with a greater variety of literary forms than many adults will accept—from poetry to folk tales, to adventure, to fantasy.

The many discoveries that children can make through literature might be sought in other ways by adults. Adults might discover human motivation through a study of psychology, or the nature of society and its institutions through a study of sociology, or the impact of nature upon human behavior through a study of anthropology. However, literature can do all of these things for children. Literature is more than a piece of writing that clarifies; literature gives to the child pleasure as well as understanding. Throughout the pages that follow we will refer to literature as "a significant truth expressed in appropriate elements and memorable language."[2] As we shall discover, the ideas expressed in poetic form, and the truths of theme and character explored through the elements of fiction, and the style of the artist with words constitute literature.

SUMMARY

Literature at its best gives both pleasure and understanding. It explores the nature of human beings, the condition of humankind. If these phrases seem too pompous and abstract for children's literature, rephrase them in children's terms:

> What are people like?
> Why are they like that?
> What do they need?
> What makes them do what they do?

The answers, or the mere glimpses of answers to these questions, are made visible in poetry or in fiction by the elements of plot, character, point of view, setting, tone, and style of an imaginative work; together they constitute literature. Words are merely words, but real literature for any age is words chosen with skill and artistry to give the readers pleasure and to help them understand themselves and others.

Notes

[1] A touchstone is a test, criterion, or standard; the meaning is derived from the use of a stone as comparison to detect the purity of silver and gold. Matthew Arnold, using the term in literary criticism, wrote: ". . . there can be no more useful help for discovering what poetry belongs to the class of the truly excellent, and can therefore do us most good, than to have always in one's mind lines and expressions of the great masters and to apply them as a touchstone to other poetry."

[2] Bess Porter Adams makes a similar statement in the introduction to *A Book of Children's Literature,* Lillian Hollowell, ed., New York: Holt, 1966, p. 2.

2 Genres in Children's Literature

Like adult literature, children's literature offers variety. It is not uniform, created with cookie-cutter sameness. We recognize rhymes and fairy tales, fantasies and lyrics, and realistic stories about other countries as well as our own. These and other kinds of literature we sometimes call "genres."

A discussion of genre in literature must begin with an effort to define the term—not a simple task. A *genre* is a kind or type of literature in which the members share a common set of characteristics. As soon as we have said this, however, we face the fact that we can identify as many differences and variations among those members as we can find similarities. Classification is easiest when each class or group possesses clear-cut, unchanging characteristics. The chemist's chart of the elements provides a helpful analogy. In fact, when an element is found that lacks the qualities to fit it into any category, or possesses additional qualities, a new class must be added. While this may work for classification in chemistry, it does not work so clearly in literature. If, for example, we divide literature into prose and poetry, where do we place rhythmic but non-metrical writing spaced on the page in "poetic" line length? Is this work poetic prose because it lacks meter? Or prose-poetry because it is filled with sensory appeals and figurative language? Furthermore, if we decide that a work is poetry we might go one step further since, for example, both lyric and sonnet are themselves genres. Yet both are poetry. Must we subdivide?[1] Genres are not always clear-cut and easily distinguished; the terms are often used loosely. Today genre distinctions, although helpful, are sometimes regarded as arbitrary.

Opinions differ about classifications, although each of us may have several reasons for our opinions. Some people may find it unnecessary even to mention genres; others like the sense of order that genre classification provides. For our purposes, the term "genre" can be very useful in organizing our discussion of children's literature. First, it helps us to be aware that there is more literature for children than one finds in the familiar genres of stories and nursery rhymes. Second, the literary

11

elements we will be talking about in the following chapters—tone, setting, and others—function differently in different genres. And third, we should be sensitive to the broad and rich variety of literature available to children so that we can help them sample it.

For our purposes we will try to use "genre" in a way that is clear and useful, discussing here the kinds of literature that are most commonly written for or read to children and that are complete art forms when read. Since drama is complete only when staged and viewed, it is not discussed here. In Chapter 10, "From Verse to Poetry," we note kinds of poems from folk rhyme to lyric, but in this chapter we look at the kinds, types, or genres of fiction: realistic fiction, with subgenres of problem and social issues realism, historical, animal, and regional realism; fantasy with subgenres of high fantasy and science fiction; and traditional stories with subgenres of folk tales, fables, myths and legends and folk epics.

All of the elements of literature are included in each of the major genres of fiction, but within each type one element may be more significant than another. In some cases the genre demands that a particular element be strong or well developed, and without that strength the credibility of the story may be in question. For example, animal realism requires an objective point of view, for we cannot know what an animal —a real animal, not a personified one—is thinking. Historical fiction, to cite another example, relies for credibility upon a clear sense of setting in a past time. And again, since folk tales have been told orally from one generation to another, descriptions of setting or details of a character's past or a character's thoughts are unnecessary because they delay the telling. When we listen to a folk tale, flat characters seem appropriate, because we recognize them immediately and can move quickly into the action.

The genres, then, are both distinct and overlapping; they contain all elements but in varying combinations and degrees. The chart at the end of this chapter is a helpful guide, showing how elements relate to the specific genres. Refer to it cautiously, however, knowing that literature is not governed by inflexible rules.

REALISM

Realism means that a story is possible, although not necessarily probable. Effect follows cause without the intervention of the magical or supernatural. Charley in *Did You Carry the Flag Today, Charley?* by Rebecca Caudill is rewarded because he helped out in the library, not because a fairy godmother intervened. The outcome seems reasonable and plausible; the story is a representation of action that seems truthful. Realistic stories have in common several characteristics: they are fictional narratives with characters that we know much or little about, involved in some kind of action that holds our interest, set in some possible place and time. Once again, keep in mind that if we divide realistic fiction into subgenres the divisions may at times seem overlapping.

Problem Realism and Social Issues Realism

Problem realism and social issues realism, which are similar in their focus upon problems, are relatively recent subgenres; their situations are realistic or possible. The problems in *problem realism* are not universal like searching for friendship, but personal and particular like having a physical handicap such as cerebral palsy in *Mine for Keeps* by Jean Little, or a retarded sibling as in *Summer of the Swans* by Betsy Byars. Novels about *social issues* show the character, usually the protagonist or central character, encountering a kind of problem engendered by society, like discrimination because of race in *Mary Jane* by Dorothy Sterling, or gender in *The Real Me* by Betty Miles, or social position in *Cotton in My Sack* by Lois Lenski.

In these kinds of realism the protagonist's problem is the source of plot and conflict, and that conflict may be with self, society, or another person. In a well-written book, character and conflict are both well developed and interrelated. In a poorly written novel, the character may either be stereotyped or seem to be made up only of problems. The physical handicaps, the problems with drugs or sex, the divorce situations, the minority or gender issues become so overwhelming that they may blot out the credibility of the character as a whole human being made up of a mixture of feelings and thoughts, emotion and intellect. Furthermore, in poor fiction of these kinds, the protagonist's problems may be solved in too pat a manner: We see that black Charley of *Call Me Charley* by Jesse Jackson solves his problem of acceptance by being more capable than other children. Such fictional solutions can be not only simplistic and sentimental, but also lacking in reality and justice. In real life, difficulties are not solved so quickly or easily. Readers who identify with the characters may find false hope for their own solutions; readers who observe the problem-ridden character may become condescending. "What's bothering my friend? Look how easy it is in this book!" Such simplistic solutions may then result in false themes or ideas like "Any problem is easily solved," or "Work hard and everything always comes out all right." Difficulty, after all, is natural to a complex problem. *A Hero ain't nothin' but a Sandwich* by Alice Childress, in which Benjie struggles with drug addiction, provides an example of a more credible truth: "Despite love and care, a big problem is not easily solved."

Tone or attitude are also affected when the novel is poorly written. Works become sensational when, to hold readers' interest, the writer so loads the story with problems that the situation is incredible, as it is in this nonexistent novel: Black Keith lives with his divorced father, an alcoholic who decides to push drugs because his teen-age lover does; sister Ann, overweight and suicidal, enlists the local hit-man, and Keith must save himself and his father from being encased in concrete and dropped into the Susquehanna River. Such a "realistic" novel is sensational and unbelievable.

While all elements are important in problem realism and social issues realism, we notice particularly the elements of theme, character and conflict. If such fiction is to help us understand ourselves and others, we must find soundly-developed characters and believable conflicts.

Animal Realism

Nonfiction should deal accurately with animals, telling the details of their appearances, their habitats, and their life cycles. Animal realism, as fiction, adds another dimension by giving continuity and conflict or adventure to the story. The setting includes details of the seasons, the geographical regions, and the influence of the elements on the animals. Within the restrictions of scientific accuracy, the fictional portrayal of animals shows them in conflict of some kind. Some are the most important characters in the story, like the three pets of Sheila Burnford's *The Incredible Journey* which determinedly battle with nature to return to their masters through the wilds of Canada. While they may be thought of as characters, they are not given human traits or anthropomorphized. Such novels as *Watership Down* by Richard Adams or *Wind in the Willows* by Kenneth Grahame cannot then be considered animal realism because the animal characters behave, think, and talk not like animals but like human beings. Accuracy about animal life requires an objective point of view when the principals are animals, but a human character when telling the story, like Billy telling about owls in Farley Mowatt's *Owls in the Family*, may report interpretations of the animals' behavior. If the point of view falters, and we "get into the mind" of the animal, the story may become not only unrealistic but also sentimental in tone, as is Felix Salten's *Bambi* where we know not only Bambi's thoughts but even those of the autumn leaves. There is usually some discovery about animals or about their relationships to human beings made in the course of an adventure.

Historical Realism

Historical fiction is placed in the past, and the time and place in the past determine setting. Details about vehicles, clothing, or food preparation, for example, must fit the time and the place. Sometimes little is known of the period, and at other times much is known; it is possible to write historical fiction about the Vikings, like *Hakon of Rogen's Saga* by Erik Haugaard, as well as about the American colonies, like *The Witch of Blackbird Pond* by Elizabeth Speare. The integral setting demonstrates how the characters live and how families support themselves. Often the setting is a period when living was markedly different, as in the pioneer days of *Caddie Woodlawn* by Carol Brink, or the Revolutionary War time of *Johnny Tremain* by Esther Forbes. Since characters, and particularly the central character, are caught in the events of the time, setting therefore influences plot. When the writer exaggerates the bad or the good of the times, the resulting historical fiction may suffer from sensational or sentimental tone. Although themes are often universal, they may relate clearly to a particular time; a story might easily be united by themes about how in times of civil war brothers fight brothers and families are torn apart as *Across Five Aprils* by Irene Hunt exemplifies, or how in pioneer days the family unit was important to survival as it is in the *Little House* stories of Laura Ingalls Wilder. Style may focus particularly upon descriptions that draw for us time and place, the dress and homes, the work and recreation of the day. Language should be appropriate to the time; obviously such slang words as "neat," "keen," or "swell" would be out of place in dialogue of Americans during the Revolution.

History presents facts. To turn facts into fiction, the writer must combine imagination with fact, bringing about an integrated story with a fictional protagonist in a suspenseful plot. As the twentieth century draws to a close, matters that not long ago were current events become the materials of a historical period. Today, for example, writers are seeing with increased objectivity the events of World War II, as does Bette Greene in *Summer of My German Soldier,* and of the Great Depression as does Mildred Taylor in *Roll of Thunder, Hear My Cry.* Such novels show the impact of the times upon the people living in them.

FANTASY

Fantasy, in the phrase of Coleridge, requires "the willing suspension of disbelief." The writer of fantasy (sometimes called "literary fantasy" to distinguish it from folk fantasy which is of unknown authorship) creates another world for characters and readers, asking that readers believe this other world could and does exist within the framework of the book. The acceptance of this other world requires of the writer an ability to make the imaginary universe so credible that we wish it were all true; for sheer pleasure, we believe. High fantasy and science fiction are two identifiable subgenres of fantasy.

High Fantasy

Successful high fantasy captures our belief in two major ways: first, by the internal consistency of the new world, like the categories or strata of small, non-human beings in *The Hobbit* by J.R.R. Tolkien; and second, by the protagonist's belief in his or her experiences, a belief exemplified by Nina in Eleanor Cameron's *The Court of the Stone Children* who is sure that her counterpart in the distant past does exist.[2] High fantasy often appeals to the intellect and raises thoughtful questions. Often it has serious purpose and may make us feel detached and philosophical about human nature.

Once again we are drawn into the story by character. We say "This character thinks, feels, and acts like me or someone I know; therefore I believe." Hans Christian Andersen has ably shown how even personified animals or inanimate objects can involve us in a story, as his stories about the ugly duckling and the darning needle demonstrate. Contemporary fantasy frequently portrays full and complete human beings like the hero of Otfried Preussler's *The Satanic Mill.* Point of view influences our acceptance of the character. We so successfully get into the mind of Will Stanton in Susan Cooper's *The Dark Is Rising* that we are convinced that Will Stanton is an Old One, a fighter for good in every age.

Plot structure may vary from the series of episodes about the wild community of Kenneth Grahame's *The Wind in the Willows* to the plot with a central climax like that of E.B. White's *Charlotte's Web.* Setting varies, but is most often integral because credibility may depend upon a created world different from our own. Time becomes flexible; sometimes it "wrinkles" as in *A Wrinkle in Time* by Madeleine L'Engle. Sometimes it balloons out and returns, as it does in C. S. Lewis's "Narnia" books and in Maurice Sendak's *Where the Wild Things Are.* At other times it is globe-shaped, as Eleanor Cameron says, "holding in equilibrium all tenses" of past, present and future.[3] Tone may be whimsical, humorous, sympathetic, awed—anything. From the vast variety of fantasies comes a multitude of themes: No one appreciates the contributions of the humble. A family may be disrupted by one person's greed. Defying a parent may ultimately improve relationships. Imagination can get people into trouble. The themes of pure or high fantasy frequently encompass a broad concern for humanity; high fantasy seems particularly effective in objectifying and universalizing the ultimate conflict in human life, that between good and evil.

There are different sub-genres of high fantasy, just as there are sub-genres of realism. Talking animals of *Charlotte's Web*, personified toys of Hans Christian Andersen's "The Little Tin Soldier," and tiny races in Mary Norton's *The Borrowers* exemplify three of such sub-genres.

Science Fiction

Science fiction is a type of fantasy, and it is often difficult to decide whether a particular work is pure fantasy or science fiction. Perhaps when we realize that our enjoyment of *A Wrinkle in Time*, for example, is neither increased nor diminished by our decision to call it fantasy or science fiction, we may decide that such distinctions are unimportant. Yet, for the sake of some kind of order when we think in genres, we might say that science fiction stresses scientific laws and technological inventions—like gravity and the speed of light and the contrivances with which to deal with these forces and limitations. This focus on science and technology sometimes overshadows the developing of human characters.

In poor science fiction, characters, committed largely to the scientific process of investigation and invention, are often governed solely by intellect. Their concerns are the products of their minds; they expend their physical energies and mental powers mainly upon inanimate objects. Their intellects invent rays and forces, intricate machines and fantastic creatures. Intellect also governs the characters' relationships with other people. Their cooperation seems to be a union of intellects to control or use a force that is either natural or mechanical; associates share a common, mind-directed goal, rather than a kinship.

Much of science fiction relies primarily upon conflict to hold the reader's interest. Such conflicts are frequently persons against societies alien to us in form and in values, like the Tripods in John Christopher's series. When the conflict is person versus nature as it is in *The Time of the Great Freeze* by Robert Silverberg, the battle, again an intellectual one, seems weighted with odds on the side of the natural force. Suspenseful plots carry most of this genre. Tricky turns and evasions caused by faulty judgment or mechanical failure often pull the reader through the story. Settings are often worlds of mechanical-scientific contrivances quite different from what we know. In fact, setting sometimes seems almost interchangeable from book to book. Long tunnels and ramps with elevators and hatches, mysterious power plants and instrument panels with dials and gauges, levers and valves—all appear regularly. Sometimes a fresh kind of setting can help to distinguish one story from another. Themes arise from conflict and character. In science fiction these themes, often rooted in intellectual issues rather than in emotional yearnings, seem to fall into similar statements. Among the most common are "The will to survive is strong," or "Good constantly battles encroaching evil." Tone, like tone in other genres of course, may become didactic: "If we don't care for our environment . . .!"

While many readers find that scientific invention carries and holds their interest, others who look for subtlety or for understanding of human motives may be disappointed until they find books by writers like Ray Bradbury, William Sleator and John Christopher, whose interest in human beings is as great as it is in scientific invention. While, for the most part, British writers with their roots deep in the faerie and folklore of northern Europe concentrate on fantasy, American writers create their specialty—science fiction that relies upon technology and conflict with the laws of nature. No other genre or subgenre generates such a sharp division of readers into those who love it and those who do not care for it. Awareness of this division as well as the maturing of the genre is bringing to readers more completely developed characters and more varied themes. It seems probable that science fiction will win more readers if the trends continue.

TRADITIONAL LITERATURE

The term "traditional" or "folk literature" implies that the form comes to us from the ordinary person, an anonymous storyteller, and exists orally rather than in writing—at least until some collector finds, records, and publishes the stories or rhymes, thus setting them into temporary form. There is then no final and definitive version of a piece of folk literature. Folktales have been called the "spiritual history" of humankind, the "cement of society," binding a culture together. They seem to express the universality of human wishes and needs. Five hundred versions of the same story, "Cinderella" for example, occur in countless cultures and show almost infinite variations, but are similar in their focus on human yearning for social acceptance and material comfort. Because of scholarly collecting, folktales that once flourished only in

communities where people did not read or write have become the prop-
erty of all people.

Folktales

In form the folktale relies on flat characters, bad ones and good ones,
easily recognized. Since folktales were heard by the teller and then
retold in the teller's own words, there was hardly time for subtle character development. A brief phrase, which may be often repeated, serves
to draw character, since the teller cannot risk losing the audience by
departing from the fast-paced narration of action to describe thoughts
and feelings.

   Stock characters like the fairy godmother and the wicked stepmother frequently appear, as both do in "Cinderella." Conflicts are
often between people or personified animals in person versus person
conflict, like Jack and the ogre in "Jack and the Beanstalk." Plots are
progressive, with the climax coming at the very end and the closing as
brief as "They lived happily ever after." Action, fast and lively, is at the
heart of the folktale. Incidents can occur singly, in threes as they do in
"The Billy Goats Gruff," or occasionally in more repetitions. The setting
is usually a backdrop for the action, a background that creates universality by its vaguely recognizable qualities rather than pins the story
down, thus limiting its significance and appeal. Point of view is rarely
first person, since the tales are told about flat characters in fantastic
situations. Tone varies; it may be sentimental as in "Beauty and the
Beast," objective as in "The Little Red Hen," or humorous as in "The
Squire's Bride." Themes also vary but they comment on human needs
and wishes, like the theme in "The Fisherman's Wife": "People are
never satisfied."

   Although themes may be explicit, they tend not to be didactic or preachy like the morals of the fables. Frequently good con-
quers evil in a short battle and the story concludes with the optimistic view that a just victory is possible. Justice is absolute; it is
never sentimentalized. Good is rewarded and evil punished; the
wicked witch goes into the oven with no regrets on our part. G. K.
Chesterton's statement that adults are wicked and therefore love
mercy while children are innocent and therefore love justice may
throw light on the popularity of folktales with children. Adults' desire for mercy over justice may account for recurrent adult misgiv-
ings about folktales and the violence done to the wicked in them.
The style of the folktale relies upon recurring images like "no bigger
than my thumb" and often includes short rhymes like those in

"Snow White": "Mirror, mirror, on the wall,/ Who is fairest of us all?" The cadenced prose fits the rhythm of oral telling.

Sometimes folktales are subdivided into tales of magic, romance, cumulation, religion, sillies, talking beasts, tall tales, and realistic situations. These categories often overlap; the subgroups only emphasize the richness and variety of the genre.

Fables

The fable is a very brief story, usually with animal characters, that points clearly to a moral or lesson. The moral, an explicit and didactic or preachy theme, is usually included at the end of the story and is the reason for the existence of the fable. The fable makes visible and objective some lesson like that we see in "The Tortoise and the Hare": "Slow but sure wins the race." Brevity dictates that one or two characters each have single traits. It also dictates that conflict is sharp and clear—as it is in "The Dog in the Manger." The setting is a backdrop for the action, and the action has no interpretive narrator telling extra details of characters' thoughts or feelings. Style is crisp and straightforward. Everything in the fable exists to make an abstract point, to make a lesson clear, as clear as the moral in "The Milkmaid": "Don't count your chickens before they hatch."

Myths and Legends

Myths are stories that originate in the folk beliefs of nations and races and present episodes in which supernatural forces operate. Because they, too, are handed down by word of mouth, they have no right or wrong form. Myths, like that of the god Thor and his hammer of thunder, are stories which interpret natural phenomena. Some myths try to make visible and concrete the ways that human beings see nature, like the division of the year into seasons caused by the story of Ceres and her daughter Persephone who is kept for part of the year in the underworld by Pluto. They may show people's relationships with each other, like the generosity demonstrated in the myth of Baucis and Philemon, a myth in which hospitality is rewarded by an eternally filled oil cruse and an endless supply of meal. Myths show the ways that human beings see the forces that control them, like the separation of day and night caused by Appollo's crossing the sky in his sun chariot. Myths explain creation, religion, and divinities; they guess at the meaning of life and death, or at the cause for good and evil as made clear in the myth of Pandora's box.

Characters represent very few qualities in the way that the

goddess Ceres or Demeter represents fertility and thus is linked to the supernatural, or the unexplainable issues of seasons and growth. Plots are often single incidents or a few incidents linked by characters. "Long ago in ancient Greece" is sufficient for setting. Since the abstract issues or themes that myths explore are broad and universal, their tone is dignified and somewhat mystical. The effective telling of a folk myth has dignity and simplicity, for it tries to recreate the spirit and intention of the original. When myths are badly told, as they are by Nathaniel Hawthorne in *Twicetold Tales,* they condescend or even insult the efforts of earlier societies to find meaning in life. When myths are well told, as they are by Grace Coolidge or Charles Kingsley, they appeal to something deep and primitive in all humankind.

Legends are similar to myths because both are traditional narratives of a people; sometimes the two subgenres are interwoven. Legends, however, often have more historical truth and less reliance upon the supernatural. When, for example, we read the legends of the Trojan War, we are aware of the actual seige of the city as well as of legendary heroes and actions. There was a King Arthur, but his legend is not historical truth; Robin Hood is based upon an historical figure, but the legends that surround him are not accurate. Such figures as Abraham Lincoln, a national hero, accumulate legends that are rooted in the authenticity of the character but fictional in detail.

Folk Epics

The folk epic is a long narrative poem of unknown authorship about an outstanding or royal character in a series of adventures related to that heroic central figure. This character or hero is, like Beowulf, bigger than life, grand in all proportions, and superhuman in physical and moral qualities. The action may involve journeys and quests, and show deeds of great courage and valor coupled with superhuman strength; the forces of the supernatural intervene from time to time. The setting is vast, including a nation, a continent, or even the universe. Point of view is objective, for the story is so grand that a protagonist of such remarkable accomplishments seems to need no interpretive narrator. The tone is dignified, and the style is therefore elevated. Often the story, which begins in the middle of things, includes long lists or catalogs of warriors, treasures, gifts, or ships, for example. Extended comparisons called epic similes frequently occur. Like the best retellings of myth, those of epic do not condescend in any way; they show the values of the society and awe the reader with the possibility of great courage and moral strength.

ACROSS GENRE LINES

What is there left to consider?

There are some books which we cannot put neatly into genres because, although they have qualities in common, they cross genre lines. Some books we group together not because of subject matter, but because they rely upon pictures to extend the story—picture books, of course. Other books are singled out for another reason; they are placed in a loose and overlapping group called classics. These works come from all genres and are works that have lasted for some time.

Picture Books

Picture books cross all genre lines. Here, of course, we consider the quality of the illustrations and how they extend the meaning of the text. We expect color and style and story to be compatible. We ask that the placement of text and pictures moves our eyes from left to right. The pleasing visual effect of the double-spread pages results from balance and rhythmic movement. Perhaps what we value most highly is the artist's unique personal style, style that does not duplicate the "art" of greeting cards nor the comic distortions of every Saturday morning cartoon show.

We are often deceived into thinking that because the text for picture books is brief, the writer of the text need not be judged by the standards of literary excellence. When we see, however, that it is possible to develop surprisingly full characters like Peter Rabbit, to create an engaging plot as Maurice Sendak so skillfully does in *Where the Wild Things Are,* to show with words as well as pictures an integral setting like that in *The Spooky Tail of Prewitt Peacock* by Bill Peet—when we see all this, we realize that a good picture book is not so simple as it looks. Our appreciation grows when we notice that words make comparisons and sound resembles meaning—that style is important. Since the picture book functions fully only when it is read aloud as well as looked at, fresh comparisons, vivid sensory appeals, and the writer's intelligence and wit make the most successful story. Some slight conflict holds our interest, and theme, like "We need food for the spirit as well as for the body" in *Frederick* by Leo Lionni, ties it all together. The elements of literature, then, are important here too, just as they are in the other genres. By pinning pictures to words, and words to ideas, the best text enlarges the world of the small child in ways that even the most careful observation of pictures cannot do.

Wordless picture books are something else. They are complete in their effect or impact only when the small child has the benefit of a highly effective communicator, an older person who verbalizes—and thus creates a text—asking questions, and speculating about pictured actions, filling in, building, intriguing, prodding and piquing the imagination of the small child. "Reading" a wordless picture book with a small child is a highly creative act and not to be minimized. It presents a great challenge. Here, however, we are concerned with literature, a term that implies words and text.

Classics

Classics are books that have worn well, attracting readers from one generation to the next. They cross all genre lines; they are historical fiction, regional literature, and high fantasy. What seems to keep them in continuous circulation may be the significance of theme, the credibility of character, the continuing reality of the conflict, or the engaging quality of style. The classics are often imitated. The success of the mischievous Tom Sawyer, for example, has resulted in periodic spates of books about mischievous boys. What seems apparent, however, is that mischief is not what keeps *Tom Sawyer* alive but far more complex and universal matters like Twain's perceptive portrayal of the adults in the community; his mixture of the experiences, emotions, rites, and yearnings of childhood; the significance of ideas like sacrifice and courage for the sake of other people, as well as Twain's lively variety of tones and his artistry with words.

A work may be popular for a time, as were *A Dog of Flanders* and *Seventeen,* and then fade. What seemed the height of ingenious wordplay at one time may at another seem dull and trite; the wit in *The Peterkin Papers,* for example, seems now to be heavy-handed and dull. *Alice in Wonderland,* on the other hand, remains an incomparable work of nonsense; readers have never outgrown Carroll's wit, and his playful inventiveness remains unsurpassed. If the diversified family farm becomes extinct, E.B. White's finest novel *Charlotte's Web* may come to be seen as a piece of historical fiction. But White's thorough portrayal of character, his choice of life and death conflict, his affectionately humorous tone, and his universal themes about friendship, satisfaction, and death are elements that identify classics. The classics of one generation may be supplanted by later works, but the appeals of other books may remain for a surprisingly long time.

To summarize the similarities and differences in the genres, there is a chart on the following pages. If we keep in mind the dangers of generalizing about all the stories in a category, it may prove helpful. Literature, since it is not so easily classified as the chemical elements, will often be elusive, refusing to fit neatly into a genre, but the chart may keep us aware of the great breadth of fiction available to children.

REALISM

Genre	Character	Plot	Setting	Theme	Point of View	Style	Tone
Problem Realism and Social Issues Realism ex: *Mine for Keeps, Roll of Thunder, Hear My Cry*	Best novels have round central characters. Poor ones load protagonist with problems, or have flat or stereotyped characters.*	Any kind of conflict, but problem is usually source. If problem is solved too easily, story is flawed.	Any.	Any, though usually related to solution of problems. Sentimentality, sensationalism, didacticism are flaws.*	Any.	Uses all devices.	Any, but sentimentality or sensationalism are flaws.*
Animal Realism ex: *Incredible Journey*	Realistic portrayal of animals, without personification.*	Conflict is usually animal versus nature.	Usually integral.*	Usually related to some discovery about animals or their relationships to human beings.	Objective in respect to the animal character; human characters may be shown in other points of view.*	Uses all devices.	Any, but if point of view falters tone may become sentimental.*
Historical Fiction ex: *Johnny Tremain, The Witch of Blackbird Pond*	Protagonist has universal human traits, but is a product of the time and place.*	Any, but conflict more often person versus society or self, as well as another person.	Integral setting with focus on particular time and place, usually time of stress or crisis, or of social change.	Any universal theme.	Any.	Uses all devices. Relies for credibility on accurate descriptions of place—costumes, activities, etc.	Any, but flawed if past is recreated sentimentally or sensationally.*
Regional Realism and Stories of Other Lands ex: *The Loner, Heidi*	Protagonist has universal human traits, but is a product of the time and place.	Conflict often related to the region, whether topography, livelihood, or mores of area.*	Integral and essentially so.*	Any universal theme.	Any.	Uses all devices.	Any.

FANTASY

Genre	Character	Plot	Setting	Theme	Point of View	Style	Tone
High Fantasy ex: *The Borrowers, The Lark Is Rising*	Realistically portrayed people, as well as personified animals, toys, or other inanimate objects often with special powers.*	Any kind of conflict, often person versus self.	Often a "special world," an integral setting where time and space have special qualities of expansion or limitation.*	Important and universal. In high fantasy, may deal with ultimate conflict of good and evil.*	Any.	Any and all devices, often highly sensory.	Any.
Science Fiction ex: *Flight of Exiles*	Round protagonist. Flawed stories often have inadequately developed central characters.*	Any kind of conflict; often mechanical or natural forces are antagonists. Plots usually progressive and suspenseful.	Often distinguishes one story from another; set in future time on unexplored planets.	May be subtle, implicit, but flawed stories have didactic theme.*	Any.	All devices; often much description in concrete terms.	Often objective, factual, but flawed story may be heavily didactic.*

TRADITIONAL TALES

Genre	Character	Plot	Setting	Theme	Point of View	Style	Tone
Folk Tale ex: *Cinderella*	Flat, even the protagonist; bad and good characters easily identified; stock characters like the wicked stepmother and the fairy godmother.	Person versus person or person versus personified nature conflicts. Often single incident, or incidents by three's. Action moves rapidly to a climax and stock closing.	Backdrop setting: "Long ago and far away. . . ."	Either implicit or explicit. Often strongly focused on justice.	Usually omniscient or limited omniscient.	A few recurring images; often short verses; cadenced prose.*	Varied. May be sentimental, humorous, objective, but is not often didactic.
Myth and Legend ex: "Narcissus" "King Arthur"	Myth: gods and heroes with traits linked to supernatural powers Legend: historical figures with fictional traits and situations	An incident or incidents linked by character.	Backdrop: "Long ago in ancient Greece. . . ." "When Arthur was king. . . ."	Explanations of natural phenomena or human relationships.	Usually objective.	Significant symbols, abstract terms, little or no dialog; brief descriptions of action.	Myth: Dignified, perhaps mystical. Legend: Often objective. Sentimentality flaws either myth or legend.*
Fable ex: "The Boy Who Cried Wolf"	Flat and stock; often personified animals with single traits.	Person versus person conflict; extremely brief; usually a single incident.*	Backdrop.	Explicit and didactic.	Objective or dramatic.	Terse, lacking imagery or connotative language.	Straightforward, didactic, and moralizing.
Folk Epic ex: *Beowulf*	Protagonist is heroic, superhuman.*	Begins in middle of things (*in medias res*); conflict is person versus person, society, or nature. Usually three incidents showing hero victorious against supreme odds.*	Undefined long ago, but set in the vast world or the universe.	Good can be victorious over evil, but only after great struggle against superhuman odds and with assistance of gods.*	Objective or dramatic.	Long, cadenced lines of oral language; symbols and images; epic grandeur and simplicity; similes and elaborate comparisons; extended formal speeches.	Dignified; grand; awesome.

*Represents elements that have special importance in a genre, or elements that are frequent sources of inadequacy in a book.

Notes

[1]In *Hamlet*, Shakespeare in Polonius's speech praising the actors (Act II, Scene 2), makes fun of the genres of drama in such phrases as "pastoral-comical" and "tragical-comical-historical-pastoral."

[2]For an enlightening discussion of the narrator and the reader/audience in fantasy, see "Some Presumptions About Fantasy" by Perry Nodelman in *Children's Literature Quarterly*, Summer, 1979.

[3]*The Green and Burning Tree*, Boston: Little, 1969, p.72.

Recommended Books Cited in This Chapter

Adams, Richard. *Watership Down.* New York: Macmillan, 1975.

Aesop. *Fables.* New York: Dutton, 1963.

Andersen, Hans Christian. *The Ugly Duckling; The Little Tin Soldier.* New York: Macmillan, 1963.

Asbjörnsen, Peter Christian, and Jörgen Moe. *East of the Sun and West of the Moon.* New York: Macmillan, 1939.

Brink, Carol. *Caddie Woodlawn.* New York: Macmillan, 1946.

Burnford, Sheila. *The Incredible Journey.* Boston: Little Brown, 1961.

Byars, Betsy. *The Summer of the Swans.* New York: Viking, 1970.

Cameron, Eleanor. *The Court of the Stone Children.* New York: Dutton, 1973.

Carroll, Lewis. *Alice's Adventures in Wonderland.* New York: Dutton, 1954. (first published 1865)

Caudill, Rebecca. *Did You Carry the Flag Today, Charley?* New York: Harper & Row, 1970.

Childress, Alice. *A Hero ain't nothin' but a Sandwich.* New York: Coward, 1973.

Christopher, John. *White Mountains.* New York: Macmillan, 1970.

Coolidge, Olivia. *The Golden Days of Greece.* Boston: Houghton, 1949.

Cooper, Susan. *The Dark Is Rising.* New York: Atheneum, 1973.

Forbes, Esther. *Johnny Tremaine.* New York: Dell, 1969.

Grahame, Kenneth. *The Wind in the Willows.* New York: Scribner's, 1953. (first published 1908)

Greene, Bette. *Summer of My German Soldier.* New York: Dial, 1973.

Grimm, Jacob and Wilhelm. *Grimm's Fairy Tales.* New York: Grosset, 1962.

Haugaard, Erik. *Hakon of Rogen's Saga.* Boston: Houghton, 1973.

Hunt, Irene. *Across Five Aprils.* New York: Follett, 1964.

Jacobs, Joseph. *English Fairy Tales.* New York: Dover, 1898.

Kingsley, Charles. *Heroes.* New York: Macmillan, 1954.

L'Engle, Madeleine. *A Wrinkle in Time.* New York: Farrar, 1962.

Lenski, Lois. *Cotton in My Sack.* New York: Lippincott, 1953.

Lewis, C. S. The *Narnia* Books. New York: Macmillan, 1951.

Lionni, Leo. *Frederick.* New York: Pantheon, 1966.

Little, Jean. *Mine for Keeps.* Boston: Little, 1962.

Miles, Betty. *The Real Me.* New York: Knopf, 1974.

Mowatt, Farley. *Owls in the Family.* Boston: Little, 1961.

Norton, Mary. *The Borrowers.* New York: Harcourt Brace, 1965.

Peet, Bill. *The Spooky Tail of Prewitt Peacock.* Boston: Houghton Mifflin, 1973.

Potter, Beatrix. *The Tale of Peter Rabbit.* New York: Warne, 1902.

Preussler, Otfried. *The Satanic Mill.* New York: Macmillan, 1973.

Sendak, Maurice. *Where the Wild Things Are.* New York: Harper, 1963.

Silverberg, Robert. *Time of the Great Freeze.* New York: Harper, 1964.

Speare, Elizabeth. *The Witch of Blackbird Pond.* Boston: Houghton, 1958.

Sterling, Dorothy. *Mary Jane.* Garden City, N.Y.: Doubleday, 1959.

Taylor, Mildred. *Roll of Thunder, Hear My Cry.* New York: Dial, 1976.

Tolkien, J. R. R. *The Hobbit.* Boston: Houghton, 1973.

Twain, Mark. *The Adventures of Tom Sawyer.* New York: Macmillan, 1966. (first published 1866)

White, E. B. *Charlotte's Web.* New York: Harper, 1952.

Wilder, Laura Ingalls. The *Little House* Books. New York: Harper, 1953. (first published 1932–1943)

3 Character

"I like stories where the people are one way at the beginning of the book, and different at the end."

We often have the superior notion that children are too immature to recognize what makes a whole human being, or to see how people can be one thing at one time, and become something else with the passage of time or events. Also, we falsely assume that children have neither the experience nor the training to relate to fictional people and their differences. As a result of our assumptions, we may cheat children by choosing for them stories that merely recite daily routine like *About a Bicycle for Linda,* or that rely for interest almost entirely on excitement and suspense like *The Hardy Boys* or *Nancy Drew.*

Children can catch many of human nature's subtleties. They care about human beings, are sensitive to them, and can know them. Even an infant responds to differences in people. The infant may hide in a protective shoulder to avoid a noisy stranger, lean out of a crib to be snuggled by a familiar friend. The smallest child, furthermore, knows and expects consistency in people. Try to persuade a child that the usually brusque and irritable Aunt Amy is—this time—friendly and kind. By turning away from what he or she regards as Aunt Amy's fakery, the child clearly demonstrates not only sensitivity to personality but also an expectation of consistency.

It seems to follow that if even the smallest children are aware of personality in the people around them and can detect their differences, children are able then to recognize personality in stories they read. It also seems natural that the child who responds to real people will respond to people in a story and will be sensitive to consistency in their actions. If the functions of literature include the giving of pleasure and the discovery and understanding of ideas and of other human beings, then character development in literature makes its own contribution to these ends.

Character as the term is generally used means the aggregate of mental, emotional, and social qualities that distinguish a person. In literature, however, the term **character** is used to mean a person, or in the case of children's literature, sometimes a personified animal or object. Each of the living beings in a story, play, or poem is a character.

When we add to the word *character* the word *development,* we have a literary term **character development,** which also has a special meaning. In life the development of a person's character or personality is a matter of growth and change. In literature, however, character development means showing the character—whether a person or animal or object—with the complexity of a human being. Each of us in real life is three-dimensional; that is, we are a mixture of qualities. None of us is completely generous; we have our limits. None of us is completely selfish; we have other traits. In the full development of character in the literary sense, the writer shows the whole, composed of a variety of traits like those of real human beings.

The writer has privileges and responsibilities in this matter of character development. Since we are following a central character in a story, it is the writer's obligation to make this person's thoughts and actions believable. On the other hand, if the character is less important, the writer has the privilege of making the character two-dimensional or even a representative of a class—for example, the bossy older brother, or the impish little sister. The importance of a character in a story—primary, secondary, minor, or background importance—determines how fully the character is developed and understood. The closer the character comes to the center of the conflict—and therefore the more important the character is—the greater is our need to know the complexity of the character's personality. Conversely, the more the character functions merely as background, the less likelihood that the character needs to be developed.

REVELATION OF CHARACTER

In life we become acquainted with people in many ways. We see our new neighbors from a distance and draw tentative conclusions about age, occupation, and social status. We hear the diction of the educated, the twang of the Texan; even the precision or the explosiveness of short sentences indicates something about temperament. From their public actions we decide that the neighbors seem to be neighborhood assets, since they prune their shrubs and walk their dog in the proper places. Finally, if the new neighbors are known to our friends, we listen to their opinions. We have come to know these neighbors by how they look, what and how they speak, how they act, and what others say about them.

In literature the process of coming to know a character is comparable. In literature, however, the writer has another alternative: the author may choose to tell what the characters are thinking. In this case, the writer may fill in details about the characters' innermost anxieties and dreams, the patterns of childhood behavior, and early home life.

By Actions

Templeton in *Charlotte's Web* is an example of a character whose actions help to define his nature. After Wilbur moves to the barn, we meet Templeton, who creeps up cautiously to the goslings, keeping close to the wall. Templeton's furtive manner arouses our curiosity; we are as suspicious as the barn animals. Twice in the story, Templeton grins, first when Wilbur lands with a thud, hurt, crushed, and with tears in his eyes after his unsuccessful web-spinning efforts. Templeton grins a second time as he takes Wilbur's tail and bites it as hard as he possibly can. Gleefully savage, Templeton delights in slinking about and nipping at his friend; he is surly, sneaky, and ill-tempered, pleased at others' discomfort. He is self-centered and gluttonous, going to the Fair only to scavenge in the garbage and litter. Templeton's actions create a picture of Templeton's character.

By Speech

Accompanying Templeton's actions are his predictable sarcasm and ill-tempered outbursts as he gripes to Wilbur in sneering tones. He crawls into Wilbur's crate as a stowaway and grumbles:

> "kindly remember that I am hiding down here in this crate and I don't want to be stepped on, or kicked in the face, or pummeled, or crushed in any way, or squashed, or buffeted about, or bruised, or lacerated, or scarred, or biffed. Just watch what you're doing, Mr. Radiant. . . ."

At the fair when Wilbur is optimistic that he may avoid becoming bacon, Templeton cannot resist commenting that when Zuckerman hankers for smoked ham, he will take the butcher knife to Wilbur. Templeton boasts about every grudging action and every carefully bought favor; he even pretends his motives are kind when he bites Wilbur's tail or saves the rotten egg. Complaining, "What do you think I am, anyway, a rat-of-all-work?" Templeton resentfully orders the directors' meeting to break up because meetings bore him. He grumbles at his commission—finding words for the web; he is not spending all his time rushing over to the dump after "advertising material." Templeton characterizes himself by what he says, showing himself to be cynical and selfish, resenting any intrusion on his own pursuits.

By Appearance

Gluttony is one of Templeton's most obvious traits, and his appearance shows it. He returns after his night of gorging at the fair, swollen to double his usual size. Only an appeal to appetite will tempt Templeton to fetch the egg sac, and as he eats first at Wilbur's trough every day, he grows fatter and bigger than any other known rat. Templeton's appearance verifies and supplements what we know of his character; gluttony and self-interest are the essence of Templeton.

By Others' Comments

Templeton is characterized by what he does and what he says and by the way he looks. However, there is more to be learned from the comments of others about him. The animals carefully watch his furtive actions since they neither like nor trust Templeton. The old sheep enlists Templeton's help in finding words, saying that the rat can be persuaded only by appeals to "his baser instincts, of which he has plenty." Since the sheep is on our side, the side of saving Wilbur, we trust his judgments. And we distrust those characters who are on the wrong side of our sympathies. We are less accepting of their judgments, just as we would doubt Templeton's opinions on any character because we know how deceitful he is. The comments of the other characters, like the comment of the old sheep, help to show character.

By Author's Comments

White's comments also add to the picture we have of Templeton's character. He calls Templeton a crafty rat who does as he pleases, even his tunnel showing his cunning. White's thoroughly negative description of Templeton verifies the goose's and gander's feelings about the rat who

> had no morals, no conscience, no scruples, no consideration, no decency, no milk of rodent kindness, no compunctions, no higher feeling, no friendliness, no anything. He would kill a gosling if he could get away with it. . . .

Templeton becomes a character we know so well that we know what to expect of him in almost any situation; he is consistent.

UNITY OF CHARACTER AND ACTION

The writer creates the whole cast of characters for the story—some important, some minor, some complex, some relatively simple—through the use of these techniques. As we come to know these characters, we respond to them.

Most of us respond to other human beings as we see similarity to ourselves, or if not similarity, recognizable traits and responses. We may say we "identify with" someone. Reading a story, we make the same demands of character—not that every character be exactly like ourselves, but that a character be credible.

In real life we know that change occurs in ourselves and in those we know well. We recognize that change only if we see a person before and after. We say that a child has grown, but even that statement implies a comparison between what *was* his or her height and what is *now* that height. If we must know both the *was* and the *is* to see growth, so it is with a character's change. If the impact of the events shapes or reshapes the personality of the character, the author is obligated to show how that change has come about.

Implicit within the acceptance of change is, of course, the idea of cause, and cause involves the story—its action. Given this complex character and adding these events, the combination may result in change. In life we say, "Just what you'd expect of her," or "It could only happen to him," and by these words we admit that character and action are inseparable. The phrase "unity of character and action" may not mean much to you at first glance, but it expresses an important idea, one of the most important in understanding any fiction. In the best fiction, according to Henry James, "What is character but the determination of incident? What is incident but the illustration of character?"[1] *This character* because of *this personality* provokes *this action;* this action by its nature demonstrates this character. In literature the skillful writer shows characters by means of actions and speeches so that character, incident, and outcome seem interwoven—and, at the end, inevitable. Think of Ben Wen in *The High King* or Karana in *Island of the Blue Dolphins* or Claudia in *From the Mixed Up Files of Mrs. Basil E. Frankweiler.* Can you think of these characters apart from the actions they take part in? (When we say "actions," we are also talking about plot, of course, the subject of the following chapter.)

Look at Hans Christian Andersen's "The Ugly Duckling" as an example of James's view on the unity of character and action. Notice how we come to know the central character. The Duckling's *appearance* seems of primary importance, since that is the basis for his being excluded. He is big and ugly, clumsy and grayish black throughout the story. However, at the end of the story his strong wings, white ruffled feathers, and slender neck have replaced his earlier awkwardness with beauty and grace. As for the dejected Duckling's *actions,* he does not look up when he is bitten and ridiculed in the duckyard. In the old woman's cottage, his panic sends him into the milk dish, the butter trough, and the flour barrel. But at the end of the story he floats gracefully upon the water, his modest head tucked under his wing. What the Duckling *says* is equally revealing of his character; several times he says sadly, "I'm so ugly," or "even the dogs won't bite me." The Duckling is sure that he is an inferior nothing, and he never resists his enemies. At the end of the story, the Duckling shows by his speech that he is still modest when he says joyously, "I never dreamed of so much happiness when I was the ugly duckling."

As for what *others say* about the Ugly Duckling, his mother says he is not pretty, his brothers and sisters that they will not put up with him for he is too big, and some wish that the cat would get him. The old woman's hen calls him a fool and finds him no fun. However, at the end of the story, the children call him the prettiest, "so young and lovely!" Finally Andersen the *writer* has kept us informed about the Duckling not only by describing appearance and actions and re- porting speeches, but also by his writer's comments, the result of his knowing everything. Andersen calls him a poor duckling, tells us he is miserable, exhausted, unhappy, terrified, the laughingstock. He calls the Duckling "poor thing!" and informs us of the Duckling's strange desire to float on the water, of his mysterious yearning to join the migrating swans. Finally, at the end of the story, Andersen tells us of the Ugly Duckling's beauty that combines with his shyness, his hap- piness without pride as the Duckling speaks "from the depths of his heart."

Through all the means at his disposal, Andersen has shown us the character of the Ugly Duckling. The result is that we know this character well, and know that the story is the result of the character's traits combined with the actions that occur. The two are inextricably intertwined; together they demonstrate the unity of character and ac- tion. The character of the Ugly Duckling lives because the trials and harassments he goes through in the course of growing up determine his personal change and are his character; the story identifies the reality of maturing. Family rivalry, rejection, fear of failure, inability to find friends, or to relate to others, even the feelings of ugliness and wishing one were dead are included in Andersen's story of the self-doubt of childhood.

On the other hand, not all writers are as successful in integrat- ing or unifying character and action. Perhaps one of the biggest disap- pointments to a perceptive reader of Judy Blume's novels is the inade- quate portrayal of characters: even the main characters in such novels as *Then again, maybe I won't* seem shallow and unbelievable. Speaking in clichés, possessing little self-understanding, and acting in stereotypical fashion, the young people and the adults contribute little to our understanding of human motivation, or to the integral nature of human beings and their actions.

TYPES OF CHARACTERS

There are certain terms that describe the degree of character development and that refer to change or lack of it in a character in the course of a story. Briefly, a ***round character*** is one that we know well, who has a variety of traits that make him or her believable. A ***flat character*** is less well developed, and has fewer traits. A ***dynamic character*** is a round character that changes, while a ***static character***—either round or flat—is one that does not change in the course of the story.

Flat Characters

Let us begin with the less important characters. They are essential to the action, but since they are not fully developed, we call them ***flat.*** In most stories, we must have these flat characters to help carry the action, to show how the central character behaves or relates to others, to make the setting a believable place because in this setting live these people. Flat characters are quickly made known to the reader, and quickly assume their necessary places in the narrative so that the story can then focus on the central characters.

Fern in *Charlotte's Web,* for example, is a flat character, a child with an intense interest that absorbs her for a time. She treats Wilbur like a doll, listens to the animals' conversations, and reports them to incredulous parents. She plays and quarrels, loves the Ferris wheel, and the freedom of the Fair. However, Fern has few traits that distinguish her from other little girls. She remains a believable little girl but not a special one with extraordinary traits that distinguish her from the large class of characters known as "little girls." Wilbur's relationships and worries are the focus of the story, and the conflict goes on without Fern's being totally aware of all that spiders and pigs mean to each other. Because this is Wilbur's story not Fern's, she needs no greater development.

When a character has very few individual traits, the character does not seem to exist as an individual human being. When the character seems only to have the few traits of a class or of a group of people, the character is called a ***stereotype.*** Each of us has a few mental stereotypes: for example, of politicians, mothers, athletes, or poets. When we examine these mental pictures and compare them to individuals we know well, we find that each stereotype is inaccurate and unjust. In literature, however, the stereotype, like the stock character who appears in many stories, is useful, since he or she quickly settles into background position and performs there in an easily understood role.

In *Charlotte's Web* Lurvy is an example of a stereotype—in this case of a hired man. Lurvy has only the expected traits and does only the expected things. He nails down the loose board on Wilbur's pen, he slops Wilbur, he discovers the exploded dud. Lurvy is neither eloquent nor imaginative:

> "I've always noticed that pig. He's quite a pig." "He's long, and he's smooth," said Zuckerman. "That's right," agreed Lurvy. "He's as smooth as they come. He's some pig."

As Lurvy's speech shows, stereotypes describe themselves by what they say as well as how they say it.

Occasionally the writer may use a ***character foil,*** a minor character whose traits are in direct contrast to a principal character, and thus highlight the principal. The snobbish lamb is as young and naive as Wilbur, but she is smug instead of humble. Pigs are little or nothing to her. Since the lamb is consistently disdainful, her behavior contrasts sharply to Wilbur's, and in this way she acts as a foil.

Stereotyping, or compressing people into flat caricatures that eliminate individual differences, is useful in literature for particular background figures that fill narrow roles. Flat and stereotyped characters, however, are not suitable protagonists; we should be particularly watchful for them in literature about minorities, because they do great injustice. (We will discuss the flat characters of folk literature shortly.) We have noted the necessity for character and action to be unified. However, flat and stereotyped characters do not truly grow out of action, and action cannot grow out of their less-than-full human natures. It seems more descriptive of flat characters and action to say that they coexist; flat characters and stereotypes move over the surface of the action, rather than being integrated with the action. Flat characters, furthermore, make little contribution to our understanding of human nature. In fact, if we read only about stereotypes, our perceptions about people may be narrowed rather than expanded. While stories for adults do occasionally make their points by careful stereotyping, these protagonists are reaching a more sophisticated readership, one that is capable of seeing a point by contrast to what is already known of the complexity of human nature.

Round Characters

A *round character* is one that is fully developed; we know this character well. The many traits of the round character are demonstrated in the action of the story. We know appearance and actions, speeches and opinions, what others say and think about the character, and oftentimes what the writer thinks about him/her. The character is so fully developed that we may even be able to predict actions and reactions. Yet, like a real person, the character may surprise us or respond impetuously on occasion. It is as though we know the character so well that the character has become a real person, one we wish we could meet or might enjoy knowing.

In children's literature there are a great many round characters that we may feel we know. However, in order to help us see clearly what is meant by a round character, compare the many traits of Wilbur, for example, to the few traits of Fern, or the stereotype Lurvy. From the first words of the first page when Fern asks where her father is going with the ax, we are anxious about Wilbur's fate. We soon discover that Wilbur's struggle is the conflict, and that he is therefore the *protagonist,* or central character. Tiny, dependent Wilbur has almost no life of his own at the opening of the story, except to amuse himself like a toddler, finding the mud moist and warm and pleasantly oozy. When he goes to live in the barn, he is bored, unable to dream up anything exciting to do. Friends must introduce themselves to him. When he squeezes through the fence and is pursued, he has no idea what to do with freedom; and his constant appetite makes him captive again, since Lurvy's pail of slops is irresistible. Wilbur plans his day around his body: sleeping, eating, scratching, digging, eating, watching flies, eating, napping, standing still, eating. On the day that Wilbur wants love more than comfort and food, he has grown. But now he wonders uncertainly about friendship, which seems such a gamble. After Wilbur makes a friend, life becomes more exciting and he becomes confident enough to try spinning a web. Cheerfully, he tries and fails; humbly he admits that Charlotte is brighter and more clever. Wilbur's innocence and dependence are clear when he pleads for a story or a song, for a last bedtime bite, a last drink of milk, and calls out the series of quiet good-nights to Charlotte. Panic is Wilbur's reaction to news of his destiny—the Arable's dinner table. But once he is assured that Charlotte can perform miracles, he calms down to be patient, trusting, and humble. The congratulatory words in Charlotte's web make Wilbur an exemplary pig; he decides that if he is called "radiant," he must act radiant, and in his way he becomes radiant. Despite all the admiration Wilbur attracts, he remains modest. Happy and confident, he honestly admires Charlotte's peach-colored egg sac and gazes lovingly into the faces of the crowd.

He looks both grateful and humble. Wilbur has enough traits to classify him as a round character.

CHANGE IN CHARACTER

If there is a unity of character and action such as James spoke about, then the character is not only affected by the events, but his or her nature may bring about various events. Frequently, the events of the story may change a character.

When the word *dynamic* is used in ordinary conversation it may mean forceful, or perhaps exciting. However, in the context of literature, the word has special meaning, since a **dynamic character** is one who changes in the course of the action. He or she may change from being shy to being poised or even domineering; or from cowardly to brave, from selfless to selfish. The character may demonstrate a new realization about himself or herself, or about his or her personal values. He may show that he is now able to take care of himself, or she may show that she has become able to care for others as well as herself. Somehow, the events of the story and qualities of the character have effected some basic character change. The variety of possibilities for change is huge.

The character, of course, may grow older by an hour or by a decade in the course of the novel's action. However, the mere passage of time is not sufficient evidence of character change. Some people are as immature at thirty-five as they were at seventeen. On the other hand, we know some people who have been changed by a single event—a traumatic experience or a simple and joyous one that has brought a realization of some kind. It is not then the passage of time that is important in character change, but the impact of events on the character —the unity of character and action—creating new traits to supplant or alter the old. The character may not necessarily be aware of his or her own change, just as looking back we may see that we are different from what we once were, but cannot necessarily account for the *where* or *when* of our change. The essential matter is that we are different.

Wilbur changes. He is a believable character early in the story, although he is young and immature. The experience of receiving self-less friendship makes him able to give selfless friendship. Slowly, as we watch this change occurring, Wilbur is altered by his part in the action, by his receiving so much. Now he is the same Wilbur, and yet not the same. To his early qualities of humility and naiveté are added dependability and steadfastness, sacrifice and purpose. Even Wilbur's vocabulary matures. When first he hears the bad news, he is a panicky child:

"I can't be quiet," screamed Wilbur, racing up and down. "I don't want to die. Is it true . . . Charlotte? Is it true they are going to kill me when the cold weather comes?"

By the end of a summer of maturing, Wilbur responds to news that his dearest friend will die, and he knows that he must save the egg sac. Notice how his vocabulary has changed to adult words, and his tone has changed to reasonable persuasion:

"Listen to me! . . . Charlotte . . . has only a short time to live. She cannot accompany us home, because of her condition. Therefore, it is absolutely necessary that I take her egg sac with me. I can't reach it, and I can't climb. You are the only one that can get it. There's not a second to be lost. . . . Please, please, please, Templeton, climb up and get the egg sac."

Wilbur does not scream; he uses "please" liberally. His desperation does not arise from his own need, but from the need of another. Once Charlotte had said to the screaming Wilbur that he was carrying on childishly. The new Wilbur tells Templeton to "stop acting like a spoiled child." Wilbur—who once planned his day around his slops— can now, out of deep concern for Charlotte, promise solemnly that Templeton may eat first and take his choice of all the goodies in the trough.

During winter Wilbur warms the egg sac with his breath in the cold barn. By the end of the story, it is Wilbur who offers the first mature greeting, a cheerful Hello! for the baby spiders. The change is significant, and it occurs slowly. It is convincing. Little by little events have molded a self-centered child into responsible maturity; we believe in Wilbur's maturity just as we believed in his childishness.

Perhaps one example of a round and dynamic character is not enough. Try another. E. L. Konigsburg, in *Jennifer, Hecate, Macbeth, William McKinley, and Me, Elizabeth,* has created a round character, one we really know. Elizabeth, a lonely new arrival, walks to school by herself, speaks to no one, is embarrassed to come in late, afraid that her eyes will "leak" as she walks down the aisle. When Elizabeth first meets Jennifer, she is so glad to find such a fascinating and unpredictable friend that she docilely follows every suggestion Jennifer makes—eat raw oatmeal, hotdogs, and an onion a day. After a few weeks, Elizabeth gets mad, but she retreats when she finds Jennifer doesn't back down. Elizabeth weighs the promised pleasure—learning to fly—and decides it's worth it. Under the spell of witch-Jennifer's self-confidence, Elizabeth gives up using the telephone, eating candy and party cake, and playing musical chairs. During the long winter months, the girls discover they have interests in common and discover each other in new ways. Now Elizabeth enjoys being different. Jennifer does not give all the orders and Elizabeth take them: "we" gather magic ingredients for flying ointment. Elizabeth actually defies Jennifer and names their pet toad both Hilary and Ezra. By the end of the story, she can sort out her feelings for Jennifer into jealousy and admiration. She can be assertive enough to tell her mother that Cynthia is a phony, and say, "All in all, I was feeling very competent." Elizabeth, now laughing with Jennifer at the things they have been so serious about, has changed. The two have moved from master witch and apprentice witch to equals. Elizabeth is a dynamic character.

It seems apparent from this example as well as that of *Charlotte's Web* that only the character most involved in the conflict is likely to change. This is Elizabeth's story. She has told the action as she saw it, related her own and Jennifer's speeches, her own personal feelings and thoughts. She is the round central character, or protagonist. Since less important characters are not so closely focused upon, and may even remain on the fringes of the action, their change is unlikely to be important or to grow out of the events of the plot. Furthermore, their changing could even be distracting.

A *static character* is one that does not change in the course of the story. The conflict does not affect the character to make any impact upon personality or outlook. Flat characters—including stereotypes and foils—would not change; they are not well enough known for us to recognize changes or to care. A round character, too, may be unchanged by the conflict. In fact, even the protagonist may be unchanged by the action.

Although Charlotte is not the center of Wilbur's story, we know her consistent nature very well. Charlotte is not only motherly, but hard-working, and her web words prove it. She is the same wise and selfless character at the end of the story that she was at the beginning, and we therefore call her a static character.

It is not necessary that a story have a dynamic or changing character. In one story the round central character may change, and in another may not. The change or lack of it does not constitute a judgment about the quality of characterization. However, the static or dynamic nature of the protagonist does help the reader to see the action and to understand the idea behind it.

In life a person rarely changes overnight, and in literature we find such a change unbelievable. In Victor Barnouw's *Dream of the Blue Heron*, Wabus, an Indian boy, must choose between his own culture and the white man's. Wabus sees brutality, rigidity, depersonalization, and the substitution of material goals for spiritual ones, all personified in the character of Mr. Wickham, the disciplinarian in the government school. Wickham stares at Wabus, hustles him roughly, rips and tears his clothing, seizes him by the hair for a haircut, and jams a hat on his cropped skull. All the boys hate Mr. Wickham, who is suspicious of everyone, whipping them unmercifully and even cross-hatching a runaway's back with long, bleeding stripes. However, a sudden change occurs in Wickham five-sixths of the way through the story—when he finds the Indians ceremonially burying Wabus's grandfather. In minutes Wickham flashes a smile, makes an offering, reassures Wabus, springs to carry the body, seizes a shovel, and leaps into the grave to dig furiously. Although he is convinced of the innocence of Wabus's father White Sky in the death of the old man, he turns him in to the law. On the next to last page of the book, Wickham offers schoolbooks to White Sky in prison and promises to help Wabus become a lawyer. Can we believe it? The novel has tried to show an Indian youth faced with a choice between his own and the white man's culture. Because the picture of white society is totally unappealing, Wabus's choice seems insufficiently motivated. The unbelievably sudden change in Mr. Wickham's character is the source of our dissatisfaction.

By contrast, in Allan W. Eckert's novel *Incident at Hawk's Hill,* we follow the slowly and cautiously developing relationship of interdependence between Ben and Badger, and grow certain that Ben can survive living like an animal underground. Notice, too, how slowly Gilly in *The Great Gilly Hopkins* by Katherine Paterson changes from her early defiance as she drives with the social worker toward Gilly's new foster home. Slowly, in incident after incident, she grows more appreciative of Trotter, more accepting of W. E., more understanding of Mr. Randolph, until she no longer needs her illusions about her own mother.

The number of round characters depends upon the complexity of the plot, and thus there can hardly be a firm rule about number. Certainly it is not feasible that every character be round. It seems evident, furthermore, that a large number of fully developed characters becomes highly distracting in a story for children. Even *Charlotte's Web,* which has three round characters, focuses more fully on Charlotte and Wilbur than on Templeton, important as he is. Some writers, in speaking of the writing process, say that a too fully developed minor character can get out of hand and become so round as to lose his or her place as subordinate and takes over, thus changing the plot. For the sake of unity in the story, it then becomes the writer's choice between flattening out the character once again, or giving him or her new importance in what must now be an altered plot.

EVALUATING CHARACTER IN CHILDREN'S LITERATURE

While character study alone may be enough for some adults, it is not enough for most children, and for several reasons. First, the younger the child, the more limited is her or his awareness of alternatives. Young children are often prevented by their elders from making discoveries about "what happens if"; they often hear instead "Do this, so that may happen," or "Don't do this, or that might happen." Chances for exploring outcomes and discovering alternatives on their own are often denied them. A related problem for the young reader is a limited understanding of motivation. Children rarely see motives for behavior beyond what they would like to see happen. Furthermore, to the young, choices are black and white, yes and no; unaware of their own mixed motives, they rarely see those of others. With maturity—which the experience of literature increases—children become aware of unselfish motives, or of subtle and self-serving motives disguised as unselfish.

Although children may have keen interest in character, they want character involved in action and in making decisions. Children, like adults, are intent on the peace or uproar that results from the characters' decisions. Children, too, like to follow characters and their motives through their emotions and their reasoning, as they face decisions and make choices. Children are also excited by the possibility of the accidental, and perhaps even more by the inevitable. The likelihood of success or the chance of defeat keeps readers of any age involved in a story's action. While character, then, is essential, there are other considerations.

Stories for the Young Child

Whether the story is meant for the young child being read to, or for the older child reading alone, it is possible for character to be well developed. Why does a child demand that *The Tale of Peter Rabbit* be read again and again? Short as the tale is, Peter is a developed or round character.

Character and incident in *Peter Rabbit* are so closely tied to one another that we can see no separation. Peter is mischievous from the start; throughout the story he believes he knows better than he actually does. He is adventuresome, since he crawls under the gate, despite his father's accident which resulted in his being eaten in a rabbit pie. He is greedy: he gorges himself on lettuces, French beans, and radishes. He is frightened and frantic in his flight, and woebegone, he cries. As we hear that this is the second lost jacket and shoes in a fortnight, we know Peter's behavior is consistent. Uncomplaining, Peter accepts the kind nursing of his loving mother; he is a secure child. Peter is no cardboard, two-dimensional rabbit. He is instead a round and believable central character.

Can we say that *Peter Rabbit* is reread because of curiosity about the outcome of the story? Hardly, since the first reading satisfies both parents and children on that score. There must be other considerations. While detailed, delicately colored illustrations as well as suspenseful action give pleasure to the reader and the listener, the character of Peter Rabbit as the universal child is the magnet that pulls us back to read and reread. Peter's actions are inherent in his personality. The one produces the other, true to James's views on the interrelatedness of character and action.

One of the surprising discoveries about character in fiction is that a round character can emerge from a short story for a small child. Contrast *Peter Rabbit* with *Cowboy Small* by Lois Lenski. What does any child remember from *Cowboy Small?* It might be called "a ho-hum book —soonest read, soonest forgotten."[2]

Cowboy Small has a horse which he keeps in a barn, feeds, waters, brushes, and curries. He saddles, mounts, rides, dismounts, cooks, eats, sleeps under the stars, rides again, rounds up cows, eats again, ropes a calf, helps in branding, plays a guitar and sings, sleeps, rides a bronco, falls off, and rides again. No one action is more important than another; there is no selectivity. All there is to Cowboy Small as a person is his name, and even that is no name. Such a story has been written with a message in mind, namely to acquaint a child with the job description of the mythical American cowboy.

However, we never come to know Cowboy Small. (Would Cowboy Small have stuffed himself as Peter Rabbit did?) We know Peter Rabbit and the Ugly Duckling; from their actions we know a great deal about their feelings and thoughts. We understand them and come to care about them; we remember them. But we are unaffected by Cowboy Small's actions; we cannot even say that we forget him, since we never really knew him. The many actions recounted in *Cowboy Small* are not in themselves dull, but because Cowboy Small is not a person involved in the action, the action then becomes dull. A sterile relationship exists between a round-faced paper cut-out and the things he does. On the other hand, Ezra Jack Keats within a shorter text than *Cowboy Small* shows Peter of *A Snowy Day* as a real boy who is delighted at the snowfall, happy with his angel-making, sad at his snowball's melting, and wistful about joining in a snowball fight; in short, Peter is a character we know and like.

Perhaps at this point it is necessary to digress, since some adults may find rabbits and people difficult to interchange. What matters here is not that Peter, like a rabbit, moves on four legs and lives in a sandbank under the roots of a fir tree, nor for that matter that, like a child, he wears a little blue jacket with gold buttons. What makes Peter a little boy is his childlike personality and behavior.

While adults may find it difficult to attribute to animals the traits of human beings, this is not difficult for most children. The child listening to *Peter Rabbit* has no difficulty seeing Peter as a child. When an animal in a children's story is a believable human being, the *anthropomorphism* merely creates fantasy. If the fantastic but believable character is involved in action related to character, children feel very much at home with the whole idea.

A discussion of character in children's literature is incomplete without reference to still another kind, since characters are not only people or animals, but may also be inanimate objects. Winnie-the-Pooh and Piglet may once have been stuffed toys, but now they are believable characters. Paul Hazard pays high tribute to Andersen when he comments on Andersen's skill in characterizing the inanimate—from tiny soldiers to willow trees, from shirts to darning needles. The collection of countless objects

> that the indifferent call "things," stirs, moves, speaks and fills the air with its complaints or its songs. Everything is alive. . . . The arithmetic problem fidgets about on its slate, the letters grow restless in the copy book and complain at having been badly traced.[3]

Andersen, like many other writers for young children, makes characters of things, endowing them with few or many traits, depending upon the length of his story and the theme he is exploring; he can give to the old lantern will power and intelligence, to the starched collar pride, to the teapot arrogance, and to the silver shilling imagination. In the many tales Andersen has told and that are still frequently read, it is the unity of character and action that makes each story live. The Steadfast Tin Soldier and the Fir Tree, although they are inanimate objects, are convincing characters in their stories.

Traditional Literature

Traditional literature has been handed down orally from generation to generation and finally been set into print. Perhaps because of the necessity to keep the story moving with suspense, the folktale relies upon stock characters. The jealous fairy, the foolish youngest son, the girl as good as she is beautiful—these are all useful stock characters. "A wicked stepmother" calls from the listener the same set of responses each time the phrase is used. Since suspense and action carry the folktales, and the usually optimistic ending makes its comment upon life, characters need only be mentioned by a class-name to be known. In a sense, this is one of the pleasures of traditional literature; we are pleased to meet characters we have met before, and whose actions are thoroughly predictable. We are free then to concentrate on action and idea as it all moves along quickly. Our discovery of the nature of human beings comes then from the relationship of theme to action, often a discovery about universal human yearnings.

Animal Realism

In fantasy like *Charlotte's Web* and *Wind in the Willows,* the animals are people, but in a realistic story we expect animal characters to behave like real animals, to be true to their natures. Sheila Burnford in her award-winning novel *The Incredible Journey* has made the effort to discover the qualities of her animal characters and depicts them as true to family and breed. In a story filled with suspense and conflict, she has made us care what happens to her three central characters as they struggle for survival against the Canadian wilderness.

First, there is Luath the Labrador retriever, a one-man dog who is slow to warm up to anyone but his first master. Luath, a hunting dog, is at home in the wilderness. Trained to retrieve and not to eat game, he nearly starves rather than violate his generations of breeding. The most determined of the three animals, Luath leads the trek through the wilds of Ontario. Though his soft, protective mouth is no good for fighting, he can ford a river and encourage the cat and the terrier to swim.

The two followers are the Siamese cat and the English bull terrier, the independent loner and the sociable clown. The feline aristocrat also is true to family and breed: she races straight at her friends and then darts away, opens doors with a leaping twist, cries the childlike wail of the Siamese, prefers heights as vantage points, and reverts easily to predator. The English bull, always the pet, seeks out people along the way; he smiles at Indian and hermit, expecting like any pet that their dinner time is his own. While shy Luath seeks the trail, the bull terrier seeks the human habitation along the way.

Our intense interest in *The Incredible Journey* results from our involvement in the struggle of these characters as they trek across the wilderness. We believe the story because we are convinced that these characters—these pets acting true to their breeds—can and would seek their masters in any way they are capable of doing. We know from occasional news accounts that pets in the real world do make such loyal journeys; here in the fictional world of animal characters we come to believe that this is how such a journey is possible.

As we shall note in a later chapter (Point of View), animal realism is at its best when the animals act only like animals. The temptation for the writer is to guess and to report what thoughts and feelings the animals are having. However, the writer does not really know what animals think or feel, and must draw conclusions from what he or she observes in their appearance and behavior. And, of course, when the writer permits the animals to talk with one another in human speech, realism is destroyed. Burnford, however, has developed the characters of her animals primarily through observation of their behavior, and we therefore believe in their reality.

Science Fiction

It is possible to write convincingly both about animal characters behaving like people, and about animal characters behaving in a manner true to their real animal natures. But at the other end of the scale are stories about human characters who have lost all of their human warmth and emotion and become the pure intellects sometimes found in science fiction. In poor science fiction the characters are often mere shadows of men. They aren't real, warm, or human, and readers cannot care about them. Such objections to character development verify what Sheila Egoff, in speaking of the tradition in humanism that characters develop gradually, says of science fiction: it is "little concerned with the complexities of human character."[4] In essence, this shallowness in character portrayal suggests that the central character or protagonist should be a round character, and his character unified with the action. The result of all this is that the character of the person governed in every relationship by intellect alone becomes one-dimensional, all mind. Surely, the idea that a scientist is only partly human is questionable. However, the characters of inferior science fiction do seem to be disproportionately governed by mind and mind's creations to the neglect of the remainder of human nature. Such protagonists are not people but inventiveness personified—stereotyped scientists.

Notice the characters of Ben Bova's *Flight of Exiles,* for example. First, the situation: 20,000 exiled scientists have been en route for fifty years to another planet in a deteriorating space ship. While the ship is in the hands of amateurs, fifty cryosealed people are burned to death, the one all-knowing scientist is killed, and astronomical data are erased. Who is the murderer? By page 45 we have met thirteen characters of almost equivalent development, names rather than people. We can scarcely be expected to identify the murderer, since we cannot identify the protagonist with certainty. He must be one of the two nearly interchangeable men, both of whom crave power, want control, love the same girl, and think in italics. Specialists—psychotechs, cryogenists, molecular geneticists, and an astronaut—are known only by their technical jobs. They, too, are flat—jealous and sharp-tongued, or beautiful and smart; they are angry, thoughtful, violent, and bitter in rapid succession and without clear motivation. In the terms of Henry James, character and action are not fused. Unlike real people who have reasons for their emotional shifts, Bova's shallow characters are so vacillating that, inevitably, we don't care about them, not even enough to wonder about the identity of the murderer. They are described from the outside, and, as Lillian Smith says, are only stage props to carry action.[5]

If we apply the same axioms of character development to science fiction as we do to other literature, we realize that believing in the reality of character makes us believe in the experience. If the experience is fantastic, as it is in science fiction, only a believable character can make us feel that the discoveries within the story have significance. Since poor character delineation limits our discovery about ourselves, action alone is left to hold our interest. However, since the action does not grow out of the nature of character, the plot seems contrived and unimportant. The failure of such a story is simply one of failure in character development.

Read for contrast Natalie Babbitt's *The Eyes of the Amaryllis,* in which Gran and Jenny's reality convinces us of the reality of their fantastic experience on the sea coast. Or notice Madeleine L'Engle's *A Wrinkle in Time,* fantasy which uses many of the devices of science fiction, yet does not rely on its machinery to produce story. Space and time fantasy can have fully developed character, and yet retain the ingenuity we find in science fiction. Even though the characters of *A Wrinkle in Time* have special mental powers, they do not lose their humanness. Father, the brilliant scientist, through sheer human weariness has lost his fight with IT, the huge, disembodied brain. Meg struggles to hold back Charles Wallace, who—arrogantly believing in the superiority of mind—is drawn into IT's control. Meg's human stubbornness helps her rescue her father, but in the process she leaves Charles Wallace. Sustained by the strength of an indomitable human force, love, Meg returns to rescue her brother and reunite the family. We can be made to care about the action, the ideas, the characters, and their relationships—when the characters are believable.

Classics

A *classic* is a book that lasts—not because it is continually enshrined on lists and because people talk about it, but because it continues to be read.[6] The most memorable stories, those that like *Peter Rabbit* we take with us from childhood to adulthood, are those that create solid and believable characters. Frequently, what characters did—or the plot—has faded from memory, but we recall the characters themselves with vividness.

Look at two classics read perhaps by more girls and boys than any other two. They are two very different novels: Louisa May Alcott's *Little Women,* which has very little action or plot, is primarily a story of daily activity, even routine, and the thinking and doing of five females. Mark Twain's *Tom Sawyer* has many chapters of seemingly unrelated episodes, but is filled with action and suspense leading to an exciting climax and discovery.

It is the character of Jo March that carries *Little Women* and has made it one of girlhood's favorites.[7] In her family, composed of vain Amy, saintly Beth, proper Meg, and worn but cheerful Marmee, Jo is the center. Jo is alive—aggressive and tomboyish, awkward and clumsy. She invents, acts, directs, complains and teases, sings off-key, and resents any restriction that would turn her into a stereotyped girl. She makes up games, dreams of heroism in active roles, and without guilt or gloom drops her bread on the carpet, butter side down.

Tom Sawyer is a second classic example of memorable character —as innumerable imitations tend to prove. Tom, seeking freedom, goes off pirating; fear-stricken, observes a murder; ingeniously hunts treasure; smugly attends his own funeral; level-headedly finds the way out of the cave; contritely does favors for Muff Potter; and courageously gives evidence in court. We remember Tom for the variety of character traits, each demonstrated in episodes of action throughout a long and absorbing story.

Not all characters are as memorable as Tom Sawyer or Jo March, but there are others. The Ugly Duckling and Peter Rabbit have been tested and have endured. Perhaps even Wilbur will live as long as Tom and Jo. However, other characters are so real to us that we feel we would recognize them on the street—characters like the three pets of *The Incredible Journey* and Laura of *The Little House* books. Our pleasure in our earliest introduction to the characters is renewed each time we recall an event from the plots involving them. Because we have known these characters, we have not only experienced vicariously their exciting adventures, but we have come to understand something about ourselves and others.

SUMMARY

In life and in books children can sense differences in human beings and are capable of recognizing and responding to well-developed character. Even in the simplest stories it is possible to find character that verifies truth about human nature. We meet these characters in action that seems part of their natures. We learn to know them—whether they be personified objects, real or personified animals, or human beings—by their appearances, words, actions, and thoughts, and the opinions of others about them. Round characters have many traits, while flat characters have limited development. Two kinds of characters that serve as background figures or contrasts are stereotypes and foils. Central characters in the action are round, so that by believing in their reality we are led to discover something about humanity, and are thereby convinced that the conflict in the story, like conflict in life, is significant. The round characters may or may not change, but if they do, we expect such change to be convincing.

We find great pleasure in reading about people like ourselves, beings both wise and foolish, brave and cowardly, frightened and confident, lonely and secure. It is this pleasure of recognition that leads to understanding. Children as much as adults, or perhaps even more than adults, need the discovery of themselves as part of humanity. Conversely, they need the pleasure of discovering that humanity exists in themselves. If literature is to help children understand the nature of human beings, we need reality in the portrayal of character. Nothing— not style, nor conflict, nor adventure, nor suspense, nor vivid setting, nor laughter, nor tears—nothing can substitute for solid character development in creating a pleasurable and lasting literature for children as well as for adults.

Reading and Evaluating

Picture book

1. *Read six picture-story books. In which ones is the central character well-developed? Is character determined by action? Action determined by character? Find a picture-story book in which the protagonist is a flat or a stereotyped character. What is the effect on the action? On interest? Are there other elements to hold interest and compensate for the flat character?*

Historical fiction

2. *Read or reread one of the Laura Ingalls Wilder* Little House *books. Is the protagonist a round character? Compare the character of Laura with that of another child from a story of pioneers. Is the protagonist round? If dynamic, can you follow the process of change throughout the action?*

Social Issues realism

3. *Read a novel about a member of a minority group, one written in the last eight years. If the protagonist changes, is the change convincing? Is the protagonist round or flat? Does it matter whether the*

change is convincing? Might the reader's guilt about Americans' treatment of minorities interfere with judgment about literary quality? How?

Problem realism   4. Read a recent book about a character with a problem of some kind. Is the protagonist a round character, or merely a composite of traits that make the character seem flat? Can the reader follow the change —if there is change—throughout the action as it unfolds? Is there a second character, less well-developed, who seems to change? Is it a believable change? Why or why not?

Science fiction   5. Read a science fiction story by Ben Bova, William Sleator, Eleanor Cameron, Andre Norton, or another writer and examine the development of the protagonist as a credible human being. Is he or she a round character? Flat? Dynamic or static? If the protagonist changes, is the change convincing? What is the effect?

Realistic novel   6. Read either a novel you remember from later childhood or a classic you missed. Evaluate the characters. Who are flat, round, foil, stereotype, dynamic, and static? How do you come to know them? Do you discover anything about human nature that seems true or worth discovering? Do you believe this discovery has any relationship either to your remembering the novel or to its continuous popularity with your friends? Was its popularity a matter of temporary circumstances or of universal character interest?

Fantasy   7. Read a high fantasy by one of the writers mentioned in the chapter or by another writer. Is the character fully developed? Does the character believe in the reality of the fantasy world created in the story? Are you willing to suspend disbelief? Is the portrayal of character one source of your willingness?

Notes

[1]Henry James, *The Art of Fiction,* New York: Oxford University Press, 1948, p. 13.

[2]Sheila Egoff, *The Republic of Childhood,* Toronto: Oxford University Press, 1967, p. 4.

[3]Paul Hazard, *Books, Children, and Men,* Boston: The Horn Book, Inc., 1960, p. 98.

[4]Sheila Egoff, "Science Fiction," in *Only Connect,* Sheila Egoff, G. T. Stubbs, and L. F. Ashley, Editors, Toronto and New York: Oxford University Press, 1969, p. 392.

[5]*The Unreluctant Years,* New York: Viking, 1967, p. 137.

[6]For a discussion of classics and how the lists are made, see James Steel Smith, "Children's Classics," *A Critical Approach to Children's Literature,* New York: McGraw-Hill, 1967, pp. 111 ff.

[7]As we will note in the chapter on theme, the strengths of *Little Women* lie in theme as well as character.

Recommended Books Cited in This Chapter

Alcott, Louisa May. *Little Women.* New York: Dutton, 1948. (first published 1868–69)

Alexander, Lloyd. *The High King.* New York: Holt, 1968.

Andersen, Hans Christian. *The Fir Tree.* New York: Harper, 1970.

――――. *The Steadfast Tin Soldier.* New York: Atheneum, 1971.

――――. *The Ugly Duckling.* New York: Macmillan, 1967.

Babbitt, Natalie. *The Eyes of the Amaryllis.* New York: Farrar, 1977.

Burnford, Sheila. *The Incredible Journey.* Boston: Little, 1961.

Eckert, Allan. *Incident at Hawk's Hill.* Boston: Little, 1971.

Fitzhugh, Louise. *Harriet the Spy.* New York: Harper, 1964.

Grahame, Kenneth. *The Wind in the Willows.* New York: Scribner's, 1953. (first published 1908)

Keats, Ezra Jack. *The Snowy Day.* New York: Viking, 1962.

Konigsburg, E. L. *Jennifer, Hecate, Macbeth, William McKinley, and Me, Elizabeth.* New York: Atheneum, 1967.

――――. *From the Mixed-Up Files of Mrs. Basil E. Frankweiler.* New York: Atheneum, 1974.

L'Engle, Madeleine. *A Wrinkle in Time.* New York: Farrar, 1962.

O'Dell, Scott. *Island of the Blue Dolphins.* Boston: Houghton, 1960.

Paterson, Katherine. *The Great Gilly Hopkins.* New York: Crowell, 1978.

Potter, Beatrix. *The Tale of Peter Rabbit.* New York: Warne, 1902.

Twain, Mark. *The Adventures of Tom Sawyer.* New York: Macmillan, 1966. (first published, 1876)

White, E.B. *Charlotte's Web.* New York: Harper, 1952

Wilder, Laura Ingalls. The *Little House* Books. New York: Harper, 1953. (first published 1932–43)

While some adult readers may be more interested in character than in any other element in the story, most of us—and most children —cannot get involved with stories that are only character studies. We want things to move and things to happen. The order in which things move and things happen in a story is what we call *plot.* Plot is the sequence of events showing characters in action. This sequence is not accidental but is chosen by the author as the best way of telling his or her story. If the writer has chosen well, the plot will produce conflict, tension, and action that will arouse and hold our interest.

The child wants what most adults want in literature: action, happenings, questions that need answers, answers that fit questions, glimpses of happy and unhappy outcomes, discovery of how events grow and turn. For the very small child there is pleasure in finding recognition of daily routine within the pages of a book, but many people think that *all* a child needs in a narrative is the recognition in printed words of an everyday happening that they call action—an action as prosaic as going to bed at night or waking up in the morning. It is surprising that adults who would never find pleasure in a literal, hour-by-hour account of their own daily routines expect such accounts of children's daily lives to satisfy them. No matter how content the young are with daily order, children very soon expect that they should find life more exciting in a story than in their own experience. Here, in a book, children and adults alike can lose themselves in the excitement of possibility as they pose the big question of all literature: What if? This element of possibility, of possible action and reaction that confronts character, builds the plot.

TYPES OF NARRATIVE ORDER

One of the privileges of the writer is to reorder existence, to rearrange events, or in other words, to create plot. The writer may focus on one moment of a day and ignore all others, or charge one hour with significance and portent that influence months or years of a life. The writer may either ignore the segments of time that have little significance, or simply summarize those moments. The writer makes alterations and deletions that our memories are unable to make for us in our own lives. The writer's selectivity and purposeful reordering and highlighting create plot.

Narrative order in fiction, the order in which events are related, may follow several patterns, but the most common pattern in children's literature is the chronological arrangement.

Chronological Order

As we all know, our lives are one 24-hour period followed by another. This time order is simple chronology. If a story relates events in the order of their happening, the story is in *chronological order.* The story can move about with the characters from one place of action to another and still be chronological. The writer may make the story line more complex by showing action that occurs with one character in one place and then turning to action that occurs to another simultaneously, but in another place: "Meanwhile, back at the ranch. . . ." The accounts of simultaneous action follow one another in the story, but the events have occupied the same point in time; therefore, the action is still chronological.

Flashbacks

In fiction for mature readers, narrative order may involve *flashbacks.* Many readers can recall their first experience with a flashback; it was puzzling. "What happened? How come?" The writer has chosen to disrupt normal time sequence to recount some episode out of the character's past, showing how that event influences the character's response to an event in the present. Or the writer shows in flashback a past event that has brought on the present one. In either case, the writer chooses to juggle time to make a point about the character and the character's story. The small child, however, may find it difficult to follow such movement back and forth in time.[1]

The child relies on his or her own experience of time for understanding when and how events occur. Since the child knows from experience, for instance, that one falls asleep and dreams, he or she understands Maurice Sendak's *Where the Wild Things Are.* The child knows that such a marvelous adventure could happen to Max while he is asleep, since the child has had similar dreams. As the child grows in sophistication, he or she comes to comprehend the possibility in literature of mixing memory, imagination, dream, daydream, and flashback.

However, for the young child, and most likely for the child being read to, the narrative order or story line is most successful when it is chronological, that is, when it is within the limits of the child's experience of time and thus within the child's comprehension. As the child matures, the experience of literature provides growing recognition of time in its infinite variations. Jean George, for example, uses flashback effectively in *Julie of the Wolves* by plunging into the story of Miyax's or Julie's dependence upon the wolves for survival on the Arctic tundra. In a flashback Part II, "Miyax, the girl" tells us of her early life, and then Part III returns us to Miyax's struggle and safe arrival at her father's house. Television probably increases children's exposure to flashback and dream techniques, and this experience could help them to recognize the techniques in literature.

CONFLICT

Plot is a more inclusive term than narrative order or its synonym, story line, since it involves not only sequence of events, but also *conflict.* In this discussion of books for the young, tension, friction, force, alternatives, excitement, suspense, discovery, and resolution are parts of conflict. Conflict occurs when the protagonist struggles against an *antagonist* or opposing force. In short, it is conflict which, added to narrative order, makes plot.

In the following subsections we will discuss four kinds of conflict in literature: person-against-self, person-against-person, person-against-society, and person-against-nature.

Person-Against-Self

Consider, for example, the classic *Tom Sawyer,* which has a plot of such complexity that we can discover several types of conflict. Mark Twain shows Tom as he faces an internal conflict, a tension within Tom that pulls him toward either of two courses of action. Tom happens to see Injun Joe murder the doctor. He makes a pact not to reveal what he has seen, and signs it with his blood, but Tom cannot forget that the town has condemned innocent Muff Potter while Injun Joe goes free. Tom takes tobacco and matches to Muff in jail. He often speculates about how to free him. Afraid of Injun Joe's revenge, but guilty about keeping Muff's innocence secret, Tom cannot sleep. When he does, he talks in his sleep; fearful lest he tell what troubles him, Tom ties his mouth shut. Such an internal struggle is between Tom's fear and his conscience, and there is no mistaking its intensity. When Tom's conscience—his keen awareness of his moral responsibility even in the face of danger—wins the battle, he goes to the judge to tell the truth about the murder. Such an internal conflict of feelings within the protagonist is called **person-against-self.** This kind of conflict also exists for the narrator in *My Brother Sam Is Dead* as he struggles with his anger and bewilderment—to be a Tory, or to be a Rebel like his brother.

Inner conflicts may exist with far less tension. In *Jennifer, Hecate, Macbeth, William McKinley, and Me, Elizabeth* by E. L. Konigsburg, Elizabeth as the new girl in school needs to become not merely a satellite of either Jennifer or Cynthia, but a person in her own right. When Elizabeth the journeyman witch manages a few spells on her own, she "feels very competent"; from this point she continues to establish herself as an independent partner in friendship with Jennifer. Her inner conflict is then resolved.

In Evaline Ness's *Sam, Bangs, & Moonshine,* Sam the fantasizer must learn for herself the difference between good and bad moonshine. Curling up in her "chariot" to daydream is good moonshine, but sending Thomas off on a dangerous search for Sam's mermaid mother is bad moonshine. Sam discovers the difference when she worries through the rescue of Thomas and the near drowning of Bangs the cat.

Tensions and conflicts in stories vary; some seem more likely to occur in the lives of children and may, therefore, seem more real, but others may give readers glimpses of important moral issues.

Person-Against-Person

There is still another conflict that Tom Sawyer must face. Muff Potter is freed only because Tom has the courage to testify—in court and in Injun Joe's presence—that Joe is the murderer. From the moment of his testimony, Tom's life is in danger. Injun Joe disappears, and then disguised as a deaf and dumb Spaniard, he comes back to prey upon the town and to steal the buried treasure. Once again Injun Joe is a very real threat to Tom's life. As the boys hide breathlessly in the haunted house, they know that Injun Joe will viciously turn on them if he finds them there. Later, lost in the cave with Becky, Tom catches a glimpse of Injun Joe and knows that his murderous enemy is close by, hiding from the law. Here we have Tom against Injun Joe, a **person-against-person** conflict.

The terms in which we describe the conflict are not so important. What does matter is that we see clearly the protagonist and the antagonist. The strain between the two forces is what holds our continuing interest and our intense curiosity about the outcome. It is Tom's internal, growing awareness of justice opposing his fear for his life that finally forces him to take action, and this action confronts Tom with the vengeance of a villainous man, Injun Joe. Children's literature is filled with suspenseful examples of person-against-person conflict, from Peter Rabbit's evasion of Mr. McGregor or Michael's conflict with his mother to let his grandmother keep her precious box in *The Hundred Penny Box* by Sharon Bell Mathis, to Meg's defeat of IT, the disembodied brain in *A Wrinkle in Time.*

Television cartoons, too, are filled with examples, as Woody Woodpecker frantically opposes the owl or Popeye opposes Brutus. In folktales, where protagonists are usually stereotypes, the person-against-person conflict is very common. Jack climbs the beanstalk and defeats the giant. Hansel and Gretel shove the wicked witch into the oven and all is well. Both Red Riding Hood and the Three Little Pigs face wolves. In some folktales the person-against-person conflict moves quickly and vigorously to conclusion, and in others conflict travels with gentle humor to an equally satisfactory resolution, as it does in "The Squire's Bride," or even in "The Old Woman and Her Pig."

Person-Against-Society

Conflict and an unknown outcome keep us reading *Charlotte's Web.* Wilbur's struggle is serious: life and death. Although we may define the struggle as a ***person-against-society*** conflict, the child knows it simply as "Will Wilbur live? Will Charlotte save him from being made into bacon?" In this case we may regard society as the farming business, which, after all, is based on profit. A runt pig is not worth keeping. Although the child reading *Charlotte's Web* gets involved in the conflict of Wilbur-versus-dinner-table, the conflict is actually Wilbur against good business. The conflict begins immediately, page one, line one: "Where's Papa going with the ax?" Whether or not Wilbur will be saved from death commands our interest. This conflict of Wilbur against the business of farming keeps our interest from start to finish.

Person-against-society conflict is much more easily understood by adults than by children. When we read, for example, of Hester Prynne's conflict with the Puritan society in *The Scarlet Letter,* we see society's instrument of degradation—the stocks. We know the society by bits of dialogue as the crowd shouts its taunts at Hester's back, or plots to take Pearl from Hester. To children, however, society as antagonist is more clear if it is represented by definite persons within the society. Mary Jane in Dorothy Sterling's story of school integration, *Mary Jane*, faces insults from specific children in the halls, from thoughtlessness of specific teachers, and from specific rules that prohibit her going to the park. In Tien Pao's conflict with society in *The*

House of Sixty Fathers, the airplanes and the devastation they bring to sampans and thatched huts represent the antagonist society. The enemy lookouts and the horsemen on patrol are identifiable human fragments of the war-making society. They serve to make the conflict understandable.

Person-Against-Nature

Julie in Jean George's novel *Julie of the Wolves* experiences a ***person-against-nature*** conflict. Having run away from her village to the wild frozen Arctic lands, Julie faces possible death by freezing and starvation. The wolves who befriend her save her life, leaving her to continue her search for her father. *Island of the Blue Dolphins* is believable because Scott O'Dell has spent considerable time describing nature and has made it a complex antagonist. First of all, Karana's people have always lived with nature, using its bounty, conserving its offerings, and preparing for its dangers. However, when Karana is left alone, she is forced to violate the taboos accepted by the tribe in order to survive; Karana, a young woman, must make weapons to defend herself against nature, and we fear that the spirits will punish her. Around her cave she must build a whale-rib fence to keep out the wild dogs. She must fight infection from injury caused by falling on the rocks; she is defeated by the sea when her canoe is too leaky for a voyage into the morning sun. The protagonist is threatened by one element after another, each one a component of nature, the antagonist. Karana's conflict is dramatic, building up to the earthquake and its following tidal wave:

> I stood facing the rock, with my feet on a narrow ledge and one hand thrust deep into a crack. Over my shoulder I could see the wave coming. It did not come fast, for the other wave was still running out. For a while I thought that it would not come at all because the two suddenly met beyond the sandspit. The first wave was trying to reach the sea and the second one was struggling toward the shore.
> Like two giants they crashed against. . . .

Although person-against-nature conflict seems less frequent in literature for younger children, Armstrong Sperry in *Call It Courage* shows Mafatu battling his fears of nature in his effort to become a man. After his shipwreck—a defeat by the sea—Mafatu must kill the tiger shark which attacks his dog Uri, the wild boar which attacks Mafatu, and the octopus which surprises him during his dive for his lost knife. To return to his own people, Mafatu must make a canoe strong enough to keep out the sea and carry him home. Although conflict is further complison-against-self conflict is largely dependent upon his victory in his conflict with nature.

Conflict of any kind grows out of character. Peter Rabbit's character—his mischievous nature, combining curiosity with greed—brings him to Mr. McGregor's garden and keeps him eating long enough to be discovered. Karana's womanhood and the traits it implies in her culture make her struggle against nature even more suspenseful. Tien Pao's innocence and youth highlight his conflict with a society at war. Tom Sawyer's inner conflict of conscience results from his sense of loyalty and justice.

There are stories, of course, with minimally developed character in which conflict carries all of the reader's interest; some are mysteries like *Nancy Drew,* with plots so contrived and episodes so coincidental that children are finally bored. Picture-story books may also rely upon conflict apart from character, as does *Goggles!* by Ezra Jack Keats, in which setting determines conflict more than does character; we know nothing about the two playmates save that they run from bigger boys who want their goggles and that a dachshund saves the goggles. The traditional stories from folk origins do not depict fully developed protagonists, but rely upon universal human traits and dreams expressed in their themes. These themes seem to take the place of character as the origin for conflict.

Intent upon conflict, television often neglects to create a fully drawn protagonist; as a result children do not learn to see the relationship between conflict and character. Plot incidents seem merely to happen *to* protagonists, rather than to be brought about by the protagonist's personal traits; the result is a dramatic story that makes little contribution to the viewer's understanding of human beings.

PATTERNS OF ACTION

Plot is more than the sequence of actions or conflict. It is also the pattern of those actions. If we were to describe plot patterns by diagrams, we might describe them with these shapes:

The first of these patterns moves from one incident to another related incident, building upon discoveries and changes toward a final climax that brings the action to its peak. Such a pattern is most clearly demonstrated in Mary Norton's *The Borrowers.* This particular story has a *frame,* since it begins and ends with Mrs. May relating the events to Kate. The frame encloses the developing plot and within it occur the events that involve the Clock family. The borrowers change from people with simple needs to a family ruled by their possessions. Homily's materialistic grab for more and more leads to discovery, to the rat-catchers, the fumigators, and the high suspense surrounding the family's escape. In the final chapter, a return of focus to Mrs. May and Kate, we know only that the borrowers might have established a new home by the hawthorne hedge, or, perhaps, that the family might have been a figment of a small boy's imagination. The plot line of development has moved steadily upward to leave us in uncertainty.

The second of these patterns of action can be demonstrated by *Jennifer, Hecate, Macbeth, William McKinley, and Me, Elizabeth.* Action moves along with tension that does not mount to a breaking point, but that keeps us interested and concerned about the growing friendship between Jennifer and Elizabeth. The conflict—and there is conflict despite minimal suspense—exists as concern, curiosity, and pleasure in the narrator who is unraveling her story as she wonders and worries, tries to or refuses to conform to witch-Jennifer's demands. In *Little House in the Big Woods,* Laura Ingalls Wilder shows Laura's life as eventful and filled with pleasure; the security of Laura's home keeps the reader interested in day-to-day happenings, but without building anxiety. This kind of action follows a straight line plot pattern.

The third pattern of action is a bit more complex. The story rises to some climax and then trails off. **Rising action** begins with a situation that must be shown and explained; we must know what has happened before the story opens, what has created the current situation. This explanation of the situation and the condition of the characters is called **exposition.** The exposition in most stories for children is woven into early action so that attention is caught immediately and held. When, for example, on page eight of *Roll of Thunder, Hear My Cry,* Little Man is nearly run down by the school bus loaded with white children, we are aware of the situation, of the feelings between blacks and whites. Since children's stories are usually short and must move quickly, **complications** begin very soon. The elements of a story that deal with rising action are: suspense, the cliffhanger, foreshadowing, sensationalism, the climax, denouement, and inevitability. Each of these terms will be treated separately in the following subsections.

Suspense

From the first line in the first chapter of *Charlotte's Web*—"Where's Papa going with the ax?"—we know that Wilbur's fate is uncertain, and from that initial moment White holds us in *suspense,* a state that makes us read on. By tears, sobs, cries, and yells, Fern wins temporary reprieve for Wilbur and he becomes Fern's baby. Wilbur's brothers and sisters are all sold and it becomes Wilbur's turn. There goes Wilbur. But, see if Uncle Homer Zuckerman will buy Wilbur so Fern can visit him at the nearby farm. Wilbur is lonely, finding his life boring without Fern as constant companion. When he finds a friend, loneliness vanishes. Then, electrifying news comes: An old sheep spitefully tells Wilbur he is being fattened for Christmas slaughter. Charlotte to the rescue. She weaves the words "Some Pig" into her web; people come from miles around to see Wilbur. Mr. Zuckerman now admires him, and no celebrity was ever made into sausage.

As the excitement wears off, our worries revive. Charlotte, however, sends Templeton to the dump for more words. When each of the woven words miraculously appears, we have new hope. Then Wilbur's protector announces regretfully that she cannot accompany Wilbur to the Fair. Catastrophe looms again, but a ray of hope glimmers: "We'll leave it this way: I'll come to the Fair if I possibly can." Our security lasts only until we overhear Arable and Zuckerman talking about the fine hams and bacon he'll make. A huge pig called Uncle is appallingly stiff competition: "He's going to be a hard pig to beat." Wilbur's doom is sealed. Suddenly, an unprecedented award, but Wilbur faints and "We can't give a prize to a *dead* pig. . . . It's never been done before." No prize. Then Templeton bites Wilbur's tail, and Wilbur revives and wins the prize.

But Charlotte is languishing. Can Wilbur survive without Charlotte? Charlotte spins her final Magnum Opus and dies, and Wilbur, now mature, takes responsibility for Charlotte's egg sac. When spring comes, Wilbur is still alive and hearty, and life continues.

Suspense, the emotional pull that keeps us wanting to read on, involves us in conflict up to the climax in the final pages. These moments of suspense are not panic points in the story; nor at any point do we know the outcome with certainty. White controls the suspense to keep it peaking and leveling, and at every point we remain not only curious but concerned for the outcome, because either success or failure looms and we cannot be completely certain which will prevail.

Suspense has kept us reading, but White has carefully led us with optimism and never despair. Throughout the suspense, even in spite of it, we feel that all will be well, somehow. The author skillfully builds the story so that nowhere is the ending too predictable, lest we lose interest, nor too frightful, lest we give up. At the end of the book, the adult or child reader feels that the ups and downs of "perhaps he'll win, perhaps he'll lose" are finally settled. Suspense does not go beyond the story's ending. White, as he pulls us to the satisfactory end of the story, makes us heave a final, relieved sigh. The feeling that all will be well, even after the final page, results from White's skill in handling suspense. Our optimism has been justified. To cite another example, the authors of *Where the Lilies Bloom* keep us in suspense by implied questions: Will Roy Luther die? Will his death be discovered? Will the children be sent to the county home? Will Kiser honor his bargain about the house? Will they have to move into a cave? Such suspense keeps us reading.

The Cliffhanger

A form of suspense that White does not use is the **cliffhanger,** the exciting chapter ending that makes it hard to lay the book aside. Unlike the chapters in *Charlotte's Web,* wherein each contributes to the development of central conflict in the total plot, each moving to its own peak and yet managing to end quietly, the cliffhanger chapter ends with such suspense that the plea for just one more chapter is irresistible. The cliffhanger is most obvious in the series novels like *Nancy Drew* and the *Hardy Boys,* and in today's soap operas, as well as in newspaper, magazine, and Saturday movie serials of the past. Each child left the darkened theater for the afternoon sunlight, worried about the hero, left, perhaps literally, hanging by the fingernails from a sheer cliff. The hero was in mortal danger and might not survive until the following Saturday matinee.

This dramatic device for building suspense is exemplified clearly in *The Borrowers.* These tiny people live in constant fear of being seen, and many chapters end with this fear expressed. Chapter 4 ends with Arrietty's parents talking:

> "She doesn't know about Eggletina. She doesn't know about being 'seen.' "
> "Well," said Pod, "we'll tell her. We always said we would. There's no hurry."
> Homily stood up. "Pod," she said, "we're going to tell her now."

And Chapter 8 ends: "Startled, she caught her breath. Something had glittered. Arrietty stared." When the climax is close, the housekeeper says at the conclusion of Chapter 17, "The police, that's what this means

—a case for the police." Note, too, the cliffhangers of *The High King* which conclude with such lines as "Wicked Queen is gone!" or "Magg's jaws will close on them as tightly as they are closed on us," and " 'Smoke,' he gasped." The intensity of the suspense varies from chapter to chapter, but the hook that catches us at the end of one section carries us relentlessly into the next, since we must know what happens.

Foreshadowing

The writer for children must decide how much suspense the child can sustain, and how much reassurance is needed to balance suspense. To relieve the reader's anxiety and to produce a satisfying sense of the inevitable, the writer must see that there are clues about the outcome —without the suspense being destroyed. Such clues must be planted artfully and unobtrusively within the action. Not all readers will be alert to all dropped hints, it is true, but White in *Charlotte's Web* uses them to hint at Wilbur's ultimate safety and Charlotte's death, and to reassure us that finally all will be well. These planted clues indicate outcome and are called *foreshadowing.*

In Wilbur's first conversation with Charlotte, we learn that gentle Charlotte lives by eating living things, and friendship looks questionable. Feeling a need for reassurance, White adds that "she had a kind heart, and she was to prove loyal and true to the very end." The first clue suggests friendship; the second, "to the very end," has a prophetic ring.

Foreshadowing and suspense balance throughout the narrative. When in "Bad News" Wilbur hears he is being fattened for slaughter, he wails. However, his safety is foreshadowed when Charlotte asserts calmly, "I am going to save you."

Another event for which we must be prepared is Charlotte's death. If her death had been unforeseen, we would be justified in accusing White of playing with our emotions. But Charlotte's acceptance of her life span foreshadows her approaching death and prepares Wilbur and the readers. The song of the crickets foreshadows death of all kinds. "Summer is over and gone. . . . Over and gone. . . . Summer is dying, dying," they sing. Charlotte, whose life like the crickets and the seasons has a predictable cycle, "heard it and knew that she hadn't much time left." Of the word "humble," she says, "It is the last word I shall ever write." When she says that she is "languishing," she is peaceful and contented, and we are as resigned as she. *Charlotte's Web* concludes with a sense of inevitability, and even, because of the 514 baby spiders, with a sense of optimism.

Clear examples of foreshadowing occur throughout good children's stories. For example, in William Armstrong's *Sounder,* the father has been sent to prison for stealing food for his family. When at long last a figure appears in the red dust of the road, Sounder the coonhound revives. Once near death from the sheriff's gunshots, now, before the approaching figure is identifiable, Sounder pants, whines, wags his tail, and paces the dooryard. His agitation foreshadows the father's limping return.

Sensationalism

The author must drop hints about what is ahead, if the reader is to feel satisfaction as the story unfolds. In the strong life and death conflict that White creates in *Charlotte's Web,* unrelieved suspense might be too much for the small child. The skill of the writer lies in balancing two elements —suspense over the action and hints at the outcome.

Unrelieved suspense, however, makes a story *sensational;* it plays us like instruments, keeping us holding our breaths in crescendoes of anxiety. The writer for adults has greater latitude in the creation of anxiety, since adults can tolerate it. With persistent enthusiasm, some adults read **sensationalism:** mystery stories, murder thrillers, and survival adventures. The suspense absorbs them; they breathe horror and terror with the protagonist. However, they are never deceived, since they never forget that it's just a story. Other adults find themselves bored with the unrelieved suspense because they, too, know that it's just a story, and, wanting more than sensationalism, they seek some discovery of real people in suspenseful action. They demand the significance of well-developed character in a conflict that reveals something about human beings.

A situation of unrelieved suspense, on the other hand, may be more than a child can bear. Take, for example, the folktale "Snow White and the Seven Dwarfs." The storyteller, watching the expressive faces of the listeners, relieves the suspense with reassuring hints about outcome. Walt Disney in making the movie, however, turned suspense to sensationalism and many children were upset by it. The ugly witch with clawlike hands and viciously evil features roused sheer terror. Many children hid their faces and suffered nightmares long after they had seen "the great children's story come alive on the screen."

Any action may be made sensational, but important and even violent events can be described with accuracy and sensitivity, yet without sensationalism. For example, the Colliers description of Sam's execution before a firing squad at the end of *My Brother Sam Is Dead* achieves this. Sensationalism results when the writer focuses on the thrilling or startling at the expense of character and idea.

The Climax

The peak and turning point of the conflict, the point at which we know the outcome of the action, is called the *climax*. Throughout the development of plot, from initial recognition of the conflict through the critical turns and irregular progress, past reversals and discoveries, up to the point where we know who wins the conflict, we follow the plot to the climax. While we speak of the climax as the turning point in the conflict, children call it "the most exciting part," or "where I knew how it would come out." No matter which term is used, the climax is inextricably related to conflict.

Although Paula Vinson's story *Willie Goes to the Seashore* is classified as fiction in the Library of Congress listing, it lacks climax because it lacks any conflict. Instead of plot being resolved, it merely peters out. Instead of coming to a decisive conclusion, the narrative just quits. The result is disappointment.

Climax of some kind exists in any story with conflict (Hooray! Peter Rabbit made it through the gate!), although the climax may come with varying degrees of intensity or varying closeness to the end of the story. In *Sam, Bangs & Moonshine,* for example, the quiet climax comes on the final page when Sam takes her gerbil over to Thomas and tells him it is his, and its name is "Moonshine!" Sam has resolved the conflict in her mind and now knows the difference between fantasizing that is harmless and harmful, between good and bad moonshine. In *The Loner* Esther Wier shows a confrontation between David the shepherd and the bear; in dramatic action, the conflict is resolved as David discovers his courage and yet knows that he did not have to kill the bear to earn acceptance. In the three parts of *Beowulf,* there are dramatic confrontations and triumphant battles between Beowulf and Grendel, Beowulf and Grendel's mother, and finally between Beowulf and the dragon.

However, look at the quiet climax of *Charlotte's Web.* Here, in the conflict of person-against-society, Wilbur is in a life-and-death struggle. The climax logically comes when we know that he will live. Checking on suspense, we find that the high point, brought on by frequent minor crises and excitement peaks, finally comes when Wilbur revives and wins the prize—the handsome bronze medal for "attracting so many visitors to our great County Fair." The runt pig has defeated good business, since Wilbur has taken the final round of the contest. By his additional award—the special prize of twenty-five dollars—Zuckerman is rewarded with money and Wilbur is a good business investment after all; this is the climax. From here on Wilbur has nothing to worry about; the conflict is resolved.

In *The Borrowers,* where the conflict pits the family of tiny people against Mrs. Driver the housekeeper, the climax comes within a few exciting pages of the end. Mrs. Driver's discovery of "the little varmints," living amidst their borrowed luxuries below the floorboards, brings on the rat-catchers. They board up the gratings and seal the space below the floor. Then they start the gas and the fumigating bellows, hoping to kill the creatures, whatever they are. But the borrowers, with whom we have worried about emigrating since Chapter 1, have a friend in the Boy who sets out to give them ventilation:

> Pick-ax in hand [he] ran out of the door. . . . Already, when he reached it, a thin filament of smoke was eddying out of the grating . . . a flicker of movement against the darkness between the bars. . . . behind him the crunch of wheels on the gravel and the sound of the horse's hoofs. . . . [W]ith two great blows on the brickwork, he dislodged . . . the grating. It fell. . . .

Although we do not see the borrowers fleeing from the gas, we think they may have escaped. With the air-tight grating gone, their path to fresh air and freedom is open.

The Witch of Blackbird Pond poses a conflict of a young woman who emigrates from the Barbados to the witch-hunting Puritan society of New England. Elizabeth George Speare shows us how Kit's independence, her compassion, her defiance of ridiculous rules, and even her luxurious wardrobe and her swimming ability work against her to prove to the Puritans that she is a witch. Accusation and trial bring us to the climax. At the hearing, filled with the accusations of the townspeople, rising suspense keeps the reader hoping for the climax. The accuser, faced with evidence that Kit has not bewitched his child but has taught her to read, drops charges, and Kit is now free and innocent. Throughout the story we have followed each indication that Kit is different, that she is willful, and that she will not conform; we have seen the frowning and suspicious community and concluded that witchcraft charges will be brought. But it has not all been so pat. Will Prudence be brave enough to prove that Kit was teaching and not bewitching her? Will Nat's ship be in port? Will he be able to help Kit? He has been forbidden to enter the town; how can he help? Will he be able to convince the villagers of the truth? When all these questions have been answered, the climax is reached.

The final chapter of A Wrinkle in Time is filled with Meg's thoughts, and yet Madeleine L'Engle maintains suspense to the climax. When Meg the protagonist finally gathers her courage to return to Camazotz and to confront the monster brain that holds her brother prisoner, we know that the climax approaches. Meg discovers that she has love and IT has not; she adds all the love of those who surround her with all she feels for them, and love and will together defeat evil and bring joy. Only when Meg's battle with IT frees the last hostage are we satisfied about the final outcome. Conflict and suspense have been intense until the last two pages.

Because of *Tom Sawyer's* complex conflict, the turning point is difficult to determine. When Tom's conscience wins over his fears, he goes to court and by his testimony frees Muff Potter. Yet, when that is over, we have remaining a strong person-against-person conflict, since Tom is not really safe until he no longer fears vengeance from Injun Joe. Tom comes out of the cave; the public makes him a hero when they learn how he protected Becky in the crisis. The buried treasure is his, and yet we wonder about the whereabouts of Injun Joe. When we learn that he has died of hunger and thirst inside the cave, we know that Tom need no longer fear for his life.

But somehow other events have relieved our fears even before the body of Injun Joe is found. Twain does not fully describe the climactic action, since at the end of Chapter 31 he shows Tom in the cave, kitestring in hand, saying good-bye to listless Becky. Then, one page into the following chapter, after a description of the mourning families, Twain sets the village bells pealing with celebration. We are not sure how it all happened, but we are hero-worshipers, and we give Tom credit for getting himself and Becky out of the cave. The celebration seems the climax, and finding the body of the defeated villain is just part of the falling action. In his involved plot Twain holds us captive for twenty-odd pages after the celebration to conclude the story satisfactorily.

In looking back over these examples of climax, we note that each involves the final battle of the protagonist with an antagonist. Each results in victory for the protagonist, and this victory seems right in children's literature. Anti-heroes, or badly flawed protagonists, and defeated protagonists are for adults only, or more accurately, for some adults only. The child has been involved in the life of a protagonist and wanted the protagonist to win. However, the winning has not happened without a struggle. There is a difference between a climax that says with sticky sweetness, "The world is good, since right always wins," and one that says, "The forces of evil are powerful, but courage and justice together can defeat them." A conflict brought to a climax makes the idea of the story clear through plot that has tension and resolution.

Denouement

Children who are following an exciting story may have trouble pinning down what for them is the climax. Agreeing on that, however, is not as important to the success of the story as agreeing that the story ends with a sense of completeness or *resolution.*

The **denouement** begins at the climax, at the point where we feel that the protagonist's fate is known. From here the action of the plot is also called the **falling action.** In the denouement of *Charlotte's Web,* Templeton and Wilbur, the two survivors of the original trio, reach a bargain about who eats first at Wilbur's trough. Wilbur returns the egg sac to the barn, and its presence sustains the feeling that Charlotte is still there. Finally, warmed and protected by Wilbur's breath, the eggs hatch. Joy, Aranea, and Nellie, three of Charlotte's tiny progeny, stay on in the barn to keep Wilbur company, and to learn from him the ways of barn life. The seasonal cycle continues; everything is resolved. There is no question left unanswered. We say there is a resolution.

When the reader is assured that all is well and will continue to be, we say that the denouement is closed, or that the plot has a **closed ending.** In this case, the tying of the loose ends is thoroughly optimistic and satisfactory, a good conclusion for a small child's story. There is no anxiety for reader or listener on the last page of *Charlotte's Web.* The sigh is not a breath of anxiety, but one of regret that so good a story is over.

An **open ending** in plot, on the other hand, is an occasional thing in adult fiction. In the open-ended story we are left to draw our own conclusions about final plot resolution. Among enduring examples of children's literature there seem to be few with open endings, although stories do appear from time to time. The anonymously written diary of a young drug user, *Go Ask Alice*, tells us that Alice dies of an overdose, but leaves open the question of who is responsible for the dosage, Alice herself or someone else. The realistic stories of the seventies, particularly those problem realism stories for the older child, occasionally leave the end open. *Guy Lenny* by Harry Mazer is an example; we are not certain whether Guy will choose to live with mother or with father, although we are left feeling that he is mature enough to make his own decision. An urgent question leaves us wondering at the end of *A hero ain't nothin' but a Sandwich:* Will Benjie show up for the drug counseling session?

Although some adult readers are intrigued by such inconclusive mystery, others find such endings frustrating. Just as some adults find the open-ended story unsatisfactory, many more children are left dissatisfied and unsure by unsolved mystery. Depending upon the gravity of the conflict and the maturity of the readers, they may even be left frightened. Without the experience and perspective needed to supply their own endings, some children may turn away from the story with a disturbing sense of anxiety. If tension has been high and the possible outcome serious, the unresolved plot and the open ending seem far less suitable for a children's story.

Inevitability

By White's use of the device called foreshadowing, we are well prepared for Wilbur's salvation and Charlotte's death. Her life is complete, and her mission accomplished. She has saved her dearest friend and produced her egg sac to carry on another spider generation. There is no other way for the story to end. Although there may be a shadow of sadness, there is a more profound sense of the quality called *inevitability,* or "it had to be." "It was inevitable" is high praise for a writer's skill in bringing plot to conclusion.

Properly motivated action that grows out of character provides inevitability, just as Peter Rabbit's curiosity and greed bring about his inevitable squeezing into Mr. McGregor's garden, his flight, and his stomachache. At the other end of the literary spectrum, Beowulf, "mightiest yet mildest of men," is the organizer and leader of the band who sail to Hrothgar's country to liberate it from Grendel's scourge. Since Beowulf is pure valor, unsullied by any past defeat or any selfish motive, and since his motive is love for his fellow beings, Beowulf cannot lose his battle with personified evil. Despite the suspense of the epic story, we are sure that such goodness will conquer evil. The battle must be to the death, since too easy a victory demeans the godlike hero. The struggle is satisfying in its intensity, but the outcome is inevitable.

The plot that depends for resolution of conflict upon sudden and incredible changes in character fails because of lack of inevitability. In Victor Barnouw's *Dream of the Blue Heron,* Mr. Wickham, the cruel disciplinarian, strangely and without foreshadowing becomes kind and sympathetic to Wabus. Wabus will someday be a lawyer because he can count on the assistance of the unbelievably reformed Wickham. Since the resolution of the conflict depends upon unbelievable character change, the plot lacks inevitability.

TYPES OF PLOTS

The plots of *Charlotte's Web* and *A Wrinkle in Time,* with their central climaxes followed quickly by denouement, are called *progressive plots.* Apparently people have always liked suspense and climax because the progressive plot is common in traditional literature. In "The Shoemaker and the Elves," for example, we move directly into the action from a few short phrases—"once upon a time," and "the couple was very poor." The first short paragraph also includes the elves' first visit and the work they leave behind. By the end of the second paragraph, the shoemaker is rich and we are halfway through the story. The couple hides to watch; their grateful gift of clothes for the elves brings on the climax—the dance of the delighted elves who then disappear. In "The Wolf and the Kids" the climax comes three lines from the end; filled with stones, the wolf falls into the well and drowns. The Bremen Town Musicians raise a furor that frightens the robbers away; the musicians stay forever. When the Fisherman tells the fish that his greedy wife wishes to be God —they are returned to their vinegar jug. The teller of oral tales knows that once the climax comes, he may lose his audience; he must finish the story quickly and conclusively.

Some book-length stories for children have another type of plot, an *episodic plot* in which one incident or short episode is linked to another by common characters or by a unified theme. A diagram of this plot might look like this:

A clear contrast to the progressive plot of *Charlotte's Web,* which we have already discussed in some detail, is the episodic one of *The Wind in the Willows.* Like White, Kenneth Grahame uses personified animals as characters in his fantasy. The book has twelve short chapters, each a separate story and each a part of the whole. Mole meets Rat, they picnic, and they meet Toad, who can think only of motor cars; Mole, lost in the Wild Wood, is found by Rat and they visit Mole's home. Toad "borrows" a car and is jailed, but he escapes and returns to Toad Hall.

The events of *The Wind in the Willows* are quiet in total effect, although many chapters have their own suspenseful conflict. Each chapter is an episode in a community of kindly animals whose lives are intertwined by loyalty and mutual concern. The suspense within each chapter is usually resolved within that chapter. Although there are twelve chapters, only the last two contribute to the conquest of Toad Hall.

Instead of a central conflict, what holds our interest is the relationships of the group of developed characters. Rat is consistently kind and reliable; Toad is consistently inconsistent, but Mole, as his self-confidence increases, changes from follower to leader. The community life of these diverse beings, living their leisurely and unselfish lives, is the discovery of *The Wind in the Willows.* In the unhurried progress through chapters that focus alternately on Rat and Mole, then on Toad, we are further warmed by discovering among other things that one loves one's home where one's belongings are, and that even the most contented finds faraway places alluring. The episodic plot relies upon characters, theme, and tension within each chapter, rather than upon suspenseful progress to the climax, to keep readers reading and listeners listening.

Winnie-the-Pooh supplies another example of episodic plot, and its form is well suited to its young listeners. One episode follows another, each with its own high point and resolution, and with a natural stopping place at the end of chapter and episode.

There are many other examples of episodic plot development. For example, in Bette Greene's *Phillip Hall Likes Me. I Reckon Maybe,* Beth Lambert's growth in ability and confidence is shown from the day she is excluded from a party, to her catching the turkey thieves, running the vegetable stand, picketing the store, and winning the calf-raising contest. *Pippi Longstocking,* Astrid Lindgren's nonsense story of the independent girl who does as she pleases, including rolling cookie dough on the floor, is one nonsensical episode after another. Robert McCloskey's *Homer Price* amuses children with the story of the runaway doughnut machine, or Miss Terwilliger's huge ball of string that she unwinds in County Fair competition. Each chapter is a story, and many of the same characters appear throughout—Uncle Ulysses and the Sheriff, for example. Other books, like Beverly Cleary's *Henry Huggins,* imitate the mischievous-boy story that the first chapters of *Tom Sawyer* initiated.

Yearly, new stories in episodic form, both fantasy and realism, are written for children. However, without conflict building to a climax in a progressive plot, the writers of these stories with purely episodic plots seem to need to rely upon other devices to carry the reader's interest. In one case the greater emphasis is upon characters, in others upon humor or nonsense.

There is great possibility for variation and combination in plot structure. *Alice in Wonderland* combines progressive with episodic plot. The underground setting, Alice's growing and shrinking, and her increasing self-confidence provide unity and progress. We recall the many ingenuities—the pool of tears, the caucus race, the caterpillar's advice, the mad tea party, and the croquet game—without being sure of their order. However, the story concludes in a flurry of excitement and a whirl of angry cards as Alice sees the ineffectual adults at the trial and finally asserts herself. *Tom Sawyer,* too, combines elements of episodic structure with progressive plot and climactic focus. Although there are a strong conflict and a final climax, there are also many chapters that are merely episodes in the life of a small-town boy and that make little contribution to the central conflict. "The Cat and the Painkiller" and "Pinch-bug and His Prey," along with several others, remind us that a novel need not have either one kind of plot or another.

EVALUATING PLOT IN CHILDREN'S LITERATURE

Most of what we have said about plot up to this point applies to plot in adult literature as well as in children's literature. For the remainder of the chapter we will discuss some of the special problems in stories for children.

We have mentioned the dangers of sensationalism in our earlier discussion of patterns of action. While adults may choose such stories, children may find sensationalism is more than they can bear. Sensational suspense, furthermore, places the focus upon tension rather than upon human beings and ideas. If the functions of literature are pleasure and understanding, the latter is slighted by sensationalism—as well as by sentimentality.

Coincidence

The concurrence of events apparently by mere chance is *coincidence.* In real life, we well know that coincidence does occur. In literature, however, where the truths of human nature and human existence are explored, reliance on coincidence to resolve conflict weakens plot. One example in which excellence in children's literature is flawed by coincidence is in *The Incredible Journey.* Here we follow the travels of three pets across the Canadian wilderness of deep woods, rushing rivers, and lonely lakes. In their conflict with nature, three chance happenings that are not in any way foreshadowed leave us troubled, doubting the credibility of the larger plot. First, part of a handwritten note blows into the fire and leaves the housekeeper baffled. Since she therefore does not realize that the two dogs and the Siamese cat have struck out on their own, she does not start the search for them. Later, a boy, hunting for the first time with his own rifle, with one remarkably accurate shot saves the Siamese cat from a lynx. Still later, an old and crumbling beaver dam by "a twist of fate" gives way at just the right moment to sweep the frightened cat downstream. Fortunately, however, the story of the pets' struggle against the wilderness is so strong in many other ways, from characterization to style, that perhaps the coincidence is forgiveable and we choose to overlook it.

Such fictional strength is not always the case, however, since inadequate foreshadowing leads the reader to doubt the credibility of an event. The test of coincidence, therefore, is foreshadowing. We are prepared to accept the concurrence of events if the incident does not seem to be mere chance, but a previously threatened or foreseen possibility.

White might easily have fallen into the coincidence trap in *Charlotte's Web.* If, for example, the enormous and healthy Uncle, the obvious choice for first prize, had happened to take sick at the Fair, that would have been coincidence. However, had Wilbur won the blue ribbon by mere default, our pleasure in the outcome would then have been a mixed pleasure over a far less satisfying victory. Furthermore, if Charlotte had by incredible coincidence eventually lived as long as Wilbur, she would have defied the natural laws of a spider's life cycle. Charlotte may talk and write words in her web, but she is a spider leading a spider life. White, by using foreshadowing and by rejecting coincidence, has given *Charlotte's Web* an inevitable, satisfying conclusion.

Sentimentality

Nor should another negative element, called *sentimentality*, mar a well-constructed plot. We term *sentiment* a natural concern or affection for another person. When, for instance, our parents are hurt in a painful accident, our natural sentiment, called love, causes an emotional response. We are hurt with those we love. However, when our sentiments are used, or played upon as they are in soap opera, we have what we call a tear-jerker situation, or **sentimentality.**

We have all at some time left a movie theater surreptitiously wiping our eyes, knowing the movie wasn't worth tears. At other times we have been unashamed of our tears, even perhaps proud. It is the legitimacy of our emotional reaction that makes us feel honest. When we are honestly moved by art, we may weep because we suffer with the character, taking his or her sorrow upon ourselves. But the writer may cause us to weep or to exult, and we know our reactions are false. They are false because we are asked for an emotional response in excess of what the situation seems to require.

Sentimentality takes varied forms. Character may be sentimentally drawn. For instance, a saintly sweet woman who never raises her voice, who is patient, kind, loyal, true, keeps a full cookie jar and a spotless kitchen is no reality. She is a cardboard, two-dimensional figure, a highly sentimentalized picture of Mother. Sentimentality may also occur in the plot. Sidney Taylor's *All-of-a-Kind Family* is a picture of growing up poor in an Orthodox Jewish family. However, it is highly sentimental because the writer not only creates a sentimental picture of Mother, but sees family life as a continually joyful chain of events, or perhaps nonevents. Five identically dressed little girls going happily to the library in a group, living frictionless lives in a large family, accepting and making the happy best of poverty, inviting the librarian to dinner and causing a loving marriage to result from her meeting with another guest—these sentimentalized pictures challenge our knowledge of the reality of family life. Because we reject, or are dubious of, Taylor's sentimentalized view of Mother and of family life, we may, unfortunately, reject the far more important discoveries about the practice of Jewish orthodoxy.

A favorite among children of the late nineteenth century was a supposedly realistic horse story called *Black Beauty,* Anna Sewell's novel told in first person by Black Beauty himself. As we look at it now, the book strikes us with its heavy sentimentality. The pathos of Beauty's own life is comparable to that of Ginger, "Poor Ginger" as one chapter is entitled. Ginger tells Black Beauty her story, and the short chapter concludes with Black Beauty's observations:

> A short time after this a cart with a dead horse in it passed our cab-stand. The head hung out of the cart-tail, the lifeless tongue was slowly dropping with blood; and the sunken eyes! but I can't speak of them, the sight was too dreadful. It was a chestnut horse with a long, thin neck. . . . I believe it was Ginger; I hoped it was, for then her troubles would be over. O! if men were more merciful they would shoot us before we came to such misery.

While none of us would argue that people have a right to be cruel to any animal, Sewell's sentimentality is vividly apparent. The graphic description of a lolling, bloody tongue, the frequent exclamation points, and even the basic idea of a realistic story of a horse being told in first person by the horse—all are tear-jerkers. Because of the sentimentality, the reader may sob more soulfully over Ginger's death than over that of a human being—although there is little confusion in our minds as to which misused creature is more deserving of grief.

Rarely do we have sensationalism in folktales, and rarely does the storyteller stop to rouse our tears by false sentiment. The wicked wolf whose stomach is full of rocks falls into the well and is drowned; we waste no sighs. The unkind girl whose punishment is to spout toads creeps into the corner and dies. The rapid pace of the folktale plot seems to prohibit pauses for tears. We appreciate the celebration of a marriage "the very next day," and we are not anguished over the fate of Rumpel-stiltskin, who stamped his two feet so hard that he split in two and "that was an end of him." Instead of being sentimental, the tale-teller resorts to humor.

Charlotte's Web does not resort to sentimentality. Lingering sobs and whimpers from Charlotte at her own death would have destroyed credibility. Charlotte is a spider and knows it. Her spider-defined life prepares us, Wilbur and the readers, for her dignified and inevitable death. Or again, Wilbur's fainting might easily have become sentimental panic, but it is instead humorous. Or Templeton might have broken down, become a reformed rat, and committed some unselfish or heroic act. Such an incredible change would have been sentimentality. Our every response to each situation in White's story is legitimately roused, never exaggerated nor superficial, and therefore unsentimental.

What is wrong with sentimentality? A good cry never hurt

anyone. Perhaps. However, there are dangers inherent in a steady diet of forced emotion. We have all had our turns at sneering at the soap opera, but perhaps we have not really considered why we sneer. One after the other, one dramatic occurrence, one crisis, and one tragedy pushes another out of our memories. We are like pumps primed to spout tears, and then just as we have settled down, primed again.

The most destructive element in the overuse of sentiment is not boredom, but the fact that the young reader, faced with continual sentimentality, will not develop the sensitivity essential to recognize what is truly moving and what is merely a play on feelings. The use of judgment and the sense of proportion grow and mature when we see honest emotion, whether it be joy or sorrow. If, after all, we regard the death of a pet mouse with the same degree of emotional intensity as the death of a brother, we have no sense of emotional proportion.

By contrast to *Black Beauty,* notice in Katherine Paterson's story *Bridge to Terabithia* the wide range of emotions that children wrestle with. They follow Jess from shyness with other children to rivalry with his sister Brenda, from pleasure over the secret bridge to the hideaway island, to numbness and grief at his friend Leslie's drowning. Or chart the genuine sentiment that a small child, reading or being read to, experiences during the relationship with Charlotte and Wilbur. Here he or she comes to know loneliness, friendship, sacrifice, tact, patience, loyalty, and maternity—as well as death and continuity; the child meets such negative human traits as selfishness, avarice, and gluttony. Furthermore, among the more surprising discoveries is the way in which such significant human traits and experiences are explored in both books—not with bathos or sentimentality, but with seriousness or deft humor. The total impact of White's book embodies respect for animals, yes, but more importantly, respect for people, as Wilbur and Charlotte personify human beings.

The child fed only on such surface sentimentality as soap opera and Walt Disney—with their sterile and stereotyped pictures of human beings and their distorted sensationalism with simplistic solutions—this child risks developing emotional shallowness.[2] The child nourished through real literature in the breadth and depth and range of true emotion grows in understanding of human nature.

Lack of Conflict

Many of today's mass-produced story books, like those found on racks in supermarkets and drugstores, lack conflict. Events follow one another in chronological narrative. Without any struggle, the story lacks suspense, hint of alternative outcomes, a sense that it had to happen, and, therefore, satisfaction. All that the reader can say at the conclusion of such a story is "So what does that prove?" Conflict, the tension that keeps a story interesting, has never appeared. There are many other examples, of course. Look at *Hold My Hand* by Charlotte Zolotow, described on the jacket as "a moment of intensity," yet there is no tension, no intensity. For a specific example, consider *Willie Goes to the Seashore,* a picture-story book with little excitement. The family has a small cottage at the beach. In a total of seventy-five printed lines, they unpack, roll in the sand, swim, hunt shells, build a sand castle, rebuild the sand castle, and splash in the water. They hang seaweed around their necks and go to bed. Next day Willie finds an old boat, explores the rocks, sees a crab dart off, collects firewood, and puts weiners on roasting sticks. Willie "never had such fun." Willie does everything—and nothing. Look at *Margaret's Birthday* by Jan Wahl and note the similarities to the random activity of Willie's seashore experience.

Suppose instead, Willie had built an elaborate sand castle, planning it, admiring it, embellishing it, and patting it into shape. Then during the weiner roast, the waves in their regular tidal shifts had destroyed the castle! Result: tension. Or suppose Willie explored the old boat, found it had oarlocks and a hollow bow, and made an imaginary fishing expedition beyond the point! Now the seashore truly becomes a place to have fun, and some tension or conflict is the cause.

Even the simplest stories for children can have conflict or tension. Will Goldilocks be caught? Will the three little pigs survive by the hair of their chinny-chin-chins? Will the troll who lives under the bridge get the Billy Goats Gruff? Suspense builds in each of these stories as a threat is repeated three times, and conflict is climaxed by defeat of the threatener. Goldilocks gets away; the wolf falls into boiling water and is eaten for dinner; the troll is crushed to bits, body and bones.

Inadequately developed conflict, like flat characterization, leaves us unconcerned about the outcome of a story. Such problems in plotting occur frequently in science fiction. Conflict holds our attention if it presents some semblance of fair fight, and if the question of outcome is open. But often in science fiction the protagonist is combatting an irresistible natural force. In person-against-person conflict, the ingenuity of the two intellects often forces the conflict to become an academic struggle with no hint of human emotions. In person-against-society conflict, the society often is remote from our experience and described in cold, technical terms. Finally, when intellect does battle with itself in person-against-self conflict, the conflict is merely a problem with a rational answer, again lacking human emotion. The reader who is uninvolved in either characters or conflict becomes apathetic: "I cannot conceive of it; I therefore cannot care."

While such inadequacy in science fiction is not necessary nor inevitable, it is frequent. *Flight of Exiles* by Ben Bova, for example, fails because of inadequate character development as well as inadequate conflict. Characters are two-dimensional and unreal; conflict is between persons, a struggle for love and power. There is, aside from intellectual exercise, little concern for the outcome.

By contrast, take once again the example of *A Wrinkle in Time,* where conflict is person-against-person. Meg battles against a disembodied brain that controls the citizens of Camazotz, whose people are programmed to be identical. Meg and Calvin struggle against IT's magnetic persuasion, but Charles Wallace, whose allegiance to mind is stronger than it is to spirit, arrogantly gives in. Pure mind, however, cannot conquer stubborn Meg, whose believable flaws make her human enough for us to care about her. When Meg sees that her strength lies in her power to love, she overcomes IT and frees Charles Wallace. These human responses of will, dependence, and love oppose the antagonist IT. We are concerned about the outcome, yearning to help Meg in a fantastic plot based upon the possible reality of opposing forces in conflict.

SUMMARY

Character study alone rarely carries the child's interest, but character becomes inextricably woven into plot by the very natures, protagonist as well as antagonist, in the conflict. Order is easier for the child to follow if it is within his or her experience; chronological order is therefore more frequent, while flashback is used more rarely. In a progressive plot, suspense pulls the reader through the rising action to the central climax, where conflict is resolved in a manner foreshadowed and thus inevitable; the last questions are usually answered in a denouement with its closed ending.

By contrast, each chapter in an episodic plot has its own small tensions and is joined to the others by theme and character. Finally, a well-plotted story relies on neither sentimentality nor coincidence for the action and resolution.

There is no right plot structure in a story for children. There are only variations of the two principal forms. The understanding of the child—reader or listener—may determine the length or structure of the story, whether that story be a single progressively arranged unit or an episode in a longer work. However, what does matter is that the piece of literature sustains interest and gives pleasure as it is read.

In considering plot development, we are most aware that without sufficient conflict or tension, accompanied by suspense, foreshadowing, and inevitability, a story is just plain dull. Few adults want to read a dull story, and certainly no children will.

Reading and Evaluating

Animal realism

1. *What is the nature of the conflict in* The Incredible Journey? *Is the conflict well-defined? How is the antagonist made believable? Do you agree that the plot is marred by coincidence? Explain. Is the plot sufficiently strong in other ways to make the coincidence unimportant? Are there coincidental actions in the story other than those mentioned? Do they mar the story? How does the fact that the coincidence involves minor characters influence acceptance of them?*

Fantasy

2. *Read a time fantasy by Eleanor Cameron, E. Nesbit, Alison Uttley, Edward Eager, or another writer, or a science fiction story by Andre Norton, Ben Bova, or another writer. What is the conflict between the protagonist and the antagonist? Is there chance of victory for the protagonist? What is the outcome of the conflict? Explain your reaction to the conflict and its outcome.*

Picture books

3. *In terms of conflict, compare the story of a personified elephant in de Brunhoff's* Babar *story with the personified rabbit in* The Tale of Peter Rabbit. *Compare the use of suspense, foreshadowing, and inevitability in the two. Test other plot elements of other picture books against* Peter Rabbit.

Other countries

4. *What is the conflict in* The House of Sixty Fathers *by Meindert DeJong? How does the writer manage to show the antagonist without turning the reader against a particular people? Is there coincidence? How does DeJong avoid sentimentality?*

Science fiction

5. *Is the criticism in this chapter of Ben Bova's* Flight of Exiles *valid? If not, why not? Does your reading of another science fiction story indicate it is possible to avoid such problems? Cite examples. How are you as a reader concerned about the climax and the outcome? What carries your interest?*

Realism

6. *From your reading of literature for children, what examples of flashback do you recall? Of open-ended conflicts? Do the stories have sound character development and plotting? What levels of maturity do the examples seem to be written for?*

Notes

[1]For a discussion of time in time fantasy, a subject in itself, see Eleanor Cameron, "The Green and Burning Tree," in *The Green and Burning Tree,* Boston: Atlantic Monthly Press, 1969, pp. 71–134.

[2]For a discussion of Walt Disney's work, see Frances Clarke Sayers: "Walt Disney Accused," in *Children & Literature: Views and Reviews,* Virginia Haviland, ed., Glenview, Illinois: Scott, Foresman, 1973, pp. 116–125.

Recommended Books Cited in This Chapter

Alexander, Lloyd. *The High King.* New York: Holt, 1968.
Armstrong, William H. *Sounder.* New York: Harper, 1969.
Babbitt, Natalie. *Knee-Knock Rise.* New York: Farrar, 1970.
Burnford, Sheila. *The Incredible Journey.* Boston: Little, 1961.
Carroll, Lewis. *Alice's Adventures in Wonderland.* New York: Dutton, 1954. (first published 1865)
Childress, Alice. *A Hero ain't nothin' but a Sandwich.* New York: Coward, 1973.
Cleary, Beverly. *Henry Huggins.* New York: Morrow, 1950.
Cleaver, Vera and Bill. *Where the Lilies Bloom.* New York: Lippincott, 1969.
Collier, James Lincoln and Christopher. *My Brother Sam Is Dead.* New York: Four Winds, 1974.
DeJong, Meindert. *The House of Sixty Fathers.* New York: Harper, 1956.
George, Jean. *Julie of the Wolves.* New York: Harper, 1972.
Go Ask Alice. New York: Dell, 1971.
Grahame, Kenneth. *The Wind in the Willows.* New York: Scribner's, 1953. (first published 1908)
Greene, Bette. *Philip Hall Likes Me. I Reckon Maybe.* New York: Dial, 1974.
Keats, Ezra Jack. *Goggles!* New York: Macmillan, 1969.
Konigsberg, E. L. *Jennifer, Hecate, Macbeth, William McKinley, and Me, Elizabeth.* New York: Atheneum, 1967.
L'Engle, Madeleine. *A Wrinkle in Time.* New York: Farrar, 1962.
Lindgren, Astrid. *Pippi Longstocking.* New York: Viking, 1950.
Mathis, Sharon Bell. *The Hundred Penny Box.* New York: Viking, 1975.
Mazer, Harry. *Guy Lenny.* New York: Dell, 1973.
McCloskey, Robert. *Homer Price.* New York: Viking, 1943.
Milne, A. A. *Winnie-the-Pooh.* New York: Dutton, 1926.
Ness, Evaline. *Sam, Bangs, & Moonshine.* New York: Holt, 1966.
Norton, Mary. *The Borrowers.* New York: Harcourt, 1965.
O'Dell, Scott. *Island of the Blue Dolphins.* Boston: Houghton, 1960.
Paterson, Katherine. *Bridge to Terabithia.* New York: Crowell, 1977.
———. *The Master Puppeteer.* New York: Crowell, 1976.
Sendak, Maurice. *Where the Wild Things Are.* New York: Harper, 1963.
Serraillier, Ian. *Beowulf the Warrior.* New York: Walck, 1961.
Speare, Elizabeth. *The Witch of Blackbird Pond.* Boston: Houghton, 1958.
Sperry, Armstrong. *Call It Courage.* New York: Macmillan, 1940.
Taylor, Mildred. *Roll of Thunder, Hear My Cry.* New York: Dial, 1976.
Twain, Mark. *The Adventures of Tom Sawyer.* New York: Macmillan, 1962. (first published 1876)
White, E. B. *Charlotte's Web.* New York: Harper, 1954.
Wier, Esther. *The Loner.* New York: McKay, 1963.
Wilder, Laura Ingalls. *Little House in the Big Woods.* New York: Harper, 1953. (first published 1932)

5 Setting

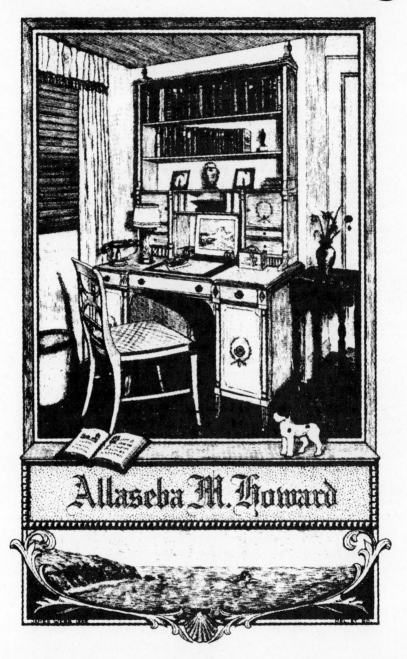

Allaseba M. Howard

Both depiction of character and working out of the plot occur, of course, in time and place. These latter elements we call *setting.* In an adult novel, action may occur anywhere, even in the mind of the protagonist, and may need little delineation of place or time. However, the story for children almost always occurs in a time and place described in some detail.

The possibilities for setting are endless. It is possible to write of a time when human beings lived in caves, and it is possible to write of a time when they may live in capsules adrift in space. As for settings in place, from cave to capsule, the spread is equally broad. When we consider all of the times and places known to us, and add to them all those we are capable of imagining, there is no limit to possibilities. Sometimes the writer wishes to make setting very clear, because the story depends upon our understanding and envisioning the particular setting. At other times, the writer deliberately refrains from closely examining and describing setting. Making the setting a specific time and place might for a particular story limit the universality of conflict, characters, or ideas the writer wishes to explore. It is the writer who determines the nature of the story, and thereby determines the setting.

Sometimes we must know the physical description of the setting, the details of what is present, how it all looks, smells, feels, and sounds. These are the relevant details that will directly influence character and conflict. Such details at other times—kinds of sounds and smells, kinds of buildings, quality of light and climate—may create the mood of the time and place and so create the atmosphere for the characters and the conflict.

You will notice from our discussion of character and plot that we found those two elements influencing and reflecting each other. This interdependence with other elements is true of setting, too. If, for example, *The Why's and Wherefore's of Littabelle Lee* were to take place not among the rivers and valleys and cliffs of the Ozarks, but on the plains of North Dakota or in glittering Miami Beach, the story would change. Aunt Sorrow's fall over the cliff on her burro, for example, could not have happened; Littabelle's wonder about what to do with her life would have included options other than teaching or woods doctoring. Such settings would create totally different novels. The Cleavers did not hit upon their choice of setting accidentally; it was *the* setting for *this* story. In evaluating a piece of literature, we should be aware of the basic kind of setting, and then decide how it functions in the story. As we analyze this relationship, we evaluate the effectiveness of the author's selection.

TYPES OF SETTINGS

In any piece of literature, whether for child or adult, there are essentially two types of setting: (1) the *backdrop* or relatively unimportant setting and (2) the *integral* or essential setting.

The importance of setting—whether it is integral or backdrop—depends upon the writer's purpose in the story. For example, in a story of internal conflict, the first-person narrator may tell the progress of the plot in narrative, dialogue, and action, or in diary form. The reader may not need to know where or when the character lives, since understanding depends upon interest in character and in the character's internal conflict as the narrator reveals the inner tension. Time and place are merely a backdrop. This kind of setting contrasts sharply with the significant integral setting in a book such as *Anne Frank: The Diary of a Young Girl.* Although this story, too, has internal conflict, where and when the action occurs are essential information if we are to understand conflict and character. In fact, setting working upon character is the essence of conflict in this book.

The writer makes the setting clear in descriptions. Each reader may have a personal catalog of mentally pictured settings—a beach, a farm, or a cabin—but the writer does not depend upon the reader's experience nor upon recollection of settings. If the writer wants to make the setting integral to this story, the writer must describe it in concrete details, relying on sensory pictures and vivid comparisons to make the setting so clear that the reader understands how this story is closely related to this particular place.

By contrast, if the unskilled writer insists that setting is significant, and yet creates a setting superficial in concept and shallow in depiction, the reader may then reject all of the story's reality, from character through action and unifying idea. A one-dimensional setting cannot be convincingly integral, and therefore little that happens seems believable.

The title *Willie Goes to the Seashore* suggests that the setting is an integral part of the action; the seashore must be so interesting that Willie will have an exciting time. The actual case is quite different. The little cottage and the sandy beach are the setting. Willie, moving in quick succession from one to another of the activities one expects at the shore, seems to move *over* the setting rather than *in* it, finding no conflict nor involvement in any of the activities the setting suggests. Although we expect that such a varied and exciting setting for play will be an integral part of the narrative tension, setting does not come alive to involve character in plot. So what is exciting about a seashore? Why would Willie want to live there all the time? The setting has failed as an integral part of the story, since it does not influence character, conflict, or idea.

Backdrop Setting

The term *backdrop* comes, of course, from the theater. Some of the action in scenes from Shakespeare, for example, or from many musicals, takes place on the apron of the stage before a featureless curtain, or before a flat, painted scene of an unidentified street or forest. Soliloquy, dialogue, action, or character confrontation concerns us; where the characters are positioned matters, but less than our seeing and hearing them, and following them in the developing conflict. Yet, while the street or forest is unidentified, it may have importance. It may have some subtle meaning that suggests the forest as a place of physical or spiritual darkness, and the busy street as a reminder of society.

A clear example of a children's story with backdrop setting is *Winnie-the-Pooh.* A. A. Milne's Christopher Robin might live anywhere at all—from England's Land's End to Lancashire, or from America's Bangor to Sacramento. Action occurs on the bank of a stream, or by a big oak tree with a honeybee nest. While time and place are not specific, they may suggest something about the action or characters when Pooh, Eeyore, Rabbit, and his assorted friends-and-relations set off on an "Expotition" to the North Pole. The Forest—with a capital *F*—is of course the proper place for Pooh and Piglet to track the fearful Woozle/-Wizzle, but there is minimal description of the beech tree beyond its being in the middle of the Forest. It is the tension in the characters that matters and dominates.

Pippi Longstocking, Astrid Lindgren's heroine, might also live anywhere. Pippi's chaotic home, Villa Villekula, figures minimally in the story action as we admire Pippi's found treasure, or as she rolls out cookie dough on the floor. Our eyes and ears focus instead on Pippi as she shows her skills as a Thing Finder, plays tag with the policeman, or tops the ladies' gossip with her own nonsensical servant problems. Pippi's house is important to us only because it must be a remarkable place; Pippi does such ridiculous things there.

In both *Winnie* and *Pippi,* setting is generalized and universal; its vividness exists in our minds merely as the place where the interesting action occurs. We do not know, for example, what Rabbit's house looks like; what matters is the memorable view of Pooh's legs serving as towel racks. Time and place, although they have importance, do not influence the character and plot in the same ways that an integral setting does.

Integral Setting

We say a story has an ***integral setting*** when action, character, or theme are influenced by the time and place, since, as Eudora Welty says, setting has "the most delicate control over character . . . by confining character, it defines it."[1] These characters, given these circumstances, in this time and place, behave in this way.

Potter's *The Tale of Peter Rabbit* is a classic example of a story for the youngest child in which setting is integral. As both author and illustrator, Potter integrates visual and word pictures; setting is so closely interwoven with character, action, and theme that we are never aware of description as such. On page one appears the family home with its soft, sandy floor—the bank under the roots of a large fir tree. Soon we are under the gate and can see the cucumber frame. In this garden, cabbages and potatoes as well as French beans and lettuces grow not far from the net-covered gooseberry bush and the toolshed, with its watering can and its three flower pots on the window sill. The stone wall has a gate and a stone step; close by are a pond and a wheelbarrow. We even hear the garden sound of the scritching, scratching hoe. Nowhere does Potter stop the action to describe setting, and yet at no point is setting unimportant. Potter's illustrations, of course, add greatly to our picture of setting. In the perfectly integrated picture book, illustration and text work together to create setting; neither stands alone.

Contemporary society, as we are reminded by the battering of advertisements, is relying less on words for communication and more upon pictures. The trend toward nonverbal communication is reflected in contemporary picture-story books which often depend entirely upon illustration to create setting. In literature for children, however, word pictures give the child an opportunity to create setting in his or her own mind, a special kind of experience which is one of the delights of literature.

Setting in *Charlotte's Web*

Our touchstone, *Charlotte's Web,* is an excellent example of integral setting literally described. This story could have occurred nowhere but on a farm, in fact only on a farm that has the traditional farm animals. This is not a sprawling ranch, nor a grain-growing industry, because such farms have concerns other than pigs and their barnyard friends. The Arable farm is near a country road, since Fern catches the school bus at her front door. There is a brook for playing in, with sticky mud that is wonderfully oozy. This farm has a dump—or how could Templeton find essential words for the web? It has meadows that show seasonal changes, maples that redden with anxiety, and a big pasture that frightens a timid piglet. This farm, with an orchard where apples fall and the gander's family feasts, is no generalized farm; there is no other farm quite like it, where fog and rain, crickets and song sparrow are all parts of the place, the setting. However, most important of all, this farm has a barn that houses a variety of animals—or how could sheep, pigs, and geese become acquainted, advising, consoling, and taunting one another? White shows the Zuckerman barn as soon as Wilbur sees it. The reader, too, knows its smells, its sights, and its warmth:

> The barn was very large. It was very old. It smelled of hay and it smelled of manure. It smelled of the perspiration of tired horses and the wonderful sweet breath of patient cows. It often had a sort of peaceful smell—as though nothing bad could happen ever again in the world. It smelled of grain and of harness dressing and of axle grease and of rubber boots and of new rope. And whenever the cat was given a fish-head to eat, the barn would smell of fish. But mostly it smelled of hay, for there was always hay in the great loft overhead. And there was always hay being pitched down to the cows and the horses and the sheep.

No one could confuse this setting with any generalized backdrop, since each item in the description shows the singularity of this setting, home of Wilbur, Charlotte, and Templeton. We know this place as well as Wilbur does, and because its description is so vivid, we are alerted to its importance in the total story.

To know the exciting Fairgrounds, we must

> hear music and see the Ferris wheel turning in the sky. . . . smell the dust of the race track where the sprinkling car had moistened it . . . smell hamburgers frying and see balloons aloft. . . . hear sheep blatting in their pens.

At night the lighted Ferris wheel revolves in the sky, the gambling machines crackle, the merry-go-round makes music, and a voice calls numbers from the beano booth. In the morning we hear sparrows stirring, roosters crowing, cows rattling chains, and cars whispering on the roadway.

The Fair is an essential part of the story, and it is therefore necessary that the reader see, hear, smell, and even touch and taste it. Wilbur's character is fully revealed at the Fair, where, experiencing threatened failure and final success, he remains humble but radiant. Wilbur's conflict, furthermore, cannot be resolved without the Fair. Wilbur must have time to grow, and then must prove himself worthy of being saved; the fall Fair is a traditional proving time for farm animals. Charlotte's efforts to prolong Wilbur's life produce no certainty of success until the Fair—he wins the prize for attracting so many visitors.

White must also show temporal change, since character growth and conflict, as well as several of the story's thematic discoveries, are dependent upon the passing of time. White must make us see the seasons as they exist, merge, and change. As we hear, see, and smell, we are aware of time passing, and of weather and landscape changing.

Spring is the time for pigs to be born; rain drips from the eaves, runs crookedly between the pigweed, and gushes from the rainspouts. Summer is everyone's holiday; lilacs are blooming, bees are dropping in on the apple blossoms, and horses are pulling the noisy mower. Birds sing and nest. However, since summer cannot last forever, the crickets' song prepares us for fall and the important Fair time. Uneasy sheep break out of their pasture, and the gander's family invades the orchard. Although little of the story's action occurs in winter, even winter is not slighted. The pasture is frozen, the cows are standing in the sun beside the strawpile, the sheep are eating snow, and the geese just hanging about. Then to complete the year's cycle, and to prove that Wilbur has survived butchering time and that Charlotte's eggs have hatched, White returns to spring and its strengthening light, new lambs, nine goose eggs, and Charlotte's old web floating away.

The time element is important here. As the year passes, Wilbur matures from a panicky child to a responsible adult. In the passing of a full year we know that his victory over society is complete. We have had time to see the truth of such themes as the growth of friendship and of maturity, and the inevitability and acceptance of death. The integral setting has helped to make all of these clear.

FUNCTIONS OF SETTING

Setting That Clarifies Conflict

As *Charlotte's Web* demonstrates, an integral setting plays an important part in conflict. In *Roosevelt Grady,* the story of a migrant family, Louisa Shotwell provides concrete details of the setting to demonstrate the Gradys' poverty and rootlessness. While as readers we are dismayed by many details describing the family's temporary dwellings, we see clearly that little things make Roosevelt happy. This discrepancy between Roosevelt's expectations and our own sharpens our awareness of his deprived life. In the shadowy attic, the roof slopes down to leave only one central place high enough for Papa to stand; even nine-year-old Roosevelt bumps his head. Jutting into the roof, right next to each other, are three bay windows that look like triplets. Even though its windows are grimy, the attic has its glories: Princess Anne can sleep in the old trunk with the tray, and the best bed is Roosevelt's—a hammock swinging from the roof rafters. Roosevelt has never slept alone before. In the bus camp, only one bus has a chimney which means a stove and winter warmth. We have been jostled in the Gradys' truck from one crop site to another; we have seen how spending a few weeks' time in one camp and a few in another deprives a family of income, medical care, education, and a sense of belonging. Understanding of setting is essential to our understanding of character and conflict as well as theme.

In *M. C. Higgins, the Great* by Virginia Hamilton, M. C. looks out from the mountain top over the land devastated by strip mining. All is still and hot, without the sounds of birds or insects. He thinks of how the scene once looked, with "ranges of hills with farmhouses nestled in draws and lower valleys." Now he sees a "gray-brown snake" curling in cuts and loops along the ridges, the hill summits "shredded away with rock and ruin which spilled down into cropland at the base of the hills." Soon he learns from the visitor Lewis that the waste heap is sliding on the oil, and that given the right steep angle the "pressure is going to build up until it crashes down" and buries his house. M. C.'s nightmare has come alive and dread sickens him. Once again, setting reveals character, suits plot, and influences theme.

Turn to the austere Puritan New England setting of *The Witch of Blackbird Pond,* into which Kit Tyler is transported from her West Indies birthplace. Author Elizabeth Speare does not rely merely on our history book knowledge of that time and place when witchcraft was feared; she clarifies setting by her description of the austerity of life among the Puritans. We see the house with burnished and hand-rubbed copper, indicative of hard work, the heavy, fortress-like door, the dim little mirror, and the severe wooden bench. Speare weaves description of the house itself into a description of Kit's tasks in a typical day. Meat must be chopped, vegetables prepared, and the pewter mugs polished with fine sand and reeds. Throughout the day Kit stirs the kettle of boiling soap with a stick, with the lye fumes stinging her eyes and the heavy stirring tiring her muscles. Even the easiest task, making corn pudding, keeps her leaning over the smoky fire which burns her watering eyes. Walking through the little town to church with Kit, we see severity in the straight, cold lines of functional buildings and punitive devices. The unpainted Meeting House, the whipping post, the pillory, and the stocks are frightening evidence that Kit is now in a rigid and uncompromising environment, one that her carefree Barbados upbringing has scarcely prepared her for.

In complex stories with multiple conflicts, the importance of setting may depend upon the nature of each conflict. For instance, while Tom Sawyer's internal conflict needs no setting, our understanding of Tom's fear of Injun Joe is dependent upon our understanding of the setting. In the nineteenth century, small-town residents were familiar with a variety of people, including riverside vagrants. A boy was free to roam the town, to spend time in the cemetery, the river, and the caves. Knowing these facts is essential to our understanding of Tom himself, his encounters and escapades, and his conflict with Injun Joe.

Sometimes we must know a mode of living or of making a living in order to understand the story's conflict. In such a case the setting is integral. *Where the Lilies Bloom,* for example, shows setting as a power shaping the lives of those who live in the Ozarks. The Cleavers create setting beautiful enough to hold the characters' loyalty, and yet so wild that it offers Mary Call's family little to subsist on. Weaving descriptions of setting into action, the writers show the slow work of wildcrafting, a tedious labor with small rewards. Action in the novel is native to this particular lush wilderness. Mary Call's struggle to keep her family together is the more convincing because we see the way of life and the setting she struggles with.

Setting as Antagonist

Sometimes setting itself is the antagonist as it is in *Julie of the Wolves.* Even fog, one of nature's milder elements, frightens Miyax, who had never given it much thought. As it streams and rolls up the wolf slope, making the wolves invisible one by one, she remembers that fog imprisons people. In fog they cannot hurt. As noted in our earlier discussion of Burnford's *The Incredible Journey,* its setting is an essential part of the story, since the Canadian wilderness is not only setting but antagonist. Without clear descriptions of the dense brush and forest land, and of the wilderness river, such a novel would have no believable conflict to hold the reader. However, Burnford on the opening page of the novel prepares us for the conflict; the rugged country is introduced on page one, line one, and the description continues for a page and a half. It is northwestern Ontario:

> a vast area of deeply wooded wilderness—of endless chains of
> lonely lakes and rushing rivers. Thousands of miles of country
> roads, rough timber lanes, overgrown tracks leading to aban-

doned mines, and unmapped trails snake across its length and breadth. It is a country of far-flung, lonely farms and a few widely scattered small towns and villages, of lonely trappers' shacks and logging camps.

Since nature is the antagonist in Burnford's story, she must show nature as strong and forceful, even threatening. If the journey of the three pet-characters is to be truly credible, we must believe in the forces they battle. The Siamese cat, bred originally for elegant court life, and Bodger the bull terrier, the comfort-loving pet, are less adaptable to living in the wilderness than the Labrador, a hunter by breeding. Their persistent trek toward their masters becomes suspenseful as we realize what these three must contend with. The conflict holds our interest because nature is not benign, but an unyielding force that threatens danger and the possibility of failure. Nature as setting and antagonist is worthy of our respect.

Setting is also the antagonist in another book discussed earlier, O'Dell's *Island of the Blue Dolphins*. We must be aware of the passing of time and of the seemingly endless period of Karana's isolation as she waits for rescue. If we did not see the dangers that threaten her survival on the island, we might find the story a happy, escape-to-the-wilderness tale. Instead, because of the many and vivid descriptions, *Island of the Blue Dolphins* is an account of a patient and determined young woman who struggles and survives against a powerful antagonist—nature, which brings hunger, thirst, injury, wild dogs, an earthquake, and a tidal wave. Setting, Karana's antagonist, is vivid. We see, hear, smell, and feel it in O'Dell's descriptions. Karana is a strong protagonist; although her adversary is also powerful, Karana is not overwhelmed.

Setting That Illuminates Character

In many of the examples we have been discussing, setting influences character. Notice the effect of isolation and crowding upon the protagonist's fear in that unusual autobiography *Anne Frank*. We must see the stiflingly cramped atmosphere of the Secret Annexe, or we cannot experience the yearning for freedom and privacy that Anne expresses during the twenty-five months of the family's hiding from the Nazi soldiers who are rounding up the Jews for imprisonment. We must see Anne's surroundings as we follow her tensions with her parents and fellow prisoners, her awakening sense of self, and her curiosity about growing up. Just two days after the family crowds into the Annexe, Anne writes as though it is an adventure:

Our little room looked very bare at first with nothing
on the walls; but thanks to Daddy who had brought my film-
star collection and picture postcards on beforehand, and with
the aid of paste pot and brush, I have transformed the walls into
one gigantic picture. This makes it look more cheerful, and,
when the Van Daans come, we'll get some wood from the attic,
and make a few little cupboards for the walls and other odds
and ends to make it look more lively.

But thirteen months later, we have another picture, this time of the
efforts necessary when bedtime approaches:

Nine o-clock in the evening. The bustle of going to bed
in the "Secret Annexe" begins. . . . Chairs are shoved about,
beds are pulled down, blankets unfolded, nothing remains
where it is during the day. I sleep on the little divan. . . . chairs
have to be used to lengthen it. A quilt, sheets, pillows, blankets,
are all fetched from Dussel's bed where they remain during the
day . . . creaking in the next room: Margot's concertina-bed
being pulled out. Again, divan, blankets, and pillows, everything is done to make the wooden slats a bit more comfortable.
It sounds like thunder above, but it is only Mrs. Van Daan's bed
. . . shifted to the window.

The setting becomes overwhelming in its effect upon every
aspect of the characters' lives. Bickering, quarrels, arguments, and rages
result from the pressures of close confinement. Then, in Anne's description of her own actions, her responses to being so long confined in this
setting, we see the impact of setting—time and place—upon the
protagonist:

I wander from one room to another, downstairs and up
again, feeling like a songbird whose wings have been clipped
and who is hurling himself in utter darkness against the bars of
his cage. "Go outside, laugh, and take a breath of fresh air," a
voice cries within me, but I don't even feel a response any more;
I go and lie on the divan and sleep, to make the time pass more
quickly, and the stillness and the terrible fear, because there is
no way of killing them.

The characters of Anne Frank's diary become more understandable, the
conflict more credible, and the themes more convincing because, in this
remarkable account by an extremely perceptive adolescent, we so
clearly see the setting.

Setting and Mood

As several of the preceding examples demonstrate, setting affects mood. Take, for example, the *Eyes of the Amaryllis* by Natalie Babbitt. In order for the reader to experience the isolation of the little house on the New England seacoast and to see how its situation affects Gran and her visitor Jenny, we must know the essential setting. We see Jenny and Gran's regular walk along the tide-washed shore at midnight, notice how the smooth sand sucks their feet into its depths as they search for some sign of the grandfather's ship wrecked so long ago. On the night of the hurricane, however, the quiet beach changes, becoming savage and threatening as the storm

> wheeled slowly north. Its eye rode far offshore, but its sweeping arms of wind and rain clawed at the nearest beaches, and the sea rose up before it in great, spreading welts that raced for miles ahead, rolling to land in the measured waves. . . .
>
> But as it swung in an upward arc to the west and north, its indignation grew, the speed of its winds increased, until at last, arriving in mid-coastal waters, it had spun itself into a rage. It was small, not more than forty miles across, but deadly: round its eye the winds were whirling ninety. . . .

Only such violent turbulence could prepare us for the lost figurehead of the Amaryllis, the sign washed up on the shore, liberating Gran from the past. Had the figurehead floated in on a benevolent wave, its significance would have been less evident and its mysterious appearance less dramatic.

Epic style is grand style, vivid and resonant; and setting—like character and action—can be pictured in elevated language. In keeping with the heroic subject, the setting of Ian Serraillier's retelling of the epic *Beowulf the Warrior* has solemn majesty; its description produces a mood of great dignity. Serraillier sketches the setting briefly with phrases that ring with grandeur. Book One begins with a description of the vast and splendid hall Heorot, scene of Grendel's monstrous deeds and of Beowulf's selfless struggle:

> Hrothgar, King of the Danes, glorious in battle
> Built him a huge hall—its gleaming roof
> Towering high to heaven—strong to withstand
> The buffet of war. . . .
>
> The long hall . . .
> The floor paved with stone, the roof high-raftered.

As Beowulf battles with Grendel in a struggle of awesome violence, this huge hall shudders. The struggle is greater, and therefore the victory is greater, because of the mood created by the splendor of setting. Book Two opens with the mother of Grendel descending upon Heorot for vengeance. The mist, the gloom, the chill, and the vast emptiness set the ominous mood and prepare us for the monster's mission:

> Over the misty moor, under the dark
> Vault of heaven a shadow came gliding—a she-monster,
> Mother of Grendel. From the chill waters of the fenland,
> Brooding on her grief. . . .

Filled with foreboding and suspense, these brief phrases describing the setting prepare us for a story of a hero and monsters. They are more than backdrop; they are a setting which creates a mood integral to the story of heroic battles and grim victories.

Setting as Symbol

Symbols may operate in setting as they may in other elements of literature. A *symbol* is a person, object, situation, or action which operates on two levels of meaning, the literal and the figurative or suggestive. When we first become aware of symbols, we have a tendency to run wild, to read into stories all sorts of fanciful overtones not legitimately supported by the story. What seems important here is that only fairly obvious symbols will be understood by most children.

The simplest of symbolic settings are those that suggest that the forest is both a literal setting and a symbol for the unknown; the garden is both a literal setting and a symbol of natural but cultivated beauty; sunlight may symbolize goodness, while darkness is evil. In such a way some of the settings in folktales have symbolic meanings. Hansel and Gretel, as well as Snow White, are lost in the fearful and unknown— the forest. The forest is also the domain of ogres and giants, mysteriously frightening creatures. Despite their backdrop qualities, these symbolic settings often set mood in traditional tales.

Symbols may be combined to create *allegory,* as they are in some stories for children. According to Northrup Frye, allegory translates into images.[2] To be a true symbol, the object must be emphasized or repeated, and supported throughout the entire story; it represents something quite different from its literal meaning. But stories for children operate on a fairly literal level. Ideas of good and evil may be translated into characters, actions, or setting, which then become symbols for ideas. In this sense the Narnia series by C. S. Lewis is allegory.

However, the Narnia books are also highly successful when read on a literal level; the young reader may or may not see the ideas symbolized by characters or setting. A child may read through the series with great excitement, think a bit, then exclaim "He's talking about good and bad!" and then reread them all, this time on an allegorical or symbolic level.

In contrast, the Forest seems a natural place for Pooh and Piglet to hunt a Woozle/Wizzle; to extend the meaning of the Forest to the point of calling it a symbol for evil is pretentious and pointless. Hannah the supposed Quaker witch in *The Witch of Blackbird Pond* does not live in the dark forest; a kind and harmless woman, she lives in the sunny meadows. Speare chooses this setting for Hannah's home to assist in creating conflict, but calling the setting symbolic seems heavy-handed.

EVALUATING SETTING IN CHILDREN'S LITERATURE

Like adults, children will accept as much or as little setting as the story seems to call for. Like adults, too, they expect that when a setting is important to understanding the story, they will be made to see, to hear, perhaps even to smell the setting—to sense the setting in any way relevant to the mood, conflict, and characters in the story. It seems reasonable, however, that younger children will be less likely to sit still for long descriptions that take them away from the conflict and characters. For them, and for many adults as well, setting interwoven with action is the most interesting and readable. Once this setting is established, any reader of any age expects the writer to be consistent. At times we all accept settings as escapes. The scene of an exotic ball or lavish banquet in a folktale undoubtedly was a satisfying escape for the poor and oppressed who heard these stories told in the past; and today setting in some adventure and science fiction stories seems to function purely as escape. But once again, we return to the principle that the essential setting should be integrated with character and conflict, and that it not be a mere digression. Since folk literature and fantasy seem to be more common in literature for children than for adults, their special considerations may need examination.

Traditional Literature

In most folktales action and theme are the focus of interest and the setting is backdrop. The action is usually brisk and little time is spent describing time and place. The setting is a vague long-ago-and-far-away that avoids pinning down time and place. Such a setting also suggests magically one of the most pleasurable aspects of the folktale: maybe-it-happened-here, maybe-yesterday! Thus such a setting also anticipates the equally pleasurable possibility that perhaps-it-could-happen-again, perhaps-here! We have noted in our discussion of character that in a folktale the protagonists are so general and universal that what happens to them might happen to anyone. Similar vagueness in setting reinforces the possibility of adventures for us, the readers.

Folktale settings often follow the "once upon a time" formula. A random sampling of tales from Grimm, for example, reveals the following settings, or lack of them, in their opening lines; little is added within the stories:

> Once upon a time there lived an old man and his wife who for a long time. . . .
>
> Once upon a time there was a king who had twelve daughters. . . .
>
> Once upon a time in deep winter, when the snowflakes were falling like feathers. . . .[3]

Occasionally we read a simple variation: "At the edge of a great forest lived a woodcutter and his wife," or another equally general definition of setting. Folktale settings from other cultures seem to vary little from the patterns of Grimm, with little more specific definition of time and place than the American Indian "My grandfather told me. . . ." It is the nature of the folktale—originally told to an audience who might become restless—to plunge into conflict and action. Such generalized settings can demonstrate more clearly a universal theme: the kindest of the daughters lives happily ever after in the palace of the prince.

Other folk literature seems equally vague about setting. The fable omits setting altogether, going immediately into action and its didactic point:

> A certain Wolf, being very hungry, disguised himself in a sheep's skin.
>
> A mischievous Shepherd's Boy used to amuse himself by calling "Wolf! Wolf!"

Many of the fables are only a few sentences long, and, since they exist to point a moral, setting is quite logically unimportant. The lesson is universal, unlimited by time or place. Myths happened "in ancient Greece," or "in the days of Thor," and designation of time and place is barely relevant. What matters is not location of specific action, but pinning down the locale to the cultural world of Greece or Scandinavia.

Here, too, simplicity in setting reinforces the universal qualities of the myths, their comments upon human vanity or greed.

Legends, those unauthenticated stories handed down from tradition and regarded by the public as historically possible or even true, are by their definition related to historical events or people. This relationship narrows somewhat their time and place. For example, Robin Hood's adventures occur in Sherwood Forest, since that is where Robin Hood, according to history, lived. Often, however, the legends refer to mystical events occurring centuries later than the lifetime of the character, and caused supposedly by the character's onetime presence. The oases of the Egyptian desert, for example, are said by legend to have sprung up wherever the fleeing Joseph, Mary, and the infant Jesus stopped to rest.

Fantasy and Science Fiction

Setting in fantasy is a special consideration, since fantasy often begins in a setting of reality and moves to the setting of a fantasy realm, then back again. Such a book as *Alice in Wonderland* moves easily from the real to the fantastic by the device of a dream; *Where the Wild Things Are* does so by daydream. *And to Think That I Saw It on Mulberry Street* is a fantastic daydream, a parade which is framed by what the narrator actually saw on the way home from school. Other transitions are more complex. In Susan Cooper's *The Dark Is Rising,* the world that Will enters is filled with the mysterious and the supernatural—integral parts of the setting and essential to the story. The castle where Will meets the Old Ones, who for centuries have been battling evil, is the setting for Will's discovery that by the exercise of his will power he can actually bring change. Reluctantly, he learns that he must accept his power in order to use it for good. He looked

> across the room at the light and shadow dancing side by side across the rich tapestries on the stone walls, and he thought hard, in furious concentration, of the image of the blazing log fire in the huge fireplace behind him. He felt the warmth of it on the back of his neck, and thought of the glowing heart of the big pile of logs and the leaping yellow tongues of flame. *Go out, fire,* he said to it in his mind, feeling suddenly safe and free from the dangers of power, because of course no fire as big as that could possibly go out.

The fire goes out. Next Will sees that each of the many tapestries on the castle walls has its own frightening image, some as terrifying as "the empty-eyed grinning white skull of a horse, with a single stubby broken

horn in the bony forehead and red ribbons wreathing the long jaws."
Threatened by the rising of evil, the Dark, Will sees clearly his responsibility to use the special power given him.

In *Alice in Wonderland* Lewis Carroll sets all logic awry, including
the logic of setting. A rabbit hole extends deep into a strange, unboun-
daried world, and time moves in all directions to create a setting essential to our experience of the story. To us as well as to Alice, time and
place are illogical and confusing; they influence nonsensical behavior
which defies every rule. In defiance of time and the related laws of
growth, Alice grows and shrinks; the Mock Turtle's lessons lessen; the
tea party murders time by going on forever; the White Rabbit tries
fruitlessly to catch up with time. As for place, nothing seems either to
be where it is expected to be, or can be counted upon to be in the same
place at another moment. The great hall with glass table and tiny door
vanishes, and Alice finds her way into a tidy little room. Turning her
back on the tea party, Alice walks through a door into a tree—only to
find herself back in the long hall with the glass table and the tiny door.
Finally, cause and effect—which occur in that order and are logically
related to time—defy time to appear in nonsensically reversed order:
sentence first, verdict later.

SUMMARY

Setting is of two principal types. First, it may be a backdrop for the
plot, like the generalized backdrop of a city, street, or forest against
which we can see some of the action of a play. Or it may be an integral part of the story, so essential to our understanding of this
plot, these characters, and these themes, that we must experience it
with our senses. Setting is usually backdrop in traditional folk literature, so generalized that it becomes universal. Depending upon the
theme, conflict, and characters, the setting and its description may
be either backdrop or integral; the choice is the writer's. The integral
setting not only may clarify the conflict, but also may help the
reader understand character, may be cast as the antagonist, may influence mood, or perhaps act as symbol. Often the sense of place
prepares the reader to accept the story and the writer's personal
view of life and its significance.

Deciding that setting is integral or backdrop does not constitute a judgment for or against the quality of a piece of writing.
What is important, however, is that understanding may develop
only when we realize that this particular setting is essential to this
story. And, if setting is essential to our understanding, the writer
must make the reader see, hear, touch, and perhaps even smell the

setting. It is as much the writer's task when writing for child as for adult to evoke setting, described either in paragraphs or in phrases woven into action, by the details of color, sound, figurative comparisons, and other stylistic means.

Reading and Evaluating

Other lands

1. *Read* The Master Puppeteer *and examine the relationship of setting to story. How is the reader acquainted with life in Japan? What details make setting distinctive? Are setting and its resultant life patterns related to the story? How? Of what significance is historical period in the story? Must time be pinned down? Explain.*

Picture books

2. *Read six recent picture-story books. Is the setting integral or backdrop in the stories? Explain. How is setting made clear? By illustrations? By word pictures? A combination?*

Folktales

3. *Read four folktales from each of three cultures—for example, German, Japanese, and American Indian. Is it possible to generalize about the folktale's backdrop setting? What variations do you see in depiction of settings? Are there symbolic settings?*

Epic

4. *Read an epic like a child's version of the* Odyssey, *another version of* Beowulf, *or* Gilgamesh. *Is setting integral? Backdrop? Does it establish mood? Do more than that? Explain.*

Historical fiction

5. *Read a historical novel for children and check the data about setting against what you know of the period and place. Does action occur in setting? Explain. Does the protagonist live in the setting, or does he or she move over it? Are action and character superimposed upon time and place?*

Fantasy/ Nonsense

6. *Read* Alice in Wonderland. *Does Carroll make use of setting as an element of his fantasy-nonsense world? Explain. How does he define Wonderland? Is it part of the nonsense? Extraneous to it?*

Notes

[1]Eudora Welty, *Place in Fiction,* New York: House of Books, 1957, p. 22.

[2]Northrup Frye, "Theory of Symbol," in *Anatomy of Criticism,* Princeton, N.J.: Princeton University Press, 1957, pp. 71–128.

[3]*The Twelve Dancing Princesses,* Alfred David and Mary Elizabeth Meek, eds., Bloomington: Indiana University Press, 1974.

Recommended Books Cited in This Chapter

Babbitt, Natalie. *The Eyes of the Amaryllis.* New York: Farrar, 1977.

Burnford, Sheila. *The Incredible Journey.* Boston: Little, 1961.

Carroll, Lewis. *Alice's Adventures in Wonderland.* New York: Macmillan, 1963. (first published 1865)

Cleaver, Vera and Bill. *Where the Lilies Bloom.* New York: Lippincott, 1969.

————. *The Why's and Wherefore's of Littabelle Lee.* New York: Atheneum, 1973.

Cooper, Susan. *The Dark Is Rising.* New York: Atheneum, 1973.

David, Alfred, and Mary Elizabeth Meek. *The Twelve Dancing Princesses.* Bloomington: Indiana University Press, 1974.

Frank, Anne. *Anne Frank: The Diary of a Young Girl.* Garden City, N.Y.: Doubleday, 1967.

George, Jean. *Julie of the Wolves.* New York: Harper, 1972.

Hamilton, Virginia. *M. C. Higgins the Great.* New York: Macmillan, 1974.

Keats, Ezra Jack. *The Snowy Day.* New York: Viking, 1962.

Lewis, C. S. The *Narnia* Books. New York: Macmillan, 1951–56.

Lindgren, Astrid. *Pippi Longstocking.* New York: Viking, 1950.

Milne, A. A. *Winnie-the-Pooh.* New York: Dutton, 1926.

Norton, Mary. *The Borrowers.* New York: Harcourt, 1965.

O'Dell, Scott. *Island of the Blue Dolphins.* Boston: Houghton, 1960.

Potter, Beatrix. *The Tale of Peter Rabbit.* New York: Warne, 1902.

Sendak, Maurice. *Where the Wild Things Are.* New York: Harper, 1963.

Serriallier, Ian. *Beowulf the Warrior.* New York: Walck, 1961.

Shotwell, Louisa. *Roosevelt Grady.* New York: Collins-World, 1970.

Speare, Elizabeth. *The Witch of Blackbird Pond.* Boston: Houghton, 1958.

Seuss, Dr. *And to Think That I Saw It on Mulberry Street.* New York: Hale, 1937.

Twain, Mark. *The Adventures of Tom Sawyer.* New York: Macmillan, 1962. (first published 1876)

White, E. B. *Charlotte's Web.* New York: Harper, 1952.

We each have at least one friend who tells a story by linking one anecdote to another, using slender threads of association as continuity: "And later that day. . . ." or "And then we. . . ." We have heard a more artful storyteller whose stories are involved and who keeps us in suspense: "You'll never believe what she said then," or "And what should happen next . . . !" The first of these narrators can bore us quickly; the second can hold our interest longer. However, the storyteller we especially value is someone whose stories awaken us to awareness of new meaning—of the inconsistency of people, or the mixed joys of family living, or the pain of social exclusion, for example. In telling his or her story, this storyteller has been aware of meaning and has reached for idea or theme.

In storytelling "What happened next?" is a question about chronology and narrative order. "Why did it happen?" is a question about conflict and plot. But when we ask, "What does it all mean?" we begin to discover theme.

THEME OR UNIFYING TRUTH

Theme in literature is the idea that holds the story together, such as a comment about either society, human nature, or the human condition. It is the main idea or central meaning of a piece of writing.

Ask a woman about the plot of *Little Women,* the story she loved as a child, and she looks baffled and perhaps chagrined that she cannot remember it. Setting, too, has faded from memory to become merely "in the past." Character, however, is still with her, because restless Jo, who has difficulty fitting into traditional female roles, seems to be Everywoman—or at least Manywomen. And chances are the adult's memory of the idea or theme of the novel is still strong; she can confidently say, "It's about a loving family of varied but accepting people." The characters of Louisa May Alcott's story convince us of one of its themes—the love of family members for each other is real and enduring. Theme comes alive and becomes memorable as the characters act out the plot.

Our definition of literature, you will recall, is "a significant truth expressed in appropriate elements and memorable language." The "significant truth" is an element that is essential to turn a simple narrative into literature. This truth goes beyond the story and comments on human beings. This discovery holds the story together so that long after details of plot are forgotten, the theme remains; we still remember the theme of family love and support in *Little Women.*

This significant truth unifies and illuminates a story, giving the reader pleasure. The reader gains one pleasure from the discovery of the simplest of truths, and gains another pleasure from the discovery that truth is not simple.[1] Theme provides this discovery, this understanding, this pleasure in recognizing "Yes, that's the way it is!"

TYPES OF THEMES

Explicit Theme

Sometimes the writer states theme openly and clearly—an *explicit theme.* Once again we turn to *Charlotte's Web* for examples. The devotion between Charlotte and Wilbur suggests many ideas that make the reader say, "It's true"; their relationship reveals and defines friendship and suggests other themes.

Charlotte has encouraged, protected, and mothered Wilbur, bargained and sacrificed for him, and Wilbur, the grateful receiver, realizes that "Friendship is one of the most satisfying things in the world." And Charlotte says later, "By helping you perhaps I was trying to lift my life a little. Anyone's life can stand a little of that." These quoted sentences are exact statements from the text; they are therefore called explicit themes. Consider another example, this statement from Zilpha Snyder's *The Witches of Worm:* "We all invite our own devils, and we must exorcise our own." It, too, is an explicit theme. Such explicit themes are common in children's literature because the writer may wish to be sure that the reader will find the unifying truth.

Implicit Theme

Underlying *Charlotte's Web* are certain implied or *implicit themes,* as important and almost as apparent as explicit themes. If two such different characters as a runt pig and a carnivorous spider can find friendship, others can; even a self-centered rat can be a friend of sorts. White thereby implies that friendship can be found in unexpected places.

Charlotte's selflessness—working late at night to finish a new word, expending her last energies for her friend—is evidence that friendship is giving oneself. Wilbur's protection of Charlotte's egg sac, his sacrifice of first turn at the slops, and his devotion to Charlotte's babies—giving without any need to stay even or to pay back—leads us to another theme: True friendship is naturally reciprocal. As the two become fond of each other, still another theme emerges: One's best friend can do no wrong. In fact, a best friend is sensational! Both Charlotte and Wilbur believe in these ideas; their experiences verify them. These themes are all developed through the characters, their actions, and their thoughts as we see them throughout the story's conflict.

When we think of theme as "a moral" or "a lesson," or even as "a message," we are turned away by the idea that we must learn something about moral values or about how or how not to behave. But a good story is not meant to instruct us. Its purpose is to entertain us by its action and characters; at the same time, it gives us insight into people and how they think and feel, and it enlarges our understanding. When we think of theme as the unifying idea that holds the other elements of a good story together, we are pleased to find that we have not only been entertained, but have made a discovery of some kind. Theme, then, is not a heavily instructive message, but a discovery.

It may seem unnecessary or even unwise to state theme in sentence form. Why not say, "The theme of *Charlotte's Web* is friendship"? Notice what happens if we do state the theme this simply. *Friendship* is too broad a term: "Friendship is fraudulent," or "Friendship is a useless luxury," or "Friendship is all giving and no receiving." Any of these statements concerns friendship and might reasonably be explored and proven in literature, but none is the truth of E. B. White's story. When we force ourselves to make a specific statement based upon the facts of the story, we define the theme more carefully.

Multiple and Secondary Themes

Each of us brings to a story a personal past, a present, and plans for the future. These elements shape our responses to the story. It seems absurd then to expect that diverse human beings must agree upon exactly the same ideas as being the most important, and must take from the story exactly the same themes, since the story speaks to us out of our own individual and varying experiences. It speaks a universal truth to us, but our own universal truth.

Although complexity and variety in themes may be one of the strongest proofs of the work's excellence, most literature for children seems to center upon a *primary theme.* When a story contains a variety of themes, they are often linked. For example, the central idea, the effort to defeat the forces of evil, is explored in Susan Cooper's *The Dark Is Rising*, a fantasy set in the English countryside. Will finds that he has special gifts, and that these gifts if properly used can work against the forces of the Dark. He relies on the help of others, the Old Ones. From our experience with the novel, we might settle on a variety of themes. Will is part of a happy family, none of them involved in the struggle in the way that Will is: "A loving family is made up of many kinds of people with differing interests and gifts, but each has value." Will does not want the difficult responsibility of being a select person, an Old One, but finds that because he is chosen, he must—he has no choice: "Only by determination, by the exercise of will, can we bring about change." The group who are fighting against the rising Dark of evil come from different social strata and from different settings in historical time: "In one generation after another, one society after another, there are those allied with evil and those committed to good." When the story ends, we have the definite impression that the battle has been won for now—but that it will resume: "The battle against Evil may be intermittent, but it is never conclusive." These themes are related and support the central or main theme.

Virginia Hamilton in *The Planet of Junior Brown* also suggests a variety of related themes. The story concerns Junior Brown, who is black, overweight, lonely, and without understanding or family life. He lives with a neurotic and possessive mother. Junior's friend Tomorrow Billy is also alone, but finds purpose and focus for his life by drawing together children without homes and showing them how to survive. Miss Peebs the solitary pianist lives with shreds of memory, and the janitor provides a haven for ostracized school children. The various themes emerge: "We all have problems"; "People find different ways of coping with their isolation and their differences"; "Everyone needs someone to belong to"; "There is hope for us all if someone cares."

If a story has multiple themes, some seem less important than the primary one. These we call *secondary themes.*

In *Charlotte's Web*, almost as important as the theme about the nature of friendship is a secondary one about death. It is the possibility of Wilbur's death that disturbs us; we would feel differently if he were an old boar who had lived long and well. We recognize, just the same, that "Death is inevitable and not to be feared." Charlotte, knowing her life cycle, foresees her own death, but neither dreads it nor asks for pity. Others accept death too. Seasons die when they have run their terms. Maple trees, crickets, lilacs, baby spiders, and the harvest Fair all celebrate the inevitable cycle of birth, life, and death. There is no grief, only acceptance.

A wealth of minor themes also emerges in *Charlotte's Web:* "People are gullible"; "People don't give credit where credit is due"; "The meek may inherit the earth"; "Youth and innocence have unique value." Each character accepts and maintains the simplicity of his or her own particular style of living, so "Be what you are." As for nature, "There are beauty and wonder in all things, even the simplest," "Life in nature is constant and continuous," and finally, "Nature is a miracle," from the silver forest of asparagus to the waterproof egg sac.

In one story, value lies in the explicit yet nondidactic statement of theme. In another, the fact that the theme is implied and must be stated by the reader for himself or herself is value of another kind. The only general rule that can be made is that a theme should be there. On first reading a good story, we usually see one or a few thematic ideas, both explicit and implicit. We see more perhaps on second reading. However, the wealth of a book for children often lies in the continuous discoveries about theme.

Does the child see these ideas? If we ask the child, "What is the theme?" we can scarcely expect replies like those we have mentioned. Children may discover from Randall Jarrell's *The Animal Family*, for example, that all living things are related, parts of a universal family, and yet not be able to state such a theme in their own words. Children differ, and the variety of their capacities for discovery as well as for phrasing that discovery is almost infinite. The smaller the child, the less likelihood of a coherent statement. We realize, however, that although a small child cannot define "home" or "mother," the youngest knows what each concept is. Security and love, comfort and constancy, warmth and protection are abstractions that they know, but abstractions beyond articulation by the very young. For children, knowing and saying need not be—and rarely are—the same.

EVALUATING THEME IN CHILDREN'S LITERATURE

Traditional Literature

Folktales have similar themes even though they originate in different cultures. Their presence in traditional literature, literature passed on from one generation to another, seems to be evidence that people create and respond to similar ideas about life and human nature. By noting just a few of these themes, we become aware that a simple, optimistic core of truth like "good can conquer evil" is explored in a great many of the tales. Some leave the theme as simple as that, but others explore ideas a bit more complex, clarifying the kind of good or the kind of evil. "The

Goosegirl," a German tale, explicitly identifies the conquered evil as deception; the servant girl who threatens and impersonates the princess is punished. "Snow White," another German tale, defines the defeated evil more clearly as jealousy; the queen-witch tries ceaselessly to kill the one more beautiful than she. "Drakestail," from the French, identifies the particular good as humility; the modest hero calls upon the Fox, the Ladder, and the River to save him from a tyrant king.

Other folktales, like the Norwegian "The Three Billy Goats Gruff," prove that keeping your wits about you can save you from danger. In the German tale "The Twelve Dancing Princesses," the soldier outwits the princesses and wins one for his bride. The Scandinavian "Boots and His Brothers" shows that if you have the wit to see its potential, curiosity can pay off. Both the Russian "The Little Humpbacked Horse" and the Norse "The Princess on the Glass Hill" praise the capacity of cleverness to bring success. Both "The Brementown Musicians" from Germany and "The Ram and the Pig Who Went into the Woods" from Scandinavia offer proof that each creature can use its gifts to contribute to common success. Tales told over and over, tales told in one land or another, tales complex in structure for older readers or simple in outline for younger readers, most have themes that state a universal truth.

Theme in folk literature, like conflict and characters, is usually clearly defined. Like the conflicts that so obviously set protagonist against antagonist, the themes are straightforward and easily seen. Although themes are often implicit, the conflict and the characters make them so evident that explicit statements are unnecessary. Good can conquer evil, hard work can bring success, intelligence is more valuable than physical strength, kindness brings rewards—these are basic issues that the vigorous action of the folktale makes clear. The prominence of theme in traditional stories seems to verify the human wish to know not only what happened, and how it happened, but also why it happened and what it means. According to Wayne Booth, one of the strongest of human interests is the "desire for causal completion." "Not only do we believe that certain causes do in life produce certain effects; in literature we believe that they should." This interest is distinct from the "pleasure of learning, of satisfaction of intellectual curiosity."[2]

But the themes of literature are not all optimistic. Human beings are not totally good nor completely successful; good does not always conquer evil. Hans Christian Andersen, although he uses the traditional forms of folktales, makes no effort either to be constantly optimistic or to preach about what people ought to be. He is too busy showing what people are. Many of his stories of humble people, animals, and inanimate objects demonstrate one of his most personal and optimistic themes, that of the Ugly Duckling: "Humble beginnings and painful trials can end in happiness." But Andersen's themes also frequently remind us that people are foolish; they value the artificial and the trivial more than the real, as "The Swineherd," "The Nightingale," and "The Princess and the Pea" tell us. People will do anything for vanity, as we see in "The Emperor's New Clothes." Whether we like it or not, the rogue sometimes wins the prize, as he does in "The Tinder Box." Andersen honestly admits that death is sometimes sudden and may leave children bereft; he explores serious themes and develops them into individualized and realistic comments on humankind. His stories prove that literature for children as well as for adults can make sad or even negative comments and still give both pleasure and discovery.

Didacticism

We often wish to help children by telling them what they ought or ought not to do. We give them little mottoes and short, preachy verses to hang on their bedroom walls. From our own past experience we tell them stories which really are instruction disguised as interesting reminiscence. The result may be the child's comment, "I'm sick of hearing how my dad *loved* to walk to school every day. And according to him, it was uphill both ways." No one is fooled.

Or we admire the welcome hyacinths in the springtime flower bed, but instead of comparing their varied colors, smelling their fragrance, touching curled, waxy petals, we turn our admiration into a botany lesson on stamen, pistil, and corolla. The science lesson has its place, of course, but not every flower bed must stimulate it. A growing awareness of startling beauty and perfection in nature may sometimes be stifled by a lesson from "Botany 101."

Didacticism or instruction is the function of textbooks.[3] Some literature gives a great deal of information without letting it take over from a suspenseful and exciting plot, or from well-developed characters. Other narratives are so filled with teaching details about a historical period, a geographical area, a social inequity, or a physical disability that conflict, character, and theme are lost in "what the reader ought to know." If the information displaces the understanding, then didacticism has won out. Literature, on the other hand, does not teach; it helps us understand.

Nor does literature preach. "Eat it; it's good for you," never persuaded anyone. Adults who choose stories for children that force morals upon them think that a story is good only if it contains obvious lessons. However, knowing our own adult dislike for "do this, but don't do that," we can scarcely expect children to enjoy such preaching, and we may be preventing the child from making discoveries on the child's own. We may be impeding growth rather than fostering it. Furthermore, sugar-coating a moral by surrounding it with a shallow story deficient in plot, character portrayal, and style does injustice to children. They come to a story excited by the promise of pleasure only to discover they have been tricked into a sermon. The preached-at child may come to reject all reading and thus to close off the vast discoveries about human beings and society available in literature.

The obvious purpose of some narratives, like *I Want to Be a Homemaker,* shows little imagination on the part of the writer and awakens little response from the reader; it may even stimulate resistance.[4] Everything in this narrative is commonplace information and therefore the narrative itself is commonplace. We have a sexist view of what a homemaker does: she bakes and sews and tends the baby. Why? Because that is her job. But there is no word of what a mother *is.* A real mother loves her children and finds satisfaction in providing for them —like the mothers of Peter Rabbit and the Moffats, or the mothers of the troubled children in *Sounder* or *Roll of Thunder, Hear My Cry.* In a story exploring motivation in a real mother we might come to see the dimensions of such love. This would be a story with some significance and not a narrative with an underlined message.

A selfish, tit-for-tat approach to friendship that says, "Be nice to your friends and they will be nice to you," or "Make everyday occurrences into fun," would be preachy. Throughout a story, understanding of friendship may grow and ordinary experience may be joyful, but the stories need not be reduced to neat little mottoes suitable for framing.

Nonsense

Such nonsense-fantasy stories as Kipling's *Just So Stories,* or *Pippi Longstocking,* and even *Alice in Wonderland* seem to lack theme, but each has as its core the idea of wonder and delight at the order and disorder of life. We marvel as the *Just So Stories* tell why whales have tiny throats and leopards have spots; *Winnie-the-Pooh* seems to say that people do strange and exciting things—and with such solemnity. Although adults find satire and social comment in *Alice,* Carroll in his opening poem speaks of

> The dream-child moving through a land
> Of wonders wild and new . . .
> And half believe it true.

Nonsense as a whole seems to say, "The world and all its inhabitants —thank heaven—make no sense." Nonsense, in its own way, may develop a theme. If it doesn't, it finally palls.

Theme for the Youngest Child

Some stories for young children are both humor-filled and rich with a variety of themes, but check the shelf of children's fare in any bookstore and notice how often action or situation humor is its chief element. The popularity of books like Hans Rey's *Curious George* with its exciting action and variety—the monkey's balloon flight which coincidentally ends on top of the traffic light, and his play with the telephone which coincidentally calls in a fire alarm—seems to suggest that a child can appreciate only light situations.

While *Curious George* is a pleasant narrative for a very small child, there is even greater satisfaction in a story with a real theme. The equally simple story *Frederick* by Leo Lionni has not only an interesting situation, a protagonist with some development, and a conflict that has climax and resolution, but it has thematic strength as well. Frederick is the mouse who collects—not wheat, corn, straw, and nuts—but sun's rays and periwinkle colors. He brings these out during the dull days of winter to remind the others of nature's beauty and of hope for spring's return. Frederick's poetry sustains the spirits of his friends throughout the long winter, showing that food and shelter do not alone support life; the spirit needs nourishment too.

When we read *Mr. Popper's Penguins,* we discover that inconvenience is unimportant when we care about those we sacrifice for. Richard and Florence Atwater's matter-of-fact tone, accepting Mr. Popper's ridiculous sacrifices of his refrigerator, his bathtub, and his basement, reveals a slight but significant theme. In Maurice Sendak's *Where the Wild Things Are* we have a character Max, whom we care about, acting out a conflict that interests us—and all united by a theme which can be stated in several ways: We show love in many ways; or the best place is where there is love. The story is more than a situation, more than the pleasure of its rhythmic style. The story also has a strong theme.

Many kinds of stories have their place in reading for small children: some offer the listening child laughter from a narrative with physical or situation humor, or the reassurance found in pure, day-to-day routine.[5] Other stories like Miska Miles's *Annie and the Old One,* or Lucille Clifton's *The Boy Who Didn't Believe in Spring* combine freshness in language, imagination in plot, and significance in theme, as well as distinctive illustrations.

Once again, we refer to *The Tale of Peter Rabbit,* which has its own implicit theme. Action and suspense race to the point of Peter's flopping down on the nice, sandy floor of the rabbit home, where he shuts his eyes. Mother, who is busy cooking, wonders what he has done with his new clothes, but she does not lecture, nor spank, nor compare naughty Peter to good Flopsy, Mopsy, and Cotton-tail. Although Peter didn't feel very well that evening, there is no hint of "It serves him right. He was naughty." Peter's mother puts him to bed and gives him a dose of camomile tea. Potter does not call it punitive medicine, nor describe it as tasting bad. Nor does she call Flopsy, Mopsy, and Cotton-tail's bread, milk, and blackberries reward for goodness.

Is the story didactic? Although we adults see clearly that disobedience and curiosity can get you into trouble, *Peter Rabbit,* after all, is for a small child. The theme is implied, not didactic. *Peter Rabbit* can become didactic, however, if some reteller adds a single phrase to Potter's final paragraph, saying that Flopsy, Mopsy, and Cotton-tail, "who were good little bunnies," ate bread and milk and blackberries at suppertime. Or when we see another illustrator's picture with an admonitory plaque hanging on the kitchen wall, saying, "Good bunnies obey," or, preaching a more positive lesson, "Obedience is rewarded." It seems doubtful that didactic preachments have made *Peter Rabbit* a favorite with children for several generations. It seems more likely that a possible implied theme, "Even when you're naughty, mother loves and accepts you," has kept it a much-loved story.[6]

Mature Themes in Children's Stories

Stories like those from Hans Christian Andersen may introduce children to ideas far more mature than we would expect them to grasp. From stories, they can understand ideas we find difficult to explain in other ways. Fear, for example, is very much a part of childhood. However, what one is afraid *of* is often hard to pin down. Bruno Bettelheim, child psychologist, writes of the capacity of folk and fairy tales to help the child "externalize" the fears that go on in a child's mind. Folktales confront and thus make legitimate the universal fears like that of the death of a parent in "Hansel and Gretel," the attractiveness of evil in "Snow White and the Seven Dwarfs," and the fear of going out into the world in "Dick Whittington and His Cat." Stories like *The Borrowers* can carry the child through a variety of fears that may haunt the reader in real life and yet are rarely clarified. That we fear the unknown is clearly part of the novel. Homily fears what will happen to Pod on his cup-borrowing expedition. Both parents keep Arrietty at home lest she be seen by a human being. They fear the fate of Uncle Hendreary, and what the boy will do; they fear Mrs. Driver, her friend Mr. Crampfurl, and the exterminators. Most of all, Homily fears moving, emigration to the unknown world beyond the floorboards. Moreover, there is in *The Borrowers* another idea that adults find easy to understand but hard to put into words for children: Materialism is a destructive force. Homily admits, "My mother's family never had nothing but a little bone thimble which they shared around. But it's once you've *had* a tea cup. . . ." Homily nags Pod for new blotting paper carpet, and sends him off for things to store away. Even when she is screaming with fright at the boy's appearance, she wants more possessions. Homily's materialism sends Pod to his "club" upstairs, and brings on the exterminators. Materialism has disrupted the family and brought it to disaster—a big discovery for readers too young to know the word "materialism."

In recent years, situations and themes in stories for older readers have been changing. With society today more open in its discussion of the many problems of growing up, recent novels have confronted many subjects that were once taboo. Although there are still some boy-meets-girl romances, novels now explore the growth of sexuality and its effects. Stories for older children are dealing with impotence, premarital sex, pregnancy, forced marriage, and abortion. What has been called the perfect-parent syndrome has been broken. Books for young people now show parents as imperfect and human—unreliable, perhaps, or alcoholic, or simply shallow. Other stories deal with such problems as death, divorce, drugs, and disease. These subjects attract readers partly because of their taboo status, but also because these matters do concern today's youth.[7]

Often these stories seem to have been written for the vast market that the pulp magazines once appealed to; often the quality of the writing seems comparable. Sometimes the young reader is carried along by sentimentality and coincidence; the writing is drab in style and shallow in characterization; themes are didactic and overly simplified. On the other hand, some writers are dealing with the issues of today with sensitivity and skill, writing about the problems that confront the young in ways that create suspenseful stories and make the reader care about the protagonist's problem. Style and characterization show skill and perception, while the themes show the universal truths that arise from the conflicts.

Take, for example, the following stories about young people, each with a problem. First there is *Deenie* by Judy Blume. Deenie has scoliosis and wears a back brace. While we do feel sorry for Deenie, she is so close to being a stereotyped adolescent—interested only in boys and beauty—that we soon find her uninteresting. One theme of the book, that even girls with back braces can find friends, seems didactic and unconvincing because we have little interest in or understanding of the relatively flat protagonist. In *Why Me?* by John Branfield, we have a clear description of diabetic diet, injections, and insulin shock. The theme seems to be that this is what diabetes can do to one—a discovery that is surely worth making. However, because we see the protagonist as only physically diabetic and not psychologically real, the theme seems inadequate.

By contrast, look at Fran Ellen in *The Bear's House* by Marilyn Sachs. Fran Ellen lives a completely happy life in her imagination that becomes real to her whenever she sits at the back of the schoolroom to stare into the tiny house of The Three Bears. Here in her daydreams Fran Ellen is accepted and loved; she eats turkey and lemon pie, and can have friends over whenever she wants to. In real life, Fran Ellen runs home at noon, and even at recess, to care for baby sister Flora who "loves her best." Meanwhile, her older sister is preoccupied with herself, and her alcoholic mother is too depressed to do anything. Since Fran Ellen, who tells her own story, is so believable in her feelings and in her way of expressing them, we care about her. We believe the theme: "Everyone yearns for a stable and loving home."

To cite another example, notice how the portrayal of Julius in *Luke Was There* by Eleanor Clymer works to convince us of the truth of the theme. Julius, who has been abandoned, comes to depend upon his social worker Luke. When Julius finds a small child who depends upon him, he makes a discovery that we are prepared to accept: "Others depend upon us." In another example, Katherine Paterson's *The Great Gilly Hopkins,* the protagonist is a resentful girl who enjoys keeping people around her stirred up and must move from one foster home to another. When she begins to respect Trotter, her new foster mother who will not be manipulated, and when she begins to appreciate the qualities of the blind man next door as well as to take pride in teaching W. E., the other foster child, Gilly has a new source of pleasure. The new Gilly is able to give up her fantasies about her real mother and to admit her disappointments. She then settles down to become her grandmother Nonie's child, knowing that there is satisfaction in making tough decisions and sticking with them.

Current stories that deal with realistic problems are a significant trend. They can show us real characters; they can explore the problems of today's youth. However, what is true for other literature seems to be true here, as well. When we believe in the character, we believe in the experience, and are then prepared to accept the theme. When, on the other hand, theme seems to have been the first motive for writing—"Now I'll write a story about the evils of smoking pot"— the stories may become didactic, as does *The Grass Pipe.* If we look beneath the surface of much of today's with-it realistic stories for young people, we find didacticism, even sentimentality, and such stories are likely to be a fad. The well-written stories, however, will convince us of the truth of the theme and thus contribute to the readers' growth and discovery. Mature themes can be explored in children's literature; they contribute to understanding when they meet the requirements of excellence.

SUMMARY

Theme, stated explicitly or implicitly, is essential to a children's story if it is to merit the name of literature. A narrative with action and people but without theme is a story without meaning that leaves the reader wondering at the close, "So what?" A piece of writing, a collection of words with plot, character, setting, style, and meaning (without preachment) is literature for children, as well as for adults. The theme we take to become part of ourselves is the one that enlarges our understanding and the one we discover for ourselves—not the one underlined and delivered didactically by the author.

Reading and Evaluating

Picture book   1. *First read* The Tale of Peter Rabbit *and* Frederick, *and then five more picture-story books. State the theme of each story. Is theme explicit? Implicit? Has the story a preaching or teaching purpose rather than a purpose that helps the reader understand himself or others? If there is no theme in the story, has it a unifying idea? Is the story pure situation humor?*

Historical fiction   2. *Read a historical fiction book by Laura Ingalls Wilder, Rosemary Sutcliff, or another writer and state the theme. Is it explicit? Implicit? Does the historical information seem more important to the writer than understanding of human beings? Are the historical details seen as important to our understanding of the story, or are they the purpose of the story? Is the theme relevant to today? To you? To today's society?*

Other countries   3. *Read a story about children from other lands by Meindert De-Jong, Katherine Paterson, or another writer. What is the theme? How is it made known? Given the country and its customs, are the characters believable enough to make you believe in the theme?*

Problem realism   4. *Read a book written within the last ten years that has a protagonist or central character with a physical, emotional, or social adjustment problem. Does the story convince you of its truth? Does the information seem more important than the characters and the theme they make you understand?*

Regional realism   5. *Read a regional realism book by Lois Lenski, Joseph Krumgold, Esther Wier, Clyde Bulla, or another writer and state the theme. Is the theme a truth only for these people in this part of the country, or is it a truth for all people? Explain your answer.*

Social Issues realism   6. *Read a story about a religious or ethnic minority by Virginia Hamilton, Natalie Carlson, or another writer. Is the theme about all human beings or does it prove that this group is singular and strange? Does the theme make this group more understandable to you?* Compare Bright April *(Marguerite DeAngeli)* and Jennifer, Hecate, Macbeth, William McKinley and Me, Elizabeth *(E. L. Konigsberg) for thematic value and didacticism. Or compare two other stories for their themes regarding minorities.*

Notes

[1]Wayne Booth in *The Rhetoric of Fiction* (Chicago, University of Chicago Press, 1961) makes this comment (p. 136).

[2]*The Rhetoric of Fiction,* p. 126. The satisfaction of knowing causality in children's literature is most obviously demonstrated in the cumulative tales like the humorous "Old Woman and the Pig," or the verse story "This Is the House That Jack Built."

[3]For a historical overview of didacticism, see Paul Hazard's *Books, Children and Men,* "Men Have Always Oppressed Children," Boston, The Horn Book, Inc., 1960. See, too, "Didacticism in Modern Dress," by John Townsend, pp. 33–40 and "Good Bunnies Always Obey," by Jason Epstein, pp. 70–90 in *Only Connect,* Sheila Egoff, G. T. Stubbs, and L. F. Ashley, editors, New York, Oxford University Press, 1969.

[4]*I Want to Be a Homemaker* by Carla Greene (N.Y., Children's Press, 1961) in many libraries is shelved among the picture books as JE. Commenting on the book here reminds us of the difference between real stories and instructive narrative. Others in the series of 54 books describe jobs; *Homemaker* seems to be describing role.

[5]See Edward W. Rosenheim, Jr., "Children's Reading and Adult Values" in *Only Connect,* Sheila Egoff, G. T. Stubbs, and L. F. Ashley, eds., New York: Oxford University Press, 1969, p. 24. Rosenheim speaks, too, of the overworked "principle of familiarity" and the unexciting commonplace.

[6]There are many examples of picture books with clear themes. Look, for example, at Lloyd Alexander's *The King's Fountain,* or Judith Viorst's *The Tenth Good Thing About Barney,* or Isaac Singer's *Mazel and Shlimazel,* or Anne Rose's *How Does the Czar Eat Potatoes?* Good picture books do have themes.

[7]See Robert Burch, "The New Realism," *Children and Literature: Views and Reviews,* Virginia Haviland, ed., Glenview, Ill., Scott, Foresman, 1973, pp. 281–287. See also Mary Q. Steele, "Realism, Truth, and Honesty," in the same volume, pp. 288–298.

Recommended Books Cited in This Chapter

Alcott, Louisa May. *Little Women.* New York: Dutton, 1948. (first published 1868–69)

Alexander, Lloyd. *The King's Fountain.* New York: Dutton, 1971.

Andersen, Hans Christian. *The Ugly Duckling, The Swineherd, The Nightingale, The Princess and the Pea, The Tinderbox, The Twelve Dancing Princesses and Other Fairy Tales.* Alfred David and Mary Elizabeth Meek, eds., Bloomington: Indiana University Press, 1974.

————. *The Emperor's New Clothes.* New York: Harcourt, 1959, and others.

Armstrong, William H. *Sounder.* New York: Harper, 1969.

Atwater, Florence and Richard. *Mr. Popper's Penguins.* Boston: Little, 1938.

Carroll, Lewis. *Alice in Wonderland.* New York: Macmillan, 1963, (first published 1865)

Clifton, Lucille. *The Boy Who Didn't Believe in Spring.* New York: Dutton, 1973.

Clymer, Eleanor. *Luke Was There.* New York: Holt, 1973.

Cooper, Susan. *The Dark Is Rising.* New York: Atheneum, 1973.

Hamilton, Virginia. *The Planet of Junior Brown.* New York: Macmillan, 1971.

Jarrell, Randall. *The Animal Family.* New York: Pantheon, 1965.

Kipling, Rudyard. *Just So Stories.* Garden City, N.Y.: Doubleday, 1946. (first published 1902)

Lindgren, Astrid. *Pippi Longstocking.* New York: Viking, 1950.

Lionni, Leo. *Frederick.* New York: Pantheon, 1966.

Mathis, Sharon Bell. *The Hundred Penny Box.* New York: Viking, 1975.

Miles, Miska. *Annie and the Old One.* Boston: Little, 1971.

Milne, A. A. *Winnie-the-Pooh.* New York: Dutton, 1926.

Norton, Mary. *The Borrowers.* New York: Harcourt, 1952.

Paterson, Katherine. *The Great Gilly Hopkins.* New York: Crowell, 1978.

Potter, Beatrix. *The Tale of Peter Rabbit.* New York: Warne, 1902.

Rose, Anne. *How Does the Czar Eat Potatoes?* New York: Lothrop, 1973.

Sachs, Marilyn. *The Bears' House.* New York: Doubleday, 1971.

Sendak, Maurice. *Where the Wild Things Are.* New York: Harper, 1963.

Singer, Isaac Bashevis. *Mazel and Shlimazel.* New York: Farrar, 1967.

Snyder, Zilpha. *The Witches of Worm.* New York: Atheneum, 1973.

Taylor, Mildred. *Roll of Thunder, Hear My Cry.* New York: Dial, 1976.

Viorst, Judith. *The Tenth Good Thing About Barney.* New York: Atheneum, 1971.

White, E. B. *Charlotte's Web.* New York: Harper, 1952.

When we hear the term *point of view*, we commonly think of opinion or attitude: "From my point of view, women's rights are. . . ." Sometimes we think of a personal angle or perspective: "That may be true for you, but I'm in business, and. . . ." But the term ***point of view*** has special meaning for literature. As we read a story we may be aware that we are seeing the events through the eyes—and mind—of one character. Or we may feel that we are objective observers watching the events unfold before our eyes. The writer wants to tell us this story. Whose view of the story the writer tells determines the point of view. Who sees the events determines how the story will develop.

Beatrix Potter wishes to tell a story about a rabbit whose mischievous nature gets him into trouble in a vegetable garden. How should she tell the story? Potter has several choices of point of view. She can be objective, telling just what happens, and nothing about the effect of events upon Peter's feelings. If Potter has Mother Rabbit tell Peter's story, we might see a mother weary of Peter's regular disobedience and of buying new jackets and shoes, but loving Peter just the same. If Flopsy, the good little bunny, tells the story, we might see a prim little sister who, because she is always good, thinks Peter really ought to know better. Cottontail might tell the story enviously: "If I had any courage, I'd have some excitement, too." But Potter chooses to tell her tale from a point inside Peter's feelings and thoughts. We know Peter's curiosity, his appetite as he munches on, his worry as he asks directions, his panic as he upsets the flower pots, and we are as relieved as Peter when he finds his way home and is not scolded for his adventure. Every element in the story has been affected by Potter's choice of point of view. Peter is the protagonist and Mr. McGregor the antagonist. We know the character of Peter; his conflict is determined by the setting. Because of Peter's adventure and his mother's kind care, we understand the thematic point—that although a child is naughty, he or she is still loved.

As we all know, two people to whom the same incident happens simultaneously can have different versions of the event; each responds out of past experience, or from belief in right and wrong behavior, as well as from the more obvious differences in the physical and emotional effects of the incident. Each version of the facts is a personal truth.

A similar situation exists in literature. As readers we describe point of view depending upon who sees and tells about the action. The same story is a different story, depending upon which side of the story we see. In the case of Louise Fatio's *The Happy Lion*, the story depends upon which side of the cage door the zoo lion is on. The Happy Lion thinks his visitors are pleasant, civil people. They nod, they bow, they greet him, and feed him—when he is inside his cage. But the day the keeper forgets to close the door, the Happy Lion walks out and meets his friends in their territory. One faints, one screams, and another throws a bag of vegetables in his face. Now the Happy Lion's friends have become puzzling strangers. Since the point of view is what we would call limited omniscient, and we know the Happy Lion's innocent thoughts, we are completely sympathetic to his puzzlement. When he calls the people foolish, we agree, since we know this Lion is not vicious nor predatory. He's just taking a walk. However, if we didn't know the protagonist's thoughts, we'd be as frightened as the human citizens of the Lion's town. It is all a matter of point of view—whose thoughts we know, whose view of the action we follow.

TYPES OF POINT OF VIEW

Point of view is determined when the writer chooses who is to be the narrator and decides how much the narrator is to know. The first possibility a writer might consider is the ***first-person point of view,*** used when a story is told in first person "I." In such storytelling, the reader lives, acts, feels, and thinks the conflict as the protagonist experiences and tells it, just as do Karana in *Island of the Blue Dolphins* or the narrator in *The Slave Dancer.* Occasionally the first-person narrator is not the protagonist, but a minor character who observes action and tells what the protagonist is doing.

The second possibility is the ***omniscient point of view.*** Here the writer, telling the story in third person (he, she, they), is all-knowing or omniscient about any and every detail of action, thought, and feeling —conscious or unconscious—in past, present, or future; if the writer chooses, he or she may recount any and all details. This omniscience is White's choice for *Charlotte's Web.*

A third possibility is the ***limited omniscient point of view,*** in which the writer, again telling the story in third person, concentrates on the thoughts, feelings, and significant past experience of only the central character or protagonist, as Wilder does in her *Little House* stories. Occasionally the writer may choose to be omniscient about a few characters; this choice, too, is sometimes called limited omniscient.

The fourth possibility is the ***objective or dramatic point of*** view, again using third person as, for example, Lenski does in *Cowboy Small*. The meaning of this term seems clear when we refer to the fictional reality of drama or motion picture. A camera seems to record —it cannot comment or interpret. There is no one there to explain to the reader what is going on or what the characters think or feel. The camera selects and we see and draw our own conclusions.

First-Person Point of View

The first-person narrator is limited; like us, he or she cannot tell what another character thinks unless told by that other character. Even though the narrator sees the action of another character, the narrator, again like us, can only speculate about what the other is thinking. A hasty tucking in of shirt or a nervous shaking of head gives evidence from which the narrator may draw conclusions, just as we draw conclusions. However, unless the second character says aloud what he or she thinks, the first-person narrator, again like us, can only guess.

The first-person narrator who tells the story may be either the protagonist or a minor character observing the action. The narrator in *The Slave Dancer* by Paula Fox is mortified to find that he is permitted to stare at the naked bodies of the slaves. As he stands amidst the crew on deck, he observes that they are dressed, shod, even armed. Then he notes the few ragged bits of cloth around the slaves' waists, and the crew staring fixedly.

> I felt fevered and agitated. I sensed, I saw, how beyond the advantage we had of weapons, their nakedness made them helpless. Even if we had not been armed, our clothes and boots alone would have given us power. . . .
> There was something else that held the attention of the men—and my own. It was the unguarded difference between the bodies of the men and women.

The narrator recalls his earlier childish curiosity, his window-peeking at women undressing; what he feels now that he can gaze "without restraint at the helpless and revealed forms of these slaves," is a mortification beyond imagining. With new sympathy, he dreads the coming of daylight, knowing he must bow to the screams of Cawthorne who would tie him to the topmost crosspiece of the mast if he refused to play his fife, to dance the slaves. We are convinced that the story is true partly because the narrator maintains a consistent first-person point of view limited by what he can know.

Karana, the protagonist in *Island of the Blue Dolphins*, is also a first-person narrator. O'Dell carefully maintains credible first-person point of view; at no time does Karana ever pretend to know what is in the minds of others, not her brother, the hunters, Tutok the Aleut stranger, or the animals. Karana can only draw conclusions about the feelings of Tutok from her actions. Tutok comes out from the brush quickly; Karana says, "She must have been waiting nearby." That possibility is all that Karana can know about Tutok's motives. Tutok hugs Karana when she receives the shell necklace. Karana says, "She was so pleased that I forgot how sore my fingers were." A hug—action from another character—makes Karana conclude that Tutok is pleased. Although Karana knows her dog Rontu very well, she describes only his actions, never his thoughts. Karana concludes that Rontu wishes to bark only because he always had. Rontu

> raised his ears at the sound, and I put him down, thinking that he wished to bark at [the gulls] as he always did. He raised his head and followed them with his eyes, but did not make a sound.

Had O'Dell violated the first-person point of view by telling us Rontu's feelings, we would have lost some of our concentration on Karana and the story would have been less real.

As we can see clearly from these passages, one of the strongest assets of first-person narration is its great potential for pulling the reader into what appears to be autobiographical truth. Because Karana's thoughts are interesting to us, we are sympathetic with her. She is consistently credible because she is believably limited in what she can admit to knowing. Because solitary Karana—like solitary Robinson Crusoe—tells her own realistic story, the vicarious experience of survival is a powerful reality, convincingly immediate to the reader. If the story had been filtered through an omniscient writer, the immediacy of the experience would probably have been less intense. The intervention of someone who wasn't there but who still knows and can tell it all would create an intervening omniscience between the solitary protagonist and the reader. The story would then be more remote, less immediate, and less intensely real.

Clearly the danger in first-person narration lies in the possibility of "I" ignoring his or her limitations, reporting thoughts of others, and predicting, when such prediction would not naturally fall within "I's" ability to predict. Credibility is then lost.

In *Owls in the Family*, Farley Mowat helps us discover a great deal of natural history. His story is filled with information and appreciation of animal life, but Mowat does not violate point of view to tell the thoughts of anyone but the narrator. Mowat has particular skill in combining believably youthful vocabulary with keen observation and meticulous attention to accurate detail. As a result, he writes a suspenseful story. A very personal description of the prairie of western Canada fits easily into Billy's account of his hunt on the bluffs for a baby owl:

> The cottonwood trees shed a kind of white fluffy stuff that looks like snow. Sometimes it's so thick it comes right over the top of your sneakers and you get a queer feeling that you really are walking through snow, even though the sun on your back is making you sweat right through your shirt.

Through Billy's story of his pets, the reader not only discovers Saskatchewan's bluffs and cottonwood clouds, but also how an owl looks, when its eggs are laid, where its nest is built, how the bird attacks. All of such objectively reported details come naturally into the narrative because they are relevant to the action. Mowat's young narrator is sympathetic to the many animals in his menagerie—white rats, gophers, garter snakes, pigeons, and Mutt the dog—but he never becomes sentimental by telling what they feel and think. The effectiveness of the story is due in large part to a first-person point of view which is clearly within the limitations and vocabulary of its young teenage narrator.

Matters of vocabulary and diction, too, can become restrictions, as the person telling the story is limited to vocabulary compatible with age and personality. In Emily Neville's *It's Like This, Cat*, Dave thinks to himself,

> The guy didn't really look like a burglar. And he didn't talk "dese and dose." Maybe real burglars don't all talk that way—only the ones on TV. Still, he sure picked that lock fast, and he was sure down in that cellar for some reason of his own.

Speaking his feelings as well as his thoughts, Dave looks out from Coney Island at the ships on the ocean, and the sea gulls and planes above him. "It's mine, all mine. I could go anywhere in the world, I could. Maybe I will." Even when Dave, because he sees his mother's actions, can be fairly certain of her thoughts, he only speculates, the essential limitation that Neville accepts:

> Maybe she figures I got in some gang fight, so she keeps asking me where I'm going and who with. Also, I guess she noticed I don't go to Nick's after school anymore.... Right now, I can see she's going to begin asking who is Tom and where did I meet him.

Occasionally a writer experiments successfully with different points of view, as does Alice Childress in *A Hero ain't nothin' but a Sandwich.* Using first person point of view, each of the characters tells the story from her or his own perspective of events and relationships. From the total of their stories, we see events, characters, plot, and theme, as well as setting. The story, set in the inner city, concerns Benjie's experience with drugs, and to be convincing each of the speakers must reveal self through distinctively personal diction.

> *Benjie:* My block ain't no place to be a chile in peace. Somebody gonna cop your money and might knock you down cause you walkin with short bread and didn't even make it worth their while to stop and frisk you over.

> *Grandmother:* This house is my jail, only I pay rent. I'm afraid to go out in the street alone, day or night. Bad boys will beat [us] and take away our little money.

> *Nigeria Greene, teacher:* Bernard Cohen is not to be believed. His whole mission in teaching is to convince Black kids that most whites are great except for a "few" rotten apples in every barrel. It burns me.

> *Benjie's mother:* I try to keep the neighbors out of my business because every friend has a friend, and if I can't keep a secret, how can I ask them not to tell what I told?

> *Walter, pusher:* The pusher, the pusher, that's all you hear! They don't call no other salesman a pusher, but that's what he natural is . . . a pusher, no matter what he's sellin'.

Sylvia Engdahl in *Enchantress from the Stars* also experiments effectively, using first-person narration for some chapters, an objective folk tale point of view for others, and limited omniscience for still other sections. So successful in maintaining point of view is Joan Blos in *A Gathering of Days: A New England Girl's Journal,* that we find ourselves searching for a footnote: Where did Blos discover this journal; it is no work of fiction.

Omniscient Point of View

A distinct change from the limitations of the first-person point of view occurs when the writer chooses the freedom of the omniscient point of view. The writer in this case may recount relevant information about any and every character, their thoughts, ideas, and feelings about themselves as well as others. The writer may flash back into past experiences, feelings, and thoughts, or forward into what will happen in the future. The omniscient writer may tell anything he or she believes is relevant to the story. The omniscient writer moves around, in, and through the characters, knowing everything, explaining motives, and giving the reader helpful information. We see in *Sounder*, for example, how the boy feels when his father has been taken to jail. "The loneliness that was always in the cabin . . . was heavier than ever now. It made the boy's tongue heavy. It pressed against his eyes, and they burned. It rolled against his ears. His head seemed to be squeezed inward, and it hurt." In adult fiction, details may be more subtly and less obviously related to the conflict and characters, but in children's stories, the writer concentrates on what is more essential to the reader's understanding.

White finds the omniscient point of view best for *Charlotte's Web*. The objective, third-person statement that Fern wore a very pretty dress to the Fair has little significance until the young reader has the omniscient writer's interpretation: because she thought she'd see boys. When Wilbur learns of Charlotte's bloodthirsty appetite, he thinks that although Charlotte is pretty and clever, she is everything he doesn't like —scheming and fierce. The reader is as uncertain as Wilbur until White adds that fears and doubts go with new friendships. We know why Templeton finds the dirty junkyard his favorite spot; he thinks it's a good place to hide. If we had merely heard speeches and seen actions, we might have interpreted the details quite differently. White knows and tells what is in the minds of all his characters: Fern thinks the world is blissful; Lurvy feels weak at the sight of the dew-covered words in the miraculous web; Wilbur can't bear loneliness; Templeton is miserable when his rotten egg breaks. And when Wilbur tries to spin a web, Charlotte watches him delightedly, pleased that he is no quitter. White is truly the omniscient narrator. The reader knows everything because of the point of view.

Limited Omniscient Point of View

Often a story is told from the limited omniscient point of view. Here the writer chooses to see action through the eyes of one character— occasionally several characters—and to report that character's thoughts. In children's literature, this character is usually the protagonist. The writer shows not only what the character sees and hears, but also what the character feels and believes. The writer is inside as well as alongside the character.

Although most of the story is told from Sara's point of view in Betsy Byars's novel *Summer of the Swans,* the story occasionally tells what is in the mind of Charlie, her retarded brother, as well. When we find him waiting for Sara while she is visiting a friend, we see Charlie's still body hunched over his knees: "The whole world seemed to have been turned off when Sara went into the Weicek's house." His ticking watch is his pleasure as he listens to it and watches the red second hand sweep around the dial. These are simple and credible glimpses of what is in Charlie's mind. In Wilder's *Little House in the Big Woods,* we know from limited omniscient narration what pioneer life was like to a child. First, however, Wilder shows us the universal child Laura. Laura had never had more fun than when she fell from a stump into the soft snow and made pictures shaped like herself. Like everything else in the Wilder series, the understanding of Santa Claus and the giving of Christmas gifts are suited to the child's view of reality. "Santa Claus did not give grown people presents, but that was not because they had not been good. . . . It was because they were grown up, and grown people must give each other presents." Through Laura's innocent point of view we get the literal interpretation of a Bible story. As Adam names the animals, Laura envies him his clothing:

> Adam sat on a rock, and all the animals and birds, big and little, were gathered around him anxiously waiting to be told what kind of animals they were. Adam looked so comfortable. He did not have to be careful to keep his clothes clean, because he . . . wore only a skin around his middle.

Because we see through limited omniscience that Laura is the universal child in her simplicity and innocence, we accept her account of pioneer life. In detailed description Laura tells us what butchering was like to the frontier child. As one factual detail follows another, from playing with the pig's bladder to roasting the pig's tail, the modern city child who knows only that meat comes from the supermarket is prepared to believe the truth of butchering on the frontier. Wilder is successful in large part because she chooses Laura's point of view. By recognizing the feelings of childhood, the reader accepts the particular and specific routines and actions of Laura's life—different though they are from the reader's own.

Objective Point of View

In the dramatic or objective point of view the writer does not enter the minds of any of the characters. The action speaks for itself as the action unfolds and the reader hears speeches and sees actions. The term *dramatic*, of course, comes from the drama where characters reveal themselves by what they say, what they do, and what others say about them. The drama permits the audience to see and hear, but to draw inferences only from what it sees and hears. Inner thoughts or feelings must be revealed by visible action. In most plays there is no interpreter standing at stage left to tell the audience what thoughts run through the speakers' minds. The audience must sometimes figure out for itself the meaning of the actions and speeches, deciding from a character's voice inflections or actions what—beneath or in spite of the words—may lie in that character's mind.

The objective or nearly objective point of view in stories makes heavier demands on the imagination and understanding of the reader. Adults guess that when a character looks at the floor, scuffs the dust with a toe, or twists a lock of hair, that person is shy or embarrassed. And so does the perceptive child. The ability to interpret body language is a skill few children have. It is the writer's responsibility when using the dramatic or objective point of view to describe and report action which, since it is without interpretation, must be within the child's understanding.

The *Incredible Journey* is an example of the use of omniscience for the minor human characters and of relative objectivity for the major animal characters. Realistically, we can never know what, if anything, is in the minds of the three animals. Since we cannot know, we instead must listen to the sounds they make, watch the tension in their animal bodies, note their actions and movements:

> The old dog walked gingerly into the shallow water, shivering . . . turning his head away. Once more the Labrador swam the river, climbed out . . . shook himself, and barked. There was no mistaking the command. The old dog took another reluctant step forward, whining piteously, his expressive tail tucked under. . . . again the Labrador swam across. . . .

Because we see the reluctant step of the old terrier, hear the piteous whine, and note the tucked-under tail, we draw conclusions about how the dog feels. The terrier "swam in jerky rapid movements, his head held high out of the water, his little black eyes rolling." Burnford does better than most writers of animal stories, but even she steps over the objective line when she uses animal/human comparisons, calling the terrier a white cavalier, and describing his wild actions on reaching the shore as "transports of joy"; he is like a "shipwrecked mariner after six weeks at sea on a raft."

Allan W. Eckert, in his portrayal of the badger in *Incident at Hawk's Hill,* is perhaps more successful; his objectivity falters less frequently. Eckert mentions instinct and experience as aids to the badger as she digs a tunnel five feet into the earth to a point she chooses for a nesting chamber. He describes the digging, the earth moving and scattering, and the choosing of a spot fifty feet away to start a longer escape tunnel connecting with the chamber. An incredible engineering feat accomplished with unerring skill, she wheezes with fatigue. We observe actions, but we do not know thoughts.

EVALUATING POINT OF VIEW IN CHILDREN'S LITERATURE

Maturity of the Reader

It is not possible, nor even relevant, to make authoritative statements about the best or most successful point of view for children's literature. We can make a few sensible inferences, however. The first-person point of view may present difficulties for the small child. Because the child is just learning his or her own "I" identity, he or she may have trouble identifying with the strange "I" of the story. Furthermore, first-person narration may be difficult for the young child to understand because the child is limited to knowing only what the narrator can know. "I" can transmit only limited interpretation or understanding.

There are some first-person stories among picture books for the smallest child, for example, Dr. Seuss's *If I Ran the Zoo* and others by this writer. The "I" narrator of these stories, however, is of minor significance since the focus is on the sheer nonsense of the doggerel and the delight of the sounds and rhythms, to say nothing of the stories' greatest assets, the inventive illustrations. *And to Think That I Saw It on Mulberry Street* uses first-person point of view effectively; in this case the story is not only skillful nonsense, but it also shows a child's imagination creating a fantastic parade.

Seuss's stories are among the relatively few successful first-person stories for the small child. Many, like *May I Bring a Friend?* by Beatrice de Regniers, rely more upon illustrations—of royalty accepting guests of unusual proportions and dispositions like hippo, lions, elephant, monkeys, for example—than upon our following the thinking of a child.

The older child, on the other hand, may find first-person stories exciting proof of understanding, and of the capacity to project self into another "I." First-person seems to be an increasingly popular choice of point of view in stories for older children or young adolescents. When Twain wrote *Huckleberry Finn* in first-person, he probably had adult readers in mind, but when Robert Louis Stevenson wrote *Kidnapped* and

Treasure Island, he must have wished to involve young readers in you-are-there adventures. Since that time we have had many more first-person stories for older readers, and currently there is an abundance of them. They seem to have proliferated since *It's Like This, Cat*. Like David's conflict with his father in that book, conflicts in these stories often explore the growing-up tensions in the child or adolescent. The protagonist of Theodore Taylor's *The Cay* wrestles, for example, with his feelings of racism; Paul Zindel's *The Pigman* shows youthful guilt over thoughtlessness.

As for the objective point of view, children are inexperienced in drawing conclusions from speeches and from descriptions of actions; they may find the dramatic point of view hard to understand. This necessity for objectivity, therefore, presents a particular kind of challenge to the writer whose audience is the small child. If the story relies, however, on pictures showing the characters' feelings through facial expressions, the interpretive words about emotions and thought are not so essential.

We see some successful objective point-of-view narration at picture-book level, like, for example, Ludwig Bemelmans' *Madeline*, in which minimal omniscience is present. Others seem to be inadequate stories—*Cowboy Small*, for example. Characterization is minimal; the story has nothing but action objectively related: eating, sleeping, riding, singing, and guitar playing. The reason Cowboy Small is a dull character is that he neither thinks nor feels nor reacts. When he is eating, riding, and guitar playing, the illustrations show only minute changes in his facial expression. Because Lenski writes neither reaction nor thought into text, and because the objective point of view simply relates information and the illustrations are nearly impassive, we have no sense of a real, human cowboy. On the other hand, Ezra Jack Keats's *A Snowy Day* seems at first glance to be objective. We know that Peter has a happy time in the snow because we see all his fun, and we remember our own similar pleasures. But an omniscient writer also comments that Peter thinks it might be fun to play with the big boys, and knows he isn't old enough. When Peter cannot find the vanished snowball he had tucked into his jacket pocket the night before, he feels sad. Even this simple and short story makes brief use of an interpretive omniscience. Peter is then a more developed character and we find ourselves caring about Peter's happiness in the snow. Perhaps, by the process of elimination, we can conclude that either of the omniscient points of view may be more successful in stories for the young child. While many older children enjoy the challenge of objective or first-person stories, more children will find stories they can follow and enjoy are written with some degree of omniscience.

Animal Realism

Animal realism is a popular kind of story for children that presents special problems in point of view. Look back at *Charlotte's Web*, a story in which the characters are animals. White had no intention of being realistic; he chose to portray his animals as similar to people. What actually happens is that White so successfully makes his animals into people that we have a distinct feeling that they *are* people. In fact, since they all think and worry and love and hurt and laugh and needle one another like real people, their animal natures are nearly lost in White's creation of an animal story that deals with human truths of friendship and continuity, death and maturity. It is partly White's choice of the omniscient point of view that makes these animals into human beings that we care about. But *Charlotte's Web* is not a realistic story about how pigs and spiders and rats live in barns; we know that. Such a story would have to show the animals living, moving, and making noises like animals. And such a realistic story would have to be told from a point of view that does not imagine and report the thoughts of nonhumans acting human. The objective or dramatic point of view seems, then, to be the logical choice for a realistic animal story.

We have noted how Burnford in *The Incredible Journey* is relatively successful in maintaining an objective point of view. But *Black Beauty* by Anna Sewell presents a distinct contrast. The book may give the impression of being a realistic story because the horses lead "horse lives." However, *Black Beauty*'s first-person narrator is a horse, using human language to tell us his horse emotions and thoughts. The point of view destroys any realism. The horse's feelings may be believable—if we assume that animal feelings are identical to our own, and that is doubtful, of course. It is, furthermore, inconsistent with realism that we should know the animal's feelings by anything but observation and speculation, although perhaps accompanied by a hearty dose of our sympathy. Black Beauty, speaking in the first-person "I," says,

> Day by day, hole by hole, our bearing reins were shortened, and instead of looking forward with pleasure to having my harness put on . . . I began to dread it.

Black Beauty decides to do his duty despite his harrassment. But worse things come; the sharp bit cuts his tongue and his jaw, and he froths at the mouth. He feels

> a pressure on my windpipe, which often made my breathing very uncomfortable. . . . my neck and chest were strained and painful, my mouth and tongue tender, and I felt worn and depressed.

While perhaps it is true that the story makes us feel like a horse as Frances Clark Sayers says,[1] the reverse is more nearly accurate; this horse feels the way we would feel if we human beings were living in horses' bodies. The realism is disturbed by the first-person point of view. A realistic animal story is a narrative in which we expect to find at least a relatively objective point of view, whether the story is for child or adult.

Choice of point of view, as we can see, affects the reader's acceptance of a story. Some writers of animal stories manage to avoid the temptation to sentimentality; they seek to convey the reality of animal life by picturing the animals' natural habitat, showing the relationships of predators, weather, seasons, and maturity cycles on animal lives. Such a writer is Felix Salten, author of *Bambi*. Sometimes Salten successfully evokes wonder; through the mind of Bambi, the deer, the reader watches the approach of winter, feeling the cold rain and hearing the shushing of falling leaves. It pleases Bambi

> to see the milk-white veils of mist steam from the meadow in the morning. . . . They vanished so beautifully in the sunshine. The hoar frost . . . with such dazzling whiteness delighted him too.

Salten clearly and believably carries the suspense through a winter in which Bambi's first enemy is starvation and his second is Man. However, when Salten depicts as human Bambi's affection for his doe, or his admiration for the wise owl, the other information—the accurate natural history—becomes less reliable. It is still accurate, but Salten begins to falsify when he humanizes even the leaves, which are also speaking characters. They worry and reassure, are troubled and touched:

> "What happens to us when we have fallen? . . ."
> "Do . . . we know anything about ourselves when we're down there? . . ."
> "Let's remember how beautiful it was, how wonderful, when the sun came out and shone so warmly that we thought we'd burst with life. . . ."
> "Now the nights are dreadful," the second leaf complained, "and there is no end to them."

Salten is totally omniscient; his assuming unlimited knowledge—even to the thoughts of leaves—may make us question his otherwise accurate portrayal of nature and its forces. Such complete omniscience is sentimental; it creates doubts in the reader's mind about what is really true.

Fantasy

If fantasy is to be successful, we must willingly suspend disbelief. If the story's characters, conflict, and theme seem believable to us, we find it plausible and even natural to know the thoughts and feelings of animal characters or tiny people. In fact, the story may be so good that we wish it *were* true. We wish we knew Arrietty. This persuasion that the writer wishes to bring about—persuasion that "what if" is really "it's true"—is most successful when the writer is consistent about point of view.

Point of view is an essential part of our appreciation of Mary Norton's *The Borrowers*. Norton's central characters are diminutive; we see most of the action through the eyes of young Arrietty. The Clock family is only six inches tall, and everything in the story, from postage stamps to primroses, is seen in relationship to the characters' size. If we are to believe that Arrietty is so tiny, we must enter the dimensions and scale of her world. Pushing through the grass, she is startled by something glittering and discovers, "It was an eye. Or it looked like an eye. Clear and bright like the color of the sky. An eye like her own but enormous." While "human beans" find a walk across the carpet easy, to tiny Arrietty it is like pushing through a dense field of grain. She moves off the rug to the shiny floor beside the wall where she can run: She "loved running. Carpets were heavy-going—thick and clinging, they held you up." Beneath a table is a great expanse of the unknown, dark as a cave, "a great cavern of darkness. . . . Chair legs were everywhere and chair seats obscured her view." The yard and garden are huge; here is Arrietty's first glimpse:

> A greenish beetle, shining in the sunlight, came toward her across the stones. She laid her fingers lightly on its shell and it stood still . . . when she moved her hand the beetle went swiftly on. An ant came hurrying in a busy zigzag. She danced in front of it to tease it and put out her foot. . . . Cautiously she moved . . . in amongst the green blades. As she parted them gently with her bare hands, drops of water plopped on her skirt. . . . pulling herself up now and again by rooty stems into this jungle of moss and wood-violet and creeping leaves of clover. . . . she sat down suddenly on a gnarled leaf of primrose.

No wonder that we suspend disbelief and are convinced that the Clock family lives. Not only do we know that safety pins and postage stamps have a way of disappearing, but we see everything from furniture to flowers from the point of view of Arrietty, who lives in our world, though seen from a six-inch height. The scale is relative to a tiny borrower, and point of view is thoroughly consistent.

The consistency in the point of view and the detail which is described from this point of view create a memorable miniature world in *The Borrowers*. It is this same strongly established point of view and detailed development of it that helps to account for some of the greatest successes in children's fantasy. One thinks of Carroll's *Alice in Wonderland*, Philippa Pearce's *Tom's Midnight Garden*, and many of Maurice Sendak's books.

Stories of Other Countries

Stories of children from other lands are a particular problem for the writer. Early in the twentieth century a series of books was published about children of other lands—*The Eskimo Twins, The Japanese Twins*, and others by Lucy Fitch Perkins. These stories stressed what seemed to be peculiarities of life in other countries. We read of flat and unreal children living in exotic and uninhabitable lands. Fascinating as it all was, stories about children eating whale blubber or octopus, or wearing wooden shoes or tatami sandals, may now seem condescending. We recall, however, at this point in our discussion of children's literature, that once we believe in the reality of character, we believe in the vicarious experience of the character's way of life. How can a story about other countries show how life is lived there without making the country and its people weird and wondrous, strange and unbelievable? People in other countries may, after all, eat different foods, live in homes unlike our own, or work at jobs unfamiliar to us.

One effective way in which the writer can picture the country accurately, make the story credible, and at the same time present the truth of human nature, is to make careful use of point of view. An objective point of view in a story about life in Morocco, for example, might leave a child puzzled by uninterpreted facts. Some degree of omniscience, however, achieves several results. First of all, since we can know thoughts, the character can more easily be shown as like us. Then, once we recognize these similarities, we accept the character as believable. From this acceptance of the character we can move on to believe the character's way of life is different but interesting, rather than strange or beneath us.

Children, like adults, see first the obvious differences in people: he has black hair and I have blonde; she is tall and I am short. From these outward physical traits, we shift our attention to more subtle differences, like names, houses, pets, and games—differences we all expect and look for. DeJong in *The House of Sixty Fathers* satisfies our curiosity on these scores; Tien Pao looks distinctively Chinese and wears clothing different from ours. He lives on a houseboat and has a pet pig. Once DeJong has established outward differences and similarities, he effectively uses his limited omniscient point of view to show more significant and subtle similarities. As we see the events of the conflict through Tien Pao's eyes and mind, we note that the protagonist's emotions and thoughts are like our own. Tien Pao loves and laughs, cries and fears. We are won to understanding what the people and their way of life are like, what it is like to be lost and wandering in a war-ravaged country, to be forced to find our parents on our own, to be cared for by strangers, and adopted by sixty fathers, then to be safe with our family once again.

Point of view also reveals other things about people from foreign lands. Through DeJong's use of limited omniscient point of view, American readers not only discover experiences unfamiliar to themselves and to this Chinese child, but also how familiar parts of American experience must look to a child of another land. We, who automatically peel paper from chewing gum and pop it into our mouths to chew continuously and without purpose, find the action nothing unusual, but Tien Pao is mystified. Not every child has ridden in a jeep, and yet any reader can discover the experience, since here we ourselves ride for the first time in a jeep, a small, open carriage:

> The man behind the strange wheel did things with his hands and feet. The carriage suddenly roared, shot ahead. It hopped and jumped and bounced in swiftness over the little road. It went still faster.

In consistent, child-like point of view, each aggressive action Tien Pao sees is committed by impersonal war equipment, but every kind act is done by a loving human being whom Tien Pao comes to know.

An interesting corollary to consider beside *Sixty Fathers* is *Dragonwings,* Laurence Yep's story of a Chinese immigrant boy coming to California, "the Golden Mountain." As he approaches the California coast, he is disappointed; it is only "a brown smudge on the horizon," the wooden houses "like shells of wood which terrible monsters had spun about themselves." As the narrator tries to learn the new language, the "letters keep on rearranging themselves in the most confusing patterns." Because they can use their great powers for good or evil, the Chinese immigrants call the Americans "demons"—demons whose calendars, even, are not properly arranged, not based sensibly on the movements of the moon nor on the ten-day week.

Because we are aware of their feelings, we find ourselves breathlessly involved in the Chinese family's lives, and are fearful for their safety. Although their lives are different from our own, they are themselves like us. We see people, countries, cultures and ways of life

—all through the point of view and wide eyes of a child—and are persuaded that a child is a child in any culture. The writers' use of the omniscient point of view has helped.

SUMMARY

Point of view, an integral part of storytelling, determines the view the reader gets of events, of character motivation, of suspense and climax, as well as theme. There are four major kinds of point of view: first-person with an "I" narrator, omniscient with an all-knowing writer, limited omniscient with focus on one or a few characters, and objective or dramatic with a report only of what can be seen and heard.

Since the limited experience of children makes it hard for them to draw their own inferences from objective description of action and speech, the writer often clarifies the story by use of some degree of omniscience. The pleasure of literature comes from style, character, plot —all of the literary elements. In literature for children understanding of character and the other elements is aided by a sensitive choice of point of view adapted to subject matter, type of conflict, and expected maturity level of readers.

Reading and Evaluating

Picture book   1 *Read six picture-story books and identify point of view. Does point of view help you to know character? To care about the character? What influence has point of view on other literary elements in the story?*

Animal realism   2 *Read* Blue Canyon Horse *by Ann Nolan Clark, or another animal realism story. What is the point of view? Is it suitable for animal realism? What is the effect? Compare point of view in this story to that in Smoky by Will James or to that in* Black Beauty *by Anna Sewell. What are the relative effects upon the reader?*

Regional realism   3 *Read a novel by Rebecca Caudill or Esther Wier. What is the point of view? Does it affect tone? Does it produce sentimentality? Does it alter credibility? Explain.*

Fantasy   4 *Read and compare* Paddington Bear *by Michael Bond and* Winnie-the-Pooh *by A. A. Milne. What is the point of view in each story? What effect has point of view on each of the two stories? How does point of view affect tone? Characterization?*

Realism

5 *Read a* Moffat *book by Eleanor Estes and compare it for point of view with one by Betsy Byars, or a* Betsy *book by Carolyn Haywood. What impact has point of view on characterization in each case?*

Social Issues realism

6 *Read* The Cay *by Theodore Taylor,* Dorp Dead *by Julia Cunningham, or another first-person novel. Does the writer stay within the limitations of the chosen point of view? Describe the diction. Is it believable considering the narrator's age and character? What is the effect of first person on the conflict? On characterization? Setting? Mood and tone?*

Note

[1]"Walt Disney Accused," by Frances Clarke Sayers in *Children and Literature: Views and Reviews*, Virginia Haviland, ed. Glenview, Ill.: Scott, Foresman, 1973.

Recommended Books Cited in This Chapter

Armstrong, William. *Sounder.* New York: Harper, 1969.
Bemelmans, Ludwig. *Madeline.* New York: Viking, 1939.
Blos, Joan W. *A Gathering of Days: A New England Girl's Journal, 1830–32.* New York: Scribner's, 1979.
Byars, Betsy. *The Summer of the Swans.* New York: Viking, 1970.
Childress, Alice. *A Hero ain't nothin' but a Sandwich.* New York: Coward, 1973.
Collier, James Lincoln and Christopher. *My Brother Sam Is Dead.* New York: Four Winds, 1974.
DeJong, Meindert. *The House of Sixty Fathers.* New York: Harper, 1956.
deRegniers, Beatrice. *May I Bring a Friend?* New York: Atheneum, 1964.
Eckert, Allan W. *Incident at Hawk's Hill.* Boston: Little, 1971.
Engdahl, Sylvia. *Enchantress from the Stars.* New York: Atheneum, 1971.
Fatio, Louise. *The Happy Lion.* New York: McGraw, 1954.
Fox, Paula. *The Slave Dancer.* Scarsdale, N.Y.: Bradbury, 1973.
Keats, Ezra Jack. *The Snowy Day.* New York: Viking, 1962.
Mowat, Farley. *Owls in the Family.* Boston: Little, 1961.
Neville, Emily. *It's Like This, Cat.* New York: Harper, 1963.
Norton, Mary. *The Borrowers.* New York: Harcourt, 1965.
O'Dell, Scott. *Island of the Blue Dolphins.* Boston: Houghton, 1960.
Pearce, A. Philippa. *Tom's Midnight Garden.* Philadelphia: Lippincott, 1959.
Potter, Beatrix. *The Tale of Peter Rabbit.* New York: Warne, 1902.
Seuss, Dr. *And To Think That I Saw It on Mulberry Street.* New York: Hale, 1937.
———. *If I Ran the Zoo.* New York: Random, 1950.
Stevenson, Robert Louis. *Kidnapped.* New York: Scribner's, 1913. (first published 1886)
———. *Treasure Island.* New York: Scribner's, 1911. (first published 1883)
Twain, Mark. *The Adventures of Tom Sawyer.* New York: Macmillan, 1962. (first published 1876)
———. *Huckleberry Finn.* New York: Dutton, 1955. (first published 1884)
White, E. B. *Charlotte's Web.* New York: Harper, 1952.
Wilder, Laura Ingalls. *Little House in the Big Woods.* New York: Harper, 1953. (first published 1932)
Yep, Laurence. *Dragonwings.* New York: Harper, 1975.
Zindel, Paul. *The Pigman.* New York: Harper, 1968.

ELNITA STRAUS LIBRARY

Let us now consider the literary element that makes language memorable—its style. Frequently someone asks, "But does the writer know what he or she is doing with words?" Yes. The author has added, subtracted, experimented, and substituted, creating the style that best tells his or her story. The skilled writer chooses words that illumine setting, plot, character, and theme to make a piece of literature.

Style is basically words, *how* an author says something, as opposed to *what* he or she says. From the almost infinite number of words available, the writer chooses and arranges words to create a particular story, the words and arrangement best for that story. Rufus Moffat, for example, on the first day of school

> felt a slight impulse to run home and play as he used to. Play what? . . . Mud pies? he asked himself sarcastically. Pooh! He was too old for all that business now. He was going to school. Soon he would be going home to lunch. . . .

This is Rufus, his own style—that is, author Estes's choice of the style suited to situation and character. By contrast, O'Dell's formal and restrained language and simple sentence structure constitute the style suited to the setting, conflict, and character in his story *Island of the Blue Dolphins*. The protagonist, who lives a life totally dependent upon nature, says in the opening lines,

> I remember the day the Aleut ship came to our island. At first it seemed like a small shell afloat on the sea. Then it grew larger and was a gull with folded wings. At last in the rising sun it became what it really was—a red ship with two red sails.

O'Dell uses nature comparisons throughout the story. Karana's brother Ramo has eyes "half-closed like those of a lizard lying on a rock about to flick out its tongue to catch a fly." An invader's beard is combed until it "shines like a cormorant's wing." Karana says the enemy's mouth is "like the edge of a stone knife." But a swarm of friendly dolphins dives in and out "as if they were weaving a piece of cloth with their broad snouts." The sea elephants have faces "like wet earth that has dried in the sun and cracked." Word pictures and comparisons describe characters, action, and setting, but in a style suited to this story of a protagonist who lives with her antagonist, nature. The styles of *The Moffats* and *Island of the Blue Dolphins* could not be interchanged. In each case style is right for that particular story.

In fiction, style at its best increases our belief in the characters' reality. We come to know them through the words they say, through the words that describe how they look and how they act. We are eager to believe in the characters' experiences, following the plot and visualizing the action described in the chosen words. Through words, we see, hear, and even smell the setting as we realize its effect upon characters and conflict. Style is the product of all the choices the writer makes.

These choices are, of course, an entirely personal matter, since style and writer are inextricable. Mark Twain's style is no more Ogden Nash's style than Twain is Nash. One writer deals with the nature of reality or fantasy in one way; another expresses her or his vision in quite another way. A writer does, of course, vary her or his own style. Since one story differs from another, styles will differ as the writer suits style to story. Notice how O'Dell's restrained and dignified style in the opening of *Island* differs from his brisk and active language in the opening of *The King's Fifth*. This is not Karana but a different character:

> It was eight bells of the morning watch, early in the month of June, that we entered the Sea of Cortés. On our port bow was the Island of California. To the east lay the coast of New Spain.
>
> I sat in my cabin setting down in ink a large island sighted at dawn, which did not show on the master chart. The day was already stifling hot, so I had left the door ajar. Suddenly the door closed and I turned to face Captain Mendoza.

Style is not something applied to a finished piece of writing, since it *is* the writing, conveying both the idea and the writer's view of the idea. Henry James says that each word and every punctuation mark directly contribute to meaning; the content of the story and how it is told are inseparable.[1] Tone, word choice, grammatical structure, devices of comparison, sound, and rhythm are style. All of these elements vary with the author's purpose, as the idea, the incidents, and the characters vary. Style gives the whole work its distinction and makes the story memorable.

Originality and style are not the same, but they are related in the sense that a writer is himself or herself an original. Nor should novelty be confused with style, for novelty is sometimes merely gimmickry—as it often is in Paul Zindel's novels—rather than unique and personal expression. If the writer's way of telling the story and its truth is distinctively the writer's own, then that expression has a personal mark, and the style should become the best possible one for a particular work.

DEVICES OF STYLE

The most easily identified element of style is the writer's use of certain specific devices of language. Many of these stylistic devices are listed in dictionaries of literary terms, but our chief concern here is with those most often used in children's literature.

Connotation

Connotation is the associative or emotional meaning of a word. Connotative meaning, when added to dictionary meaning, or **denotation,** adds significance and impact to a term. Charlotte, for example, is not as big as a thimble, nor as small as a fingernail, nor as round as a button —all denotative comparisons which might convey her proper size and shape but which have no emotional impact. Charlotte is, instead, "about the size of a gumdrop." Now, there's a reassuring comparison for a bloodthirsty spider. The stomach of gluttonous Templeton is not bulbous, nor enlarged, nor even like a ball. Instead, "as big around as a jelly jar" expresses comparative size and shape, but adds pleasant connotations. No spider egg sac ever had the appeal of Charlotte's; it is neither orange nor pink, but peach-colored and looking like cotton candy. The images of cotton candy, jelly jar, and gumdrop are all favorites with children; each of these comparisons describes size, color, and shape, but adds pleasant and positive emotional meaning.

Imagery

By far the most frequently used device, and the most essential, is imagery. **Imagery** is the appeal to any of the senses; it helps create setting, establish a mood, or show a character. We use imagery in our everyday conversations to describe sounds, smells, and sights. We say the sky is amethyst blue, the carpet is celery green, a jacket is fire engine red; we describe the nature of a sound as clanging, buzzing, humming, or thundering. We say that tastes are bitter, sweet, or salty, that smells are acrid or musty, and that texture is scaly or slimy.

The writer, too, relies on imagery to give the reader impressions of what the writer wishes to depict. But *verisimilitude*, or description to duplicate reality, is not the writer's only goal; suggestion and release of the imagination are important. The writer, by the choice of details and of the words used to describe the details, stirs the reader's imagination; the impact may be recognition or delight.

Charlotte's Web demonstrates the use and effectiveness of imagery. In the opening pages of the third chapter White shows us the scene of most of the action. Wilbur has just come to live in the manure pile of the Zuckerman barn, and we explore the building with him. No barn was ever more real, more suggestive of security and activity. The imagery convinces us as we smell the variety of smells, feel the warmth and coolness, and see the clutter of equipment. We may not settle down snugly in the manure pile, but we are as much at home in the barn as Wilbur is.

White describes the silence of the barn, but by sound imagery of a negative kind. The quiet itself is described by White's noting the absence of the customary noises; animals are so quiet that we hear only the weather-vane:

> The sheep lay motionless. Even the goose was quiet. Overhead, on the main floor, nothing stirred: the cows were resting, the horses dozed. Templeton had quit work. . . . The only sound was a slight scraping noise from the rooftop, where the weather-vane swung back and forth.

When Wilbur first arrives at the Fair Grounds, that setting is created for the reader by imagery. As White lists the senses one by one, a specific image appeals to each:

> they could hear music and see the Ferris wheel turning in the sky. They could smell the dust of the race track where the sprinkling cart had moistened it; and they could smell hamburgers frying and see balloons aloft. They could hear sheep blatting in their pens. An enormous voice over the loudspeaker said: "Attention, please! Will. . . ."

White relies on imagery to make the reader aware not only of setting, but also of character and action. When Wilbur gets his buttermilk bath, we see him; he stands with closed eyes, feeling the buttermilk trickling over his sides. When he greedily opens his mouth and tastes the delicious buttermilk, Wilbur's child-like character is revealed. He stands in the pig trough and drools with hunger, while White itemizes the slops, each particle a distinctly visual image with a taste of its own:

> It was a delicious meal—skim milk, wheat middlings, leftover pancakes, half a doughnut, the rind of a summer squash, two pieces of stale toast, a third of a gingersnap, a fish tail, one orange peel . . . the scum off a cup of cocoa, an ancient jelly roll, a strip of paper from the lining of the garbage pail, and a spoonful of raspberry jello.

As we visualize slops, each item has color and shape in our minds. At the same time, White appeals to taste by listing foods a child knows and likes. And finally, the variety has the distinct quality of slops, since it is punctuated by a fish tail and a bit of garbage pail liner. Imagery not only helps create setting, but pictures action and character as well.

Figurative Language

Another device of style is *figurative language.* The writer uses words in a nonliteral way, giving them meaning beyond their usual, everyday definitions, and thereby adding an extra dimension to meaning. Personification, simile, and metaphor are the most common kinds of figurative language in stories for children.

Children's stories often make use of *personification,* the giving of human traits to nonhuman beings or inanimate objects. In *Charlotte's Web* a large cast of nonhuman characters is personified, from Wilbur to the maple trees and even insects:

> The crickets sang in the grasses. They sang the song of summer's ending. . . .
> The sheep . . . felt so uneasy they broke a hole in the pasture fence. . . . The gander discovered the hole and led his family through . . . A little maple tree . . . heard the cricket song and turned bright red with anxiety.

We hear the crickets singing, rather than chirping. The sheep are "uneasy," the goose "family" eats apples, and nearby the "anxious" maple turns autumn colors. Human qualities are given to everything. Where Salten fails in *Bambi,* White is successful because his personification is fresh and he is not sentimental.

One of the simplest figurative devices is the *simile,* a stated comparison between unlike things, using *as, like,* or occasionally *than.*

Straw fluttered down "like confetti" at the exciting news from the Fair loudspeaker. When Charlotte is weary, she is swollen and listless and feels "like the end of a long day." These very specific comparisons are easy to see, since they are directly stated. Their combination of imagery and comparison makes them distinctive enough to stir the reader's imagination.

Comparisons that are implied are called **metaphors.** They are sometimes so neatly put, so recognizably clear that we scarcely notice them—like the familiar beads of water decorating Charlotte's web, a comparison of droplets to beads. As Charlotte catches and stings her insect fare, she metaphorically "anaesthetizes" them. Templeton hears the Fair is a figurative "paradise," where he'll find a "veritable treasure" of leftovers, enough for "a whole army of rats." Paradise is great happiness, treasure great wealth, and army a vast number; all are metaphors.

Hyperbole

We are so accustomed to exaggeration as humor that we scarcely recognize it as a figure of speech; we often stretch a comparison to create **hyperbole.** When, for example, Mrs. Zuckerman is scared to death, or Wilbur threatens to die of a broken heart, the author uses hyperbole that has become part of our daily conversation. But when Templeton, grousing that he did not come to the Fair to be a newsboy, refuses to "spend all my time chasing down to the dump after advertising material. . . . next thing you'll want . . . is a dictionary," his grumbling and sarcasm are hyperbole. Wilbur uses self-pitying hyperbole when he says, "I'm less than two months old and I'm tired of living." But we may laugh at the words of the sheep whose hyperbole is sheer imaginative extremism. He speaks to Templeton:

> "If Wilbur is killed and his trough stands empty day after day, you'll grow so thin we can look right through your stomach and see objects on the other side."

Understatement

The reverse of exaggeration is **understatement,** or playing down. Like hyperbole, it may be used for comic effect. When Fern bites into a raspberry with a concealed "bad-tasting bug," and gets "discouraged," we compare discouragement with our imagined response to a bad-tasting bug and know White's choice of words is deliberate—and amusing—understatement. When Avery removes the frog from his pocket—the frog that has traveled back and forth on the barn swing all morning, scrunched and dried in a tight pants pocket—we read that the frog seems tired from a morning of swinging. Merely tired?

Allusion

One figure of speech, **allusion,** probably has meaning only to the mature reader, since it relies on recognition of a reference to something in our common understanding, our past, or our literature. No adult will miss an allusion, for example, to a disastrous experience, an exam perhaps, when it is called "my Waterloo." White adds an opportunity for pleasure for the adult reader when he alludes to the call of the white-throated sparrow which must have come all the way from Boston, "Oh, Peabody, Peabody, Peabody!" Some adults may recognize reference to the Peabody sisters of Salem, but if not, no meaning is lost; it remains a New Englander's description of the bird song. Allusion is difficult for children to catch, since it relies on a background they lack. One of the delights of *Alice in Wonderland* for the Victorian reader was the wealth of allusions they could recognize, although contemporary readers, young and old, may miss them.

Puns and Word Play

An imaginative writer who enjoys the pleasure of words is tempted to **echo** words of other literary works. When White says that Templeton has no "milk of rodent kindness," we may recognize an echo from *Macbeth*. Wilbur is lured back to his pen by the promise of slops and the goose warns, "It's the old pail trick, Wilbur. Don't fall for it!" We hear echoes of the old shell game. A sly grammatical error slides in, one that parents frequently correct in their children:

> "He also has a smudge on one side where he lays in the manure."

And instead of correcting the grammar, Zuckerman corrects the facts:

> "He lays in clean straw."

Then White adds a bad *pun:*

"If that ancient egg ever breaks, this barn will be untenable."

"What's that mean?" asked Wilbur.

"It means nobody will be able to live here on account of the smell."

And finally, White plays with words in still other ways. Naive Wilbur uses faultless logic when he argues with the lamb that he is not less than nothing:

> "I don't think there is any such thing as less than nothing. Nothing is absolutely the limit of nothingness. It's the lowest you can go. . . . If there were something that was less than nothing, then nothing would not be nothing. . . ."

Devices of Sound

Many stories for children are meant not only for silent reading, but also for reading aloud. The writer who chooses words with care can increase pleasure and clarity by devices of sound.

Onomatopoeia

One sound device called **onomatopoeia,** or words that sound like their meanings, dominates an occasional paragraph of *Charlotte's Web*. For example, as White describes Wilbur's eating his slops, he uses the onomatopoeic words "swishing and swooshing" which suggest Wilbur's happy gluttony. While these slushy sounds suggest one kind of eating, the explosive sounds of "gulping and sucking" describe another.

Alliteration

Another easily recognized sound device is **alliteration,** repetition of initial consonants: "They sang the song of summer's ending." The effect of the sentence is musical, but its movement is slow and the music sad and final. By contrast, the Zuckerman dump becomes exciting as visual imagery rhythmically piles up interesting debris, layer upon layer. Alliteration then adds to the pleasure of the passage: "broken bottles . . . discarded dishmops . . . last month's magazines."

Assonance

A device that enhances meaning by the repetition of similar vowel sounds within a phrase is called **assonance.** When we hear the crickets' song, "a sad, monotonous song," not only the drawn out *a* of "sad," but also the repeated neutral *a* and the similarly sounded *o*'s, suggest the feeling of sorrow and sameness. Reading the passage aloud shows how sadness and monotony are here extended by assonance.

Consonance

The close repetition of consonant sounds is called **consonance.** In the phrase "empty tin cans and dirty rags and bits of metal and broken bottles," repetition of the abrupt, harsh *t*'s emphasizes the idea of ragged remains of unrelated items—junk. Again, reading the sentence aloud is the best test for assonance, consonance, and other sound devices, since sound rather than spelling shows how meaning is affected.

Rhythm

So closely is **rhythm**—from the Greek word meaning flow—associated with poetry and verse that we often forget that it is also part of prose. Stories that are read aloud to children can make particularly effective use of rhythm, which in prose is sometimes called **cadence.** White uses the word *and* to create rhythm as he shows the Zuckerman dump, an accumulation of one item after another, each joined to the others by *and*'s. Reading aloud is the test for rhythm as it is for other sound devices. Here is

> an astonishing pile of old bottles and empty tin cans and dirty rags and bits of metal and broken bottles and broken hinges and broken springs and dead batteries and last month's magazines and old discarded dishmops and tattered overalls . . . and useless junk of all kinds, including a wrong-size crank for a broken ice-cream freezer.

The rhythmic list slows to a halt with the last comma, and is followed by the final, jerking phrase filled with abrupt and explosive consonants: "a wrong siz*e cr*an*k* for a *br*o*k*en ice-*c*ream *f*reez*er.*" The changed rhythm brings the astonishing pile to an end.

  An unusually effective example of cadence occurs in White's description of the rope swing as it flies back and forth. The first phrases of the passage anticipate "and jumped," and then the swinging begins. Again by reading aloud, we hear each of the phrases shorten, as the arc of the swing narrows. Abruptly the words bring the swing to a halt, and the swinger jumps to the ground:

Then you got up all your nerve, took a deep breath, and jumped. . . . the rope would twist and you would twist and turn with the rope. Then you would drop down, down, down out of the sky and come sailing back into the barn almost into the hayloft, then sail out again (not quite so far this time), then in again (not quite so high), then out again, then in again, then out, then in; and then you'd jump off and fall down and let somebody else try it.

Rhythm ceases completely with the series of short, explosive words and phrases at the end of the paragraph. As the successive phrases shorten, we find pleasure in the description of action as well as in the understanding of the experience. Rhythm is the key.

Rhythm often occurs in picture-book narration. Wanda Gág's *Millions of Cats* supplies an excellent example:

> Cats here, cats there,
> Cats and kittens everywhere
> Hundreds of cats,
> Thousands of cats,
> Millions and billions and trillions of cats.

And Maurice Sendak's *Where the Wild Things Are*, as well: "And when he came to the place where the wild things are they roared their terrible roars and gnashed their terrible teeth and rolled their terrible eyes and showed their terrible claws."

EVALUATING STYLE IN CHILDREN'S LITERATURE

Trite versus Fresh Style

A story written in ***clichés*** is dull, just as a person who thinks in clichés is dull. Estes in *The Moffats* makes an ordinary situation seem unusual by the freshness of her style. Jane Moffat, making a delivery for her dressmaker mother,

> took the package and walked as carefully up the street as though she were carrying a lemon meringue pie. The Cadwalladers lived in a sleepy-looking gray house across the street from Chief Mulligan's. The shingles protruded over each window like languorous, drooping eyelids. "I bet they close like

eyes after everyone has gone to bed," thought Jane, grinning to herself as she rang the bell.

Estes's personification of the sleepy gray house, her imagery that makes us see just how Jane carries her package, her figurative comparison of the package itself to a pie—these devices make a girl approaching a doorstep a fresh experience.

By contrast, Judy Blume's books, despite the appeal of their subject matter, are often trite in style. In *Then Again, Maybe I Won't* the first person narrator has just found that his friend is shoplifting.

> The salesman told me the mitt I liked was $37.50. I thought that was a lot of money. . . . I'd have to think about it. . . . I walked back to the cash register where Joel was waiting. I wanted to know if he thought $37.50 was too much for a mitt. But I never asked him because he was smiling his crooked smile and humming some tune.
>
> I thought, oh no! Please, Joel. I don't want to be sick again. I don't want to go back to the hospital. I know what you've done. I can tell by just looking at you. What'd you take this time, Joel?

We've heard this before. Or even worse—we feel we must have, even if we know we haven't. There are no surprises. Nothing is vivid. The first person narrator gives us no sense of the person speaking because the words lack individuality and freshness. Notice next the opening of a chapter in *The Bear's House,* Marilyn Sachs's story of Fran Ellen who is trying desperately to care for her baby sister in a chaotic home.

> I don't know why, but that day I felt scared. As soon as I snuck back into the building at recess, my feet began shaking so, I didn't see how I'd ever get myself home. I shouldn't have gone, but I got to thinking about Flora. . . .
>
> I went on down the stairs through the basement and out the back door. I could hardly get my feet moving. And then I thought I heard somebody else behind me. Quick, I swung around. Nobody there, but that scared feeling got inside my mouth, and made my teeth rattle. Then I ran. My feet didn't shake so hard when I ran, but I started crying, and I couldn't stop.

We know Fran Ellen. In this short section little or nothing has happened, and yet this narrator speaks in language both fresh and personal: snuck, shaking feet, rattling teeth, scared feelings inside her mouth. Simple as the diction is, the style is expressive.

Our memories of *Tom Sawyer* include adventures and characters, as we recall Tom's runaway trip to the pirate island, his surreptitious night visit to Aunt Polly, and Tom, Huck, and Joe as they attend their own funeral. We remember hunting treasure by moonlight, and getting lost in the cave, but we may not be aware that these memories are so vivid because of Twain's style, his use of the right word in the right place.

Twain meticulously describes Tom's and Becky's wandering farther and farther away from the cave mouth, intrigued by the possibility of exciting discovery. Notice the imagery and the figurative devices in Twain's description:

> Presently they came to a place where a little stream of water, trickling over a ledge and carrying a limestone sediment with it, had, in the slow-dragging ages, formed a lace and ruffled Niagara in gleaming and imperishable stone. Tom squeezed his small body behind it in order to illuminate it for Becky's gratification.

A reteller of *Tom Sawyer* matter-of-factly substitutes monosyllables and clichés and eliminates the allusion.[2] While Twain's Tom *squeezes* behind the ruffled Niagara, the reteller's Tom *steps* behind the falls:

> Soon they came to a place where a little stream, carrying limestone matter with it, had formed a falls of beautiful stone. Since Tom was small, he stepped behind the falls with his candle so that Becky might see the lacy stone lighted in all its glory.

Twain's description is filled with imagery; he uses details to describe the cave:

> In one place they found a spacious cavern from whose ceiling depended a multitude of shining stalactites of the length and circumference of a man's leg. They . . . presently left it by one of the numerous passages.

The reteller eliminates the long words; he substitutes for stalactites a trite comparison to ice that fails to create a picture, and he turns the children's awed exploration into a pleasant walk through a hallway:

In one place they found a cave from whose top hung something that looked like ice. Parts of this were nearly the size of a man's leg, and when Tom held his candle up toward them, they shone in the light. The children walked all about this cave, wondering and admiring, and finally left by one of the halls.

Twain shows the children wondering, admiring, marveling, and being bewitched by turns. He creates mounting suspense, his imagery showing the enormous, endless caverns and corridors of the cave. His verbs change from those of appreciative awe to verbs of vigorous action that show Tom's fear, and arouse fear in the reader: seizing, hurrying, darting, striking, chasing, plunging. However, when the reteller substitutes more ordinary verbs—saw, flew, put out, hurried—the action loses its suspense. As for the cave, Twain's is a labyrinth of endless passageways and a limitless lake; we fear that Tom and Becky will never find their way out. In the reteller's version of the story, two children merely come to a small hall.

We might point out many more contrasts in the two versions of *Tom Sawyer*, each one of them showing how the loss of freshness in style results in the loss of suspense in the action, depth in the characterization, and vividness in the setting. The two stories are vastly different, even though the same events are carefully reported in the retelling. The reason for the difference is not what happens, but how the writer selects and uses his words to show what happens. This is style.

Stories of Other Periods and Places

Diction should give the reader the flavor of the time, the place, and the events; this the writer does by use of language that seems native to the period and locality of the story. Diction may be of two kinds, the diction of narration and the diction of speech.

Walter Edmonds in *Bert Breen's Barn* manages to duplicate rural, colloquial language in a convincing way. He mentions a route: the bridge by Dutch Mill, Miller's hatchery, the "turn up on the Irish Settlement Road to Kehoe's pond," and the bridge below over Crystal Creek, to where the "road's going back to brush." During the barn building, Birdy whistles all the time, not "proper" whistling, because it "came out through his teeth, half a tune, half the kind of hiss a man makes currying a horse whose hide is clogged with mud." Drawing a "snorty breath," Birdy slaps on a "dose" of mortar. By that time "he would have got some of the mortar into his mustache, turning the hairs into a gray bristle, so that . . . he made Tom think of an old otter telling the young ones to get out of his way." This is rural Pennsylvania, and these are the terms of rural people, using the language of rural life. The diction includes imagery, simile, metaphor, and personification as well as other devices. The flavor and color of the style are appropriate here, as they apply to time, place, characters, and situation. The same statement can be made of Ozark diction in *Where the Lilies Bloom.* As she works her way wildcrafting through dense weeds high as her head, Mary Call says that she "cussed" out here "alone on this blasted mountain working myself to a frazzle." She thinks she must "have moss growing inside [her] head where [her] brains should be." "Nobody but a poor dement" would take on "three snot-nosed kids to raise." "If I had the sense of a rabbit or even half that much, I'd just take off across that bald over there and go down the other side of it . . . and never look back." By their style these two novels give us universal characters whose experiences we believe in, although the times and places of their lives are different from our own.

Stories of other lands and times make special demands upon the writer. Before we can accept other times and places as believable, we must first believe that the characters are human beings like ourselves. Yet, on the other hand, to understand the new culture we must see the particular differences between our own lives and those of other people. Style makes the difference.

Picture Books

Picture books, too, need interesting style which awakens the interest of the young child in the nuances of meaning possible even with ordinary diction. In *Something on My Mind* vivid phrasing accompanies Tom Feelings's pictures: "Talking make-believe," "hanging in the park," "remembering/Grandma filling up this porch/with laughing." Contrast these phrases with the halting style of Clyde Bulla in *Mika's Apple Tree:* "They dressed and went into the house. Supper was ready. They had cabbage soup with rye bread and butter. They had pancakes with jam." Even the simple combining of short sentences would create more vitality in style, and yet, if the early reader were reading alone, would add no more difficulty to the diction.

SUMMARY

Few of us are content with a plot summary as a substitute for the story itself. What happened to Heidi or to Beowulf was not merely plot, since action alone does not make absorbing hours of reading.

Helpful as Charles and Mary Lamb are in *Tales from Shakespeare*, the book is not a substitute for Shakespeare, and a quick look at a book of plot summaries reminds us that *Tom Sawyer* or *Little Women* were never like this. Any good story is words, many words, selected and then arranged in a manner that best creates characters, draws setting, recounts conflict, builds suspense to a climax, and ties it all together with some significance. Words, the best possible words for this particular story, are not only the style of the story; they are the story.

Reading and Evaluating

Problem realism

1 *Dip into a story by Judy Blume and note the style, the imagery, and figurative language. Compare the style with that of Bette Greene's novels, or that of the Cleavers's. What effect has style on characterization? On conflict and setting?*

Epic

2 *Read two versions of* Beowulf, *one by Ian Serraillier, and the other by Robert Nye, Rosemary Sutcliff, or Dorothy Hosford. How do they compare in their effect upon you, the reader? Which account shows Beowulf as a man of more heroic stature? Why? What is the effect of the added details in Nye's version?*

Folktale

3 *Read and compare three versions of one of Grimms' folktales. Which seems to retain the style of an oral tale? Comment on traditional form, brevity of characterization, repeated images, memorable phrases, the use of motif. In oral reading, which flows with the cadence of oral telling? Why?*

Other countries

4 *Read a recent book about a child from another country. What is the importance of imagery in the depiction of setting? Of the way of life? Is imagery essential? Does the style add any special effects to the story? What are they? How are they created?*

Picture books

5 *Find six picture books that have received favorable mention for their pictures. Examine the text for style. What devices does the writer use? Would the text, if published without the pictures, have merit on its own? Why or why not? Does it matter?*

Social Issues realism

6 *Read a story about a child from a minority group, or about a social issue like sexism. Is there a difference between the diction of narration and that of dialogue? Does the dialogue disappoint by its emphasis upon ethnic or sexist language? Does the style seem to make the book preachy about the issue being explored?*

Notes

[1]*Henry James, The Art of Fiction and Other Essays,* New York: Oxford University Press, 1948.

[2]*Tom Sawyer*, adapted by Albert O. Berglund, Glenview, Ill.: Scott, Foresman, 1949.

Recommended Books Cited in This Chapter

Carroll, Lewis. *Alice in Wonderland.* New York: Macmillan, 1963. (first published 1865)
Cleaver, Vera and Bill. *Where the Lilies Bloom.* New York: Lippincott, 1969.
Edmonds, Walter. *Bert Breen's Barn.* Boston: Little, 1975.
Estes, Eleanor. *The Moffats.* New York: Harcourt, 1941.
Feelings, Tom, and Nikki Grimes. *Something on My Mind.* New York: Dial, 1978.
Gág, Wanda. *Millions of Cats.* New York: Coward, 1928.
O'Dell, Scott. *Island of the Blue Dolphins.* Boston: Houghton, 1960.————. *The King's Fifth.* Boston: Houghton, 1960.
Sachs, Marilyn. *The Bear's House.* New York: Doubleday, 1971.
Sendak, Maurice. *Where the Wild Things Are.* New York: Harper, 1963.
Serraillier, Ian. *Beowulf the Warrior.* New York: Walck, 1961.
Spyri, Johanna. *Heidi.* New York: Macmillan, 1962.
Twain, Mark. *The Adventures of Tom Sawyer.* New York: Macmillan, 1966. (first published 1876)
White, E. B. *Charlotte's Web.* New York: Harper, 1952.

ELSEWHERE

We hear the command from old cowboy movies, "When you say that, smile!" and we know what the speaker means: "If you call me your friend, a smile will say you mean it, a frown will mean the opposite." Although they might use identical words, friend or enemy can change meaning by adding a smile. The same words spoken by a teacher to a child acquire a different tone for different situations by the change in voice inflection. Pulling a rebellious child into the classroom, a teacher says, "Come on!" Encouraging a child to try out the new word puzzle, the teacher says, "Come on!" Rejecting a long-winded excuse from the child who must clear the work table, the teacher says, "Come on!" Each time the words have different meanings because inflection, or vocal tone, changes meaning.

Just as tone of voice reveals how a speaker feels about his or her subject, **tone** in literature tells us how the author feels about his or her subject. In literature, however, we cannot rely upon inflection in a writer's voice. We rely entirely upon words. Words express the writer's attitude toward his or her work, subject, and readers. Without vocal inflection to help convey tone, the writer must choose words with great care.

The author's *style* is what conveys the tone in literature. Sentence structure, word choice, patterns, arrangements, all influence style. Figures of speech are chosen for their meaning as well as for their sounds. All these choices create the style and determine the tone of the writing, revealing the attitude of the writer toward both the subject and the reader.

You may feel that tone is too subtle a literary element to be found in children's literature. But this is not so. For example, Kipling's tone in *Just So Stories* most readers would agree is humorous. Kipling's way of saying "this is the way it all happened—just so" is his own unique combination of matter-of-fact and humor:

> So the Elephant's Child went home across Africa frisking and whisking his trunk. . . . When he wanted grass he plucked grass up from the ground, instead of going on his knees

as he used to do. When the flies bit him he broke off the branch of a tree and used it as a fly-whisk; and he made himself a new, cool, slushy-squshy mud-cap whenever the sun was hot.

We suspend our disbelief and say wouldn't-it-be-fun-if, toying with the idea that it might really have happened this way. Because we like the pompous Bi-Coloured-Python-Rock-Snake, and the Crocodile with his musky tusky mouth who stretches the mere smear nose into a handy trunk, we play along with Kipling's "facts" about how the elephant got his trunk. The tone here is the feeling resulting from all the elements working together—the mock-serious situation Kipling is reporting, the tongue-in-cheek characterization, the playful language, the deliberately overplayed, pretentious style. The humorous tone is the result of all of these.

Tone in the *Just So Stories*, like tone in any writing, cannot be isolated from the words of the story. More specifically, words of all kinds, and the sounds of these words, show tone, and tone influences meaning. "Frisking," "whisking," and "plucking" are playful and light-hearted kinds of action expressed in short vowels and quick consonants. Their kinds of action are quite different from the action suggested by, for example, "slamming, banging, and breaking." If the light, rapid sounds of "fly whisk" became "fly swatter," tone would become more serious; if the Elephant's Child's "schloopy-sloshy mud-cap all trickly behind the ears" became instead an objectively described "cold, messy, runny mudpie dripping behind the ears," the harsher consonants and the longer vowels would influence and change the tone. Kipling's choice of playful words and quickly moving cadences makes his pretense of factual reporting into humorous spoof.

We have noted the literary meaning of point of view as the mind or minds through which we see the story—the voice telling the story, whether a character or an omniscient author. Tone is different. It is the author's attitude toward story and readers. By the writer's choice of materials, the writer almost inevitably reveals something about his or her own personality. If the author were telling the story orally, voice tone would reveal attitude and self; since the author is telling the story in print, the choices of words must be the means of showing attitude.

TONE IN *CHARLOTTE'S WEB*

How do we discover tone? We can often describe a writer's tone but are not aware of how we discovered that tone. Tone seems to creep into our consciousness without our being aware of its presence. However, tone, like the showing of action, depiction of character, and description of setting, is created by the writer's choice of words. If we look carefully at a few passages from *Charlotte's Web*, we may see how White's tone is revealed.

The first pages of the book are filled with kindness and affection: Mr. Arable looks at Fern "with love," and speaks to her "gently." Fern kisses her father and her mother, pleased that the runt pig is safe. White describes the setting and the characters in the same kinds of affectionate terms. The action—Wilbur spinning a web, for example, or fainting at his honors—is humorous and yet affectionate.

The chapter "Summer Days" begins with a description of setting:

> The early summer days on a farm are the happiest and fairest days of the year. Lilacs bloom and make the air sweet, and then fade. Apple blossoms come with the lilacs, and the bees visit around among the apple trees. The days grow warm and soft. School ends, and children have time to play and to fish for trouts in the brook.
>
> . . . All morning you could hear the rattle of the machine as it went round and round, while the tall grass fell down behind the cutter bar in long green swathes. Next day . . . the hay would be hauled to the barn in the high hay wagon, with Fern and Avery riding at the top of the load. Then the hay would be hoisted, sweet and warm, into the big loft, until the whole barn seemed like a wonderful bed of timothy and clover. It was fine to jump in, and perfect to hide in.

In this selection, there are nothing but pleasant sensory images—fragrant lilacs, apple blossoms visited by friendly bees, children fishing for trout. Summer work goes on, but the sights and sounds are pleasant; work is another kind of sensory pleasure—rhythmic "round and round," colorful "long green swathes," sweet smelling clover, soft timothy bed for playing in. The abstract terms "happiest," "fairest," "warm," and "soft" describe the days, while "wonderful," "fine," and "perfect" describe the fun the days bring. Both the abstract words and the vivid appeals to our five senses have pleasant connotations. Summertime is not marred by a single unpleasant image or connotation. Summer fun is also humorous; Avery carries in his pocket a stiff and warm trout to be fried for dinner, or finds a slender grass snake and pockets it. Like the rest of the story, this chapter is filled with descriptions of a serene and pleasant world. White loves the summertime, the farm, the children, and the animals. Although White later builds suspense to a strong climax, his affectionate descriptions of all that summer brings have assured us that he will not permit disaster to come. While his emphasis upon the cycle of seasons prepares us for change, he never suggests in his choice of words that the change will bring tragedy or despair. Summing up White's attitude toward his story, we can best characterize it as humorous affection. As White goes on to compare a gray spider to a gumdrop, the contours of a gluttonous rat to a jelly jar, and describes a pig as terrific, radiant, and humble, we see affection and humor in all that happens in the story. White's word choices—style— have determined tone.

HUMOR

Humor is an important tone in children's literature. Much of the humor comes from situation, that is, incongruous happenings that make children laugh. The cow jumping over the moon, the barber shaving a pig —these situations are funny to a small child. Situation or action is also the source of humor in *Pippi Longstocking* and *Homer Price*. But these stories are more than pie-throwing cartoons; they have invention and absurdity expressed in straightforward language.

Other stories depend for their humor upon style or unexpected phrasing as well as upon situation. Ludwig Bemelmans' *Madeline*, for example, in which the diction is precise and brief, not only shows a humorous situation, but also describes the situation in fresh and unexpected wording, rhythm, and rhyme. The crack upon the ceiling whose habit it is to look like a rabbit is situation nonsense; it is also humorous absurdity because of the unexpected internal rhyme and the personification that accompanies cracks having habits. The source of humor in *Winnie-the-Pooh* does not lie in the situation alone—sailing off on an overturned umbrella or disguising oneself as a black cloud. The humor rises as much from the quiet, almost solemn wording of conversations and descriptions surrounding the absurdities.

There is verbal humor in Lucille Clifton's *Don't You Remember?* as impatient Tate, tired of being put off till later for everything she wants, cries out "It's later now," and "Now is next time," as well as when she explodes with "Dag, double dag!" The quiet verbal humor of Russell Hoban's picture books has merit, too, and yet it is quite unlike the vividly phrased ironic humor in the picture books of Isaac Bashevis Singer who also refuses to give children only slapstick humor. The humor of Maurice Sendak's *Pierre, a Cautionary Tale,* keeps that story from becoming didactic. Arnold Lobel's *Frog and Toad Together* is funny not only because of situation—they are odd animals for step-ladder climbing— but also because of the understated verbal humor, a surprise in basic vocabulary.

As we have noted, the humor of Kipling's *The Elephant's Child* is not merely nonsensical, but highly witty verbal humor. Mark Twain's humor, too, is rich and varied. It ranges from situations—the hurried search for a lost pocket knife after the first smoke, the showing off on the picket fence for Becky's benefit—to humorous pokes at innumerable human foibles: the less there is to justify a tradition, the harder it is to get rid of it; the more an act is forbidden, the more enticing it becomes.[1] Often Twain understates, occasionally he exaggerates, but always his language is fresh, filled with figurative language and imagery.

When we seek out the sources of laughter in children's literature, we may be surprised at our discoveries. When, for example, Sara tries to dye her orange sneakers baby blue in *The Summer of the Swans,* it is not only the situation that makes us laugh. It is also the freshness of language. As Sara lifts her sneakers out of the sink between two spoons, she says to her friend,

> ". . . Look at that. That is the worst color you have ever seen in your life. Admit it."
>
> "I admit it."
>
> "Well, you don't have to admit it so quickly. They ought to put on the dye wrapper that orange cannot be dyed baby blue."
>
> "They do."
>
> "Well, they ought to put it in big letters. Look at those shoes. There must be a terrible name for that color."
>
> "There is," Mary said. "Puce."
>
> "What?"
>
> "Puce."
>
> "Mary Weicek, you made that up."
>
> "I did not. It really is a color."
>
> "I have never heard a word that describes anything better. Puce. These just look like puce shoes."

We expect children to laugh at situation humor, since it is easy to see. But we underestimate children when we assume that is all that they can find humorous. We limit children's discovery when we limit their exposure to the simplest and most obvious. A double row of beds, a double file of children is the situation humor of *Madeline*. However, "lived twelve little girls in two straight lines" is the sophisticated humor of style. Children deserve this source of humor, too.

Parody

Parody is usually a device for older readers, since it relies on the reader's memory of a known piece of writing or of a way of talking. It retains the form of the original but changes the words and the tone for humorous effect. "An hour of freedom is worth a barrel of slops" is a simple parody of an old saying—an ounce of prevention is worth a pound of cure. A parody reminds us of something known, then gives fresh pleasure by duplicating form which contrasts to new and humorous meaning. A clear parody for children is the bedtime story that Charlotte tells Wilbur. It has the traditional beginning, as well as the fluid phrasing, of folk or fairy tale. Within the folktale parody is a description of the struggling fish trapped in the spider web. Read the paragraph aloud and notice its similarity to a prizefight account:

> "There was my cousin, slipping in, dodging out. . . . dancing in, dancing out, throwing her threads and fighting hard. First she threw a left around the tail. The fish lashed back. Then a left to the tail and a right to. . . ."

And again, try square dancing while Charlotte spins her web:

> "Now for the R! Up we go! Attach! Descend! Pay out line! . . . Whoa, girl! Steady now! . . . Now right and down and swing that loop and around and around! O.K.! Easy, keep those lines together! . . ."

The child catches some of the pleasures of White's parody and word play, but the adult catches many more; the result is pleasure for everyone. Carroll's literary parodies are extremely witty—Robert Southey's "The Old Man's Comforts" becomes "You Are Old, Father William," for example. But with the exception perhaps of "Twinkle, twinkle, little bat," they are unknown to the child—or to most of today's adults, for that matter. White parodies word patterns from three familiar situations —folktale, prizefight, and square dancing. Wit explained loses its wittiness, and these need no explanations.

DIFFERING TASTES IN TONE

We know that we all bring to a story our own backgrounds and experiences, and that the story has a personal meaning for us because we respond out of our own emotional history and present feelings. Readers, however, can only take from a story something already put into the story by the writer; tone is the effect of the writer's words. If two readers describe tone differently, it is often the result of personal definitions of their descriptive terms, or the result of differing personal taste and experience.

The tone of *Winnie-the-Pooh* may seem to one reader whimsically affectionate. Pooh and Piglet do not converse in fragments the way we do, but in long, complex sentences filled with "that" clauses. And all the time, what they discuss so gravely is near nonsense.

> "I think that I have just remembered something. I have just remembered something that I forgot to do yesterday and shan't be able to do tomorrow. So I suppose I really ought to go back and do it now."
>
> "It isn't the sort of thing you can do in the afternoon," said Piglet quickly. "It's a very particular morning thing, that has to be done in the morning, and, if possible, between the hours of—What would you say the time was?"

One reader calls the tone whimsical and playful. Another reader, thinking the playfulness and sentiment excessive, reads Christopher Robin's words, "Oh, Bear . . . how I do love you!" and says this is not a lightly affectionate tone, but sentimentality—an adult talking the way children never talk. The same words are used by the writer; two different readers receive them. The differing opinions might be called a matter of taste. Children, like adults, have their personal preferences. They may not define their reactions in terms of tone, but they may think the Pooh stories are "funny," or "silly," or "boring." On questioning them, we may find that these children are responding to what they see as Milne's attitude toward his material and his readers —in other words, tone.

TONE RELATED TO THE AUTHOR'S CHOICE OF MATERIALS

Any kind of tone can be found in any kind or genre of children's literature. A fantasy, for example, may be serious in tone to fit its serious themes, as Ursula K. LeGuin demonstrates in *The Tombs of Atuan,* and Eleanor Cameron does in *The Court of the Stone Children.* Or the tone may be light-hearted as it is in *The Wind in the Willows,* which—with its little universe of peace, its pictures of natural beauty, and its variety of friendly and harmless animal characters in a quiet country setting— shows in its tone Grahame's attitude toward his characters and his story. In gentle and kindly acceptance, Grahame not only observes but enjoys the differences among the characters, their styles of living, their prefer- ences, and their habits. Bountiful leisure, filled with lunches, snacks, picnics, and breakfast extending into lunchtime, and all surrounded by profound good will, occupies a benevolent world.

First, notice how the setting reflects Grahame's tone. Rat loves his river. When the brown flood water drops

> "away and shows patches of mud that smells like plum-cake, and the rushes and weed clog the channels, and I can potter about dry-shod over most of the bed of it and find fresh food to eat . . ."

that is when Rat loves his river best. "Plum-cake" and "potter about" are connotative of comfort and happiness. The river is Rat's world and its banks are covered with his friends. Mole learns to love it, too, to enter "into the joy of running water." Badger is the perfect host in his house "behind comfortable-looking doors," a cozy home with "wide hearth," chairs grouped "sociably," "spotless plates" winking from the shelves, and rafters hung with stored harvest:

> The ruddy brick floor smiled up at the smoky ceiling; the oaken settles, shiny with long wear, exchanged cheerful glances with each other; plates on the dresser grinned at pots on the shelf, and the merry firelight flickered and played over everything without distinction.

Everything in Badger's house is friendly; each item is personified and made to smile, to glance cheerfully, to grin, to play and be merry. The settles, or wooden-backed benches, show by their gloss that they have made many visitors comfortable before the fire. Mole's home, too, although it is also underground, has a welcoming front yard which shows love of home and a hospitable welcome:

> A garden-seat stood on one side of the door. . . . On the walls hung wire baskets with ferns in them . . . a skittle-alley, with benches along it and little wooden tables marked with rings that hinted at beer-mugs.

Here, also, the setting shows tone: the pleasant game court, lined with spectator benches and with tables that show evidence—rings hinting of beer-mugs—of a generous host who serves his friends refreshments in leisurely comfort.

This same kindness and acceptance appear in the characters' attitudes toward one another. Of the impetuous braggart Toad, who keeps his friends in a state of constant concern, Rat says indulgently,

> "the best of animals. . . . So simple, so good-natured, and so affectionate. Perhaps he's not very clever—we can't all be

geniuses; and it may be that he is both boastful and conceited. But he has got some great qualities, has Toady."

When Mole disappears into the Wild Wood, Rat calls out "cheerfully," hunts "patiently," is joyful at hearing Mole's cry, and speaks "soothingly" when he approaches Mole—despite Mole's having ignored Rat's advice. When Rat is tempted by the Wayfarer to abandon his home and friends, Mole tactfully leads him back to his beloved River by talk of harvesttime. He slips away for paper and pencil and suggests gently that Rat do some poetry, "have a try at it." These terms, with their positive connotations of acceptance and concern, convey the tone. Among these varied characters there is no bickering nor condemning. Grahame's words instead intensify the strong feeling of community among the very different individuals. Such terms as "accepting," "kindly," "friendly," or "genial" might describe tone, but all spring from the close relationship between the idyllic country setting and the gentle accepting characters.

Ian Serraillier in his retelling of *Beowulf the Warrior* uses the language of today and yet retains the tone and qualities of the folk epic as it was first recorded 1000 years ago. The intent of the folk epic is serious, since the long narrative centers on a national hero and makes clear the values of a people. Serraillier has respected this intent by maintaining a consistently dignified tone. He keeps the elevated language, the compound synonyms or kennings, the imagery, the alliteration, and the extended metaphors. In the passage below, Beowulf and his band set sail:

> They ran up the white sail. And the wind caught her,
> The biting wind whipped her over the waves.
> Like a strong bird the swan-boat winged her way
> Over the grey Baltic, the wintry whale-road.

The voyage across the sea is no happy and light-hearted sail across the bay; Beowulf and his valiant warriors face a sea worthy of their courage.

Hand-to-hand combat with a monster has a dignity heightened by long, rhythmic lines, richly connotative terms, and alliterative descriptions with long vowels and hard consonants:

> Spilling the benches,
> They tugged and heaved, from wall to wall they hurtled.
> And the roof rang to their shouting, the huge hall
> Rocked, the strong foundations groaned and trembled.

The long sounds (extended *a*'s and *oo* sounds, slowly moving consonants—*l*'s, *g*'s, and *r*'s, for example) make the poetic lines move slowly
to create a sense of dignity that accompanies the awesome struggle.
After Beowulf defeats Grendel, Hrothgar praises Beowulf, and thereby
shows his own generous and humble nature. But here shorter vowel and
consonant sounds quicken the pace and so lighten the tone:

> the grateful King,
> All glooming gone, his countenance clear and cloudless
> As the sky in open radiance of the climbing sun,
> Gave thanks to God for deliverance. "Beowulf," he said,
> "Bravest of men, I shall love you now as my son.
> All I have is yours for the asking."

In the early lines of Part Three, we again experience awe at the
man whose life has been a "journey" of heroic deeds, suggesting that
Beowulf has been in constant movement and progress, one brave deed
following another:

> From youth of fighting and heroic deeds
> Quietly he journeyed toward the tomb, until,
> Old at last—like a mighty oak in winter,
> Flaunting no longer her green midsummer glory,
> But stripped and bare, yet splendid still—he hoped
> To die in peace.

The image and simile comparing Beowulf to a mighty oak whose summer glory is gone but whose strength remains contribute still more to
the tone. Beowulf, although he is simply described by the statement
"mightiest yet mildest," is not merely an average man doing minor
deeds of courage. His character is noble and selfless; he leads, and he is
victorious. His life exemplifies valor and sacrifice. The actions of such
a character are grand and elevated; the tone of such a tale must be
equally grand and elevated.

EVALUATING TONE IN CHILDREN'S LITERATURE

Condescension

When someone looks down upon us, treating us as though we are
unintelligent or immature, we call this attitude condescension. In the
original writings of the Greeks, Homer, Hesiod, and Pindar, the myths

conveyed religious truth; they expressed the depth and seriousness of ancient faith. As Edith Hamilton says, we know Greek mythology best through the Greek writers who believed in what they wrote. One of Hamilton's examples is the story of Perseus and the Gorgon's head, a story that moves us, its brief descriptive phrases giving horror and urgency to the tale:

> And they are three, the Gorgons, each with wings
> And snaky hair, most horrible to mortals.
> Whom no man shall behold and draw again
> The breath of life.

By contrast, in Nathaniel Hawthorne's retelling in *A Wonder Book*, the Gorgons become snake-fairy-butterfly concoctions:

> Why, instead of locks of hair, if you can believe me, they had each of them a hundred enormous snakes growing on their heads, alive, twisting, wriggling, curling, and thrusting out their venomous tongues, with forked stings at the end! . . . and they looked very dazzling, no doubt, flying about in the sunshine.

By making the Gorgons into cartoon-like characters, Hawthorne has turned the tone of the story almost into ridicule. He is condescending in his attitude toward both his subject and his readers.

In Hawthorne's descriptions of the hero himself, Perseus who slew the Gorgon Medusa, there is none of the dignity we would expect. Instead, in casual, quick-paced diction Hawthorne describes Perseus as pathetically vulnerable. His turning to stone would be a "very sad thing to befall a young man." Perseus's motives seem selfish and glory-seeking, as he "wanted to perform a great many brave deeds, and to enjoy a great deal of happiness in this bright and beautiful world." Perseus could hardly keep from crying. He felt "greatly ashamed . . . like a timid little school boy." "What would my dear mother do, if her beloved son were turned into stone?" "Dear me . . . I shall be afraid to say a syllable." All grandeur is lost in this version.

The tone of the myth in Hawthorne's retelling is not respectful but condescending. He seems to be saying to the reader, "Now, children, isn't this a silly little story about foolish people?" There is no awe at the size of Perseus's task, no admiration for a courageous and liberating act.

The myths of ancient people, myths that have come to us from those who believed in them, were filled with reverence and mystery, since by myth human beings were attempting to explain the wonders of human beings and of nature. Hawthorne, although he may have followed the traditional details, has changed the myth completely by his condescending tone.

A modern example of condescension is Walt Disney's *Wonderful World of Knowledge,* Volume 10, which does include the traditional details of the myths. Although the diction is condescending, it is not as offensive as the illustrations: Pluto is Icarus and King Arthur; Mickey Mouse is Jason, Roland, Sigurd, and Galahad; Tinker Belle is one of the ondines or water sprites from the Norse Eddas. Despite color reproductions of classic art works showing myths, the total effect is destroyed by the cartooned heroes.

Does this condescending tone matter? When a retelling so completely violates the original tone or the spirit in which it was told, the story is changed beyond recognition; a child meeting such condescension may be turned off by tone that talks down, and he or she may never be encouraged or interested enough to find a better version. In original fiction, too, literature that talks to us as "dear little readers" demeans us; we may even be insulted. No one likes condescension, and the child who meets it may reject the pleasures and discoveries of literature.

Sentimentality, or the overuse of sentiment, is a kind of condescension. Thornton W. Burgess, still in print and on the library shelves after sixty years, in telling his story *Mother West Wind's Animal Friends* is not only trite in language but also sentimental in tone. Burgess creates talking animals that have few traits to convince us either of their likeness to people or of their animal natures—except that those with wings fly, and those without, walk. Open a Burgess story and find this:

> Then old Mr. Toad picked up his cane and started down the Crooked Little Path to the Green Meadows. There he found the Merry Little Breezes stealing kisses from the bashful little wind flowers. Old Mr. Toad puffed out his throat and pretended that he disapproved, disapproved very much indeed, but at the same time he rolled one eye up at jolly, round, red Mr. Sun and winked.
>
> "Haven't you anything better to do than make bashful little flowers hang their heads?" asked old Mr. Toad gruffly.

The many capitalized nouns and adjectives, the personification of breezes, flowers, and sun, the repetition of words and phrases ("disapproved, disapproved very much indeed"), the clichés ("anything better to do"), do little to convey conflict or to make the story move. Peter Rabbit (a nod to Beatrix Potter) and the "Little meadow people and forest folk" are organizing an Easter Egg Rolling for everyone in the Green Meadows, the Purple Hills, and the Green Forest. Poor Peter, Burgess sighs:

> No, Sir, Peter Rabbit, happy-go-lucky Peter, who usually carries the lightest heart on the Green Meadows, was not happy. Indeed, he was very unhappy. . . . he saw nothing beautiful at all because, why, because his big soft eyes were full of tears. Splash! A big tear fell at his feet in the Crooked Little Path. Splash! That was another tear. Splash! Splash!

The long-winded combination of sentimentality and the omniscient point of view creates a coy tone and fails to reveal character or to describe actions. Burgess seems to lack respect for his readers, his characters, and his story; his condescension makes a shallow story.

By contrast, O'Dell in *Island of the Blue Dolphins* never condescends, never demeans Karana's life by sentimentality. Her people have always lived on a windswept island, dependent upon themselves and their own capacities to use what is provided by nature, and avoid death at nature's impersonal hands. A product of this culture, living close to the elements, Karana quietly accepts what faces her. Life is sometimes cruel; humans survive by self-control. Ramo's being killed by wild dogs does not make Karana wild in her grief; we sense instead her feeling of inevitability and of necessity for restraint:

> All night I sat there with the body of my brother and did not sleep. I vowed that someday I would go back and kill the wild dogs in the cave. I would kill all of them. I thought of how I would do it, but mostly I thought of Ramo, my brother.

O'Dell's tone of restraint makes us feel sympathy for and understanding of Karana in her isolation and loneliness; there is no sentimentality here.

Nor is there sentimentality in Katherine Paterson's portrayal of Jess's grief at the death of his friend in the flood waters. In *Bridge to Terabithia* we read that Jess's stomach "felt so odd." And yet, the morning after the news, pancakes doused in syrup taste "marvelous." Jess's sister accuses him of not caring, and he is puzzled: "The coldness curled up inside of him and flopped over." As Jess's mother and sister talk, he "could hear them talking and they were farther away than the memory of a dream." He cannot leave the table, but he doesn't know what to do. Then, his mind a blank, he mumbles, "What little girl?" Paterson's depiction is not sentimental, filled with sighs and tears and sobs; we nonetheless see that Jess is shocked and grief-stricken.

Sensationalism, which we have noted in our discussion of plot, is another kind of tone. In many places *The Slave Dancer* and *My Brother Sam Is Dead,* for example, might have been sensational. The writers, however, have carefully chosen words that convey meaning and control tone, but avoid sensationalism.

Changing Values

[Styles in writing change—for children as they do for adults. Sometimes it is tone that forces the retirement of a onetime classic.] Such, it seems, may be the case in E. Nesbit's *Five Children and It*, a book that continues to appear on lists of classics but is no longer read by many children.[2] [While an occasional child today may still respond to the playful fantasy of *Five Children and It*, it is perhaps the sentimental and condescending tone that has retired it from the active shelf.] Lamb, who is too old to be called a baby today, says,

> "Poor, poor." And he let the gipsy woman kiss him, and what is more, he kissed her brown cheek in return—a very nice kiss, as all his kisses are, and not a wet one like some babies give.

Robert, who is

> not a brutal brother, though very ingenious in apple-pie beds, booby traps, original methods of awakening sleeping relatives, and other little accomplishments which made home happy,

asks Lamb to "come and have a yidey on Yobby's back." Sentimental and stereotyped characterization combines with condescension toward gipsies, "Eyetalians," and "Red Indians."

Condescension combined with whimsy also contrasts artificially the views of children and adults on what is real and true:

> So . . . you may leave [this] book about quite safely, for no aunts and uncles either are likely to write "How true!" on the edge of the story. Grown-up people find it very difficult to believe really wonderful things, unless they have . . . proof. But children will believe almost anything, and grown-ups know this . . . they tell you that the earth is round like an orange, when you can see perfectly well that it is flat and lumpy; and why they say that the earth goes round the sun, when you can see for yourself any day that the sun gets up in the morning and

goes to bed at night like a good sun as it is, and the earth knows its place, and lies as still as a mouse.

While Nesbit's stories have been great favorites in the past, contempo-⟩ rary children may reject such talking down.

By contrast, look at Eleanor Estes's *The Moffats,* or Beverly Cleary's *Ramona and Her Father,* two other family stories. One might call the tone of such stories "wonder"—a kind of wonder that says "Aren't everyday, ordinary things remarkable?" Ramona, who has made herself a crown of burs and now must have her hair cut off in order to remove the burs, begs Daddy not to cut any more than he has to. "Does it look awful?" she asks. And her father replies with humor, "It will never be noticed from a trotting horse." Ramona lets out a "long, shuddery sigh, the closest thing to crying without really crying." When Ramona, whose father has lost his job, wishes she might earn a million dollars like the boy on the hamburger commercials, her father replies

> "I'll bet that boy's father wishes he had a little girl who finger-painted and wiped her hands on the cat when she was little and who once cut her own hair so she would be bald like her uncle and who then grew up to be seven years old and crowned herself with burs. Not every father is lucky enough to have a daughter like that."

Although the events of *Five Children and It* are fantastic and those of *Ramona* are humorously realistic and everyday, *Ramona* is far more successful in its creation of a sense of surprise. True, the children of *Five Children and It* live in an era more remote and foreign. But time distance is not the issue, since to a child time has no definition by decade. It is possible that what makes one story old-fashioned and relegates it to book lists and what may keep the other alive and read may be to a great extent tone, or how the authors feel about their subjects and readers. Our tastes in tone may change. Baby-talk was more acceptable in Victorian fiction than it is today.⏋

Didacticism

Preaching or teaching, as we have noted, is the function of textbooks and sermons. In literature it is a negative quality. Sometimes a writer makes a lesson into a story. By giving the protagonist a few personal traits and setting him or her into a narrative, the writer may seem to have created a story. (Remember our earlier discussion of *Willie Goes to the Seashore.*) Since pleasure comes from a good story told well, and understanding grows from a discovery about human nature, the story often fails as literature.

Look, for example, at the picture book *I Want to Be a Homemaker*. Jane's mother gives her advice about her doll children. She says that they need good food, and must be given milk, eggs, vegetables, meat, and so forth, and then they will grow. As Jane pours tea into her doll teacups, her mother adds that some foods will build bones and others muscles. Some will grow teeth and skin and hair, and some will help keep children warm. Others give "pep" for running, jumping, and playing. "You see, Jane, we need many kinds of food." Moments later Jane tells her visitor about her doll children who sometimes won't behave, won't brush teeth, often get wet feet, and even run into the street. And Mother replies that a good homemaker is a teacher all day long.

Such a story seems to have been conceived in the writer's mind only in order to teach. Characters are undeveloped, conflict is nonexistent, and style is dull. All that survives is a didactic or teaching message: homemakers, i.e., women, must know about child care. While *Homemaker* is an extreme example—and an unfortunate example—of sexist stereotyping [many "stories" seem to have as purpose the underlining of a moral or the teaching of a lesson to the exclusion of the elements of literature. Pleasure and understanding are buried in lessons.]

Variety of Tone

[Some writers vary tone as the situation in the story changes; they use various tones to comment on people as individuals and as social groups.] While such a story can often be read as a fast-paced, character-conflict-theme story, the perceptive reader who catches the shifts and shading of tone may find added pleasure in the story. As the readers recognize human manners and behavior, they also discover the author's attitude, and a whole new level of pleasure can be uncovered.

We can note the various tone shifts in Andersen's "The Ugly Duckling." Andersen is sometimes humorous, sometimes tender, often critical, and even, sometimes, almost cynical. The child may read "The Ugly Duckling" often during the early years because of the range of tone; at each new reading, the child discovers a new tone open and available. [The story, since it is rich in meanings, gives a richness of understanding to the reader. A good story continues to open itself to the reader for many reasons; complexity in tone is one.]

Few stories have greater variety and complexity in tone than *Tom Sawyer*, a story that offers great excitement on the level of character and plot alone. Mark Twain ranges over human attitudes from tenderness to sarcasm, from delight to cynicism. In his depiction of boyhood and adolescence, Twain admits that life is varied and contradictory; he uses tone to show its complexity and perversity. In checking passages from the novel, notice Twain's distance from, and yet smiling acceptance of, the self-deception and self-absorption of the young:

> *On crushes:* He had been months winning [Amy]; she had confessed hardly a week ago; he had been the happiest and the proudest boy in the world only seven short days, and here in one instant of time she had gone out of his heart like a casual stranger whose visit is done.

> *On ceremony:* [T]he oath was complete. They buried the shingle close to the wall with some dismal ceremonies and incantations, and the fetters that bound their tongues were considered to be locked and the key thrown away.

Twain, in commenting on human behavior, is sly and faintly satirical.

> *On theft:* [T]here was no getting around the stubborn fact that taking sweetmeats was only "hooking," while taking bacon and hams and such valuables was plain simple stealing—

> *On sermons:* The discourse . . . went lame and halting. . . . It was a genuine relief to the whole congregation when the ordeal was over and the benediction pronounced.

> *On the forbidden:* Huckleberry was cordially hated and dreaded by all the mothers of the town, because he was idle and lawless and vulgar and bad—and because all their children admired him so, and delighted in his forbidden society, and wished they dared to be like him.

Although we remember *Tom Sawyer* as a happy book, Twain is ironic, sarcastic, even cynical at times:

> *On showing off:* [The Sunday school superintendent] by bustlings and activities. [The librarian] by making a deal of the splutter and fuss that insect authority delights in. [The teachers] by bending sweetly over pupils that were lately being boxed.

> *On accusation:* [T]he public are not slow in the matter of sifting evidence and arriving at a verdict.

And finally, on public sentimentality he becomes almost sardonic:

> This funeral stopped the further growth of one thing—
> the petition to the governor for Injun Joe's pardon . . . a commit-
> tee of sappy women . . . in deep mourning . . . wail around the
> governor, and implore him to be a merciful ass and trample his
> duty underfoot . . . scribble their names to a pardon petition,
> and drip a tear on it from their permanently impaired and leaky
> waterworks.

By filling his novel with a great variety of tone, depending upon his attitude toward the particular situation or subject, Mark Twain has increased the scope and significance of his story. He has shown what pleasure can come from observing all of life and from taking a stand on any and every aspect of it. By varying tone upon dozens of different subjects and yet maintaining an overall attitude of humor and enjoy-ment of each experience, he has not only managed to create a novel of suspense and excitement, but also one that continues to amaze and de-light, no matter what the age of the reader or the number of rereadings.

There are kinds of tone that seem unsuited to children's stories. Satire with its intent to reform is often too intellectual an exercise. It demands breadth of experience and ability to see and interpret exagger-ation and understatement. There are books, however, in which the story is so strong that it carries the child's interest and the satire may be missed completely without any loss to the reader—the *Alice* books would be examples. As overall tone, sarcasm with its intent to wound is also too complex and thus questionable for children. To children, all experience is a subject for wonder. Condemnation, as well as fear and pessimism, seem to have little place in their literature; without experi-ence to place these negative tones in perspective, they may be over-whelmed and moved to despair.

Children's literature in recent years has taken increasingly hon-est looks at all areas of life, and part of the result has been more suffering, pain, and futility in stories for young readers. As long as these negative attitudes are not unrelieved, they have their place. However, children are less able than adults to defend themselves against despair and so find the pessimistic messages more meaningful if they are pre-sented within a story in which the tone is basically optimistic.

What matters is that tone for children's literature be, if not optimistic, at least positive, or perhaps objective.[3] For children, all the world is opening up; there is so much to be appreciated and marveled at—and improved upon. If limiting tone to optimism and affirmation narrows tone too much, we may consider only condescension and un-relieved despair as even worse and quite unsuitable. But if we defend these two kinds of tone, we must remind ourselves of the functions of literature. Futility and despair do not give pleasure nor necessarily increase understanding; there are dozens of other possible attitudes that may do this for young readers.

SUMMARY

Tone, the author's attitude toward subject and readers, is an integral part of story, since it is created by the writer's choice of words. It is not created by any single, deliberate decision the author makes, but is the result of all the choices he or she makes in telling the story. Tone can make the same story—one of heroes and valiant deeds, for example—either a series of trivial anecdotes or a monument to human valor. Tone can fill us with affection and acceptance, or rouse us to examine and to laugh at ourselves.

Reading and Evaluating

Myth

1 *Find three versions of the same myth and compare them. Does the tone demonstrate the purpose of myths? Is the tone consistent with the subject? Is it condescending?*

Realism

2 *Find a realistic novel written before 1940 that recurs on classics lists. What is its tone? Is the novel still being read by children? What significance has tone in the life of the work?*

Picture books

3 *Read four Caldecott-Award-winning picture books. What is the tone? Is it simple or complex? Is it possible that adults reading the story to children may catch one tone, and the listening children another tone? If so, what is the difference and what is the effect?*

Fantasy

4 *Read* Mary Poppins *by Pamela Travers or a fantasy by Eleanor Cameron, Susan Cooper, Alan Garner, or Penelope Lively and describe tone. Which situations and characters best support your choice of term descriptive of tone? Explain your reaction to the tone.*

Social Issues and Problem Realism

5 *Read a realistic story from the 1960's or later that deals with a protagonist with some kind of problem. What is the tone? What is the effect of tone upon the characterization? Upon the theme? Upon the conflict?*

Humor

6 *Find at least six humorous picture books and compare them. Which rely only upon situation for humor? Upon illustrations rather than upon language? Which have distinctive literary style? In the book you consider to have the most humorous style, which particular devices does the writer rely upon for the creation of humor?*

Notes

[1]*For a discussion of humor in children's books, see "The Hoot of Little Voices,"* in *A Critical Approach to Children's Literature*, by James Steele Smith, New York: McGraw-Hill, 1967, pp. 203–225.

[2]See note nine, Chapter 3, on classics lists.

[3]June Jordan in "Young People: Victims of Realism in Books and Life" (*Wilson Library Bulletin*, Oct. 1973) comments on children's need for some good news, for positive messages of change, for optimism. Natalie Babbitt in "Happy Endings? Of Course, and Also Joy," (*Children and Literature: Views and Reviews*, Glenview, Ill.: Scott, Foresman, 1973, pp. 155–159) comments on tone and theme in children's literature. Noting the vast range of subjects and tone, she finds that what can and might happen—joy and optimism—seem to be the special pleasure of stories for children, and rightly so.

Recommended Books Cited in This Chapter

Andersen, Hans Christian. *The Ugly Duckling*. New York: Macmillan, 1967.
Bemelmans, Ludwig. *Madeline*. New York: Viking, 1939.
Byars, Betsy. *The Summer of the Swans*. New York: Viking, 1970.
Cameron, Eleanor. *The Court of the Stone Children*. New York: Dutton, 1973.
Carroll, Lewis. *Alice in Wonderland*. New York: Macmillan, 1963. (first published 1865)
Cleary, Beverly. *Ramona and Her Father*. New York: Morrow, 1977.
Clifton, Lucille. *Don't You Remember?* New York: Dutton, 1973.
Collier, James Lincoln and Christopher. *My Brother Sam Is Dead*. New York: Four Winds, 1974.
Estes, Eleanor. *The Moffats*. New York: Harcourt, 1941.
Fox, Paula. *The Slave Dancer*. New York: Bradbury, 1973.
Grahame, Kenneth. *The Wind in the Willows*. New York: Scribner's, 1953. (first published 1908)
Kipling, Rudyard. *Just So Stories*. Garden City, N.Y.: Doubleday, 1946. (first published 1902)
LeGuin, Ursula K. *The Tombs of Atuan*. New York: Atheneum, 1972.
Lindgren, Astrid. *Pippi Longstocking*. New York: Viking, 1950.
Lobel, Arnold. *Frog and Toad Together*. New York: Harper, 1972.
McCloskey, Robert. *Homer Price*. New York: Viking, 1943.
Milne, A. A. *Winnie-the-Pooh*. New York: Dutton, 1926.
Nesbit, E., *The Story of the Treasure Seekers*. New York: Stokes, 1899.
O'Dell, Scott. *Island of the Blue Dolphins*. Boston: Houghton, 1960.
Paterson, Katherine. *Bridge to Terabithia*. New York: Crowell, 1978.
Serraillier, Ian. *Beowulf the Warrior*. New York: Walck, 1961.
Twain, Mark. *The Adventures of Tom Sawyer*. New York: Macmillan, 1966. (first published 1876)
White, E. B. *Charlotte's Web*. New York: Harper, 1952.

10 From Rhyme to Poetry

ex libris
grethel dasio

When do children first meet literature? If they are lucky, they meet it in infancy, as early as the time they are making valiant efforts to "pat-a-cake, pat-a-cake, baker's man." Because nursery rhymes or Mother Goose rhymes use the elements of literature and the devices of style, and because the rhymes are sources of pleasure and understanding, we can legitimately call them the earliest literature for the youngest child. And these rhymes are the beginning of poetry for children.

NURSERY RHYMES

Few narratives in literature for child or adult are told as economically as the nursery rhymes. Many of them, like "Pussy cat, pussy cat, where have you been?" are the most tightly constructed stories. "Sing a song of sixpence, a pocketful of rye" tells a complete tale in three short verses. "Three wise men of Gotham" could hardly be more condensed:

> Three wise men of Gotham
> Went to sea in a bowl.
> If the bowl had been stronger,
> My story had been longer.

Small children whose attention spans are limited are introduced to brief fictional tales in rhyming forms. While the rhymes are not poetry, they are the simplest and best introduction to poetry.

Literary Elements

Many of the Mother Goose or nursery rhymes are the simplest and briefest of stories. The *characters* are the Queen of Hearts who made some tarts, the old woman tossed up in a basket, and Old Mother Hubbard whose cupboard is bare. *Setting,* too, is quickly sketched in some rhymes.

The Old Woman lives in a shoe, and Jack and Jill go up the hill. The brief narratives have simple *plots*. The crooked man uses his crooked sixpence to buy a crooked cat which "caught a crooked mouse,/And they all lived together in a little crooked house" for a happy closed ending. Action in these stories varies from the simplest of tumbles taken by Humpty Dumpty to the more complex involvements of "The House That Jack Built," and "Who Killed Cock Robin?"

Ideas or themes also occur in Mother Goose rhymes, ideas a small child can grasp. Some of the simple rhymes are surprisingly clear in their insights, and oftentimes the short verse-stories have slight *themes*. "Life is a fleeting thing," we discover from

> Solomon Grundy
> Born on Monday,
> Christened on Tuesday,
> Married on Wednesday,
> Took ill on Thursday,
> Worse on Friday,
> Died on Saturday,
> Buried on Sunday,
> That's the end
> Of Solomon Grundy.

Because of Dapple Gray, we know that "A pet is worth more than money":

> I had a little pony; his name was Dapple Gray.
> I lent him to a lady to ride a mile away.
> She whipped him, she slashed him,
> She rode him through the mire—
> I would not lend my pony now
> For all that lady's hire.

A child's understanding is increased in other ways. Curiosity about the environment is roused when the commonplace is made exciting. The trip to the grocery store is time for "To market, to market, to buy a fat pig," and a walk beside the flower beds time for "Mistress Mary's garden" with "silver bells and cockle shells and pretty maids all in a row."

Style

In the pleasant or unusual beat of nursery rhymes there is *rhythm* that may correspond to breathing and heartbeat within us; rhythm is a way into poetry:

Hickory, dickory, dock.
The mouse ran up the clock.
The clock struck one,
And down he run,
Hickory, dickory, dock.

The quick movement of a rhyme makes a child jump to its beat:

Jack be nimble, Jack be quick.
Jack jump over the candlestick!

Children clap hands to "The Farmer in the Dell," and swing their arms to "London Bridge." Rhythm, which is determined by patterns of accented and unaccented syllables and by long or short vowels, moves the lines quickly and happily.

The variety of sound effects in nursery rhymes, although simple, acquaints children with poetic devices and gives pleasure. "A tisket, a tasket," or "Hey, diddle, diddle," "Hickety, pickety," or "Rub-a-dub-dub" use *internal rhymes, assonance,* and *consonance. Alliteration* occurs in "Daffydowndilly," or "Peter Piper picked a peck of pickled peppers"; consonant and vowel repetitions exist in "Tommy Snooks and Bessie Brooks went walking out one morning." There is *onomatopoeia* in "Hark, hark, the dogs do bark!" and "Bow-wow-wow, whose dog art thou?" The enjoyable sounds of tongue-twisters are endless challenges. And of course the usual *end rhyme* is a source of pleasure:

Little Boy Blue, come blow your horn!
The sheep's in the meadow, the cow's in the corn.
Where's the boy who looks after the sheep?
Under the haystack fast asleep!

Figurative language is another stylistic trait of Mother Goose rhymes. Dishes and spoons, ravens and daffodils, cats and mice and ladybugs are excitingly *personified.* "Frogs and snails and puppy dogs' tails" contrast to "sugar and spice and everything nice," *metaphors* for bad and good qualities in little boys and girls. Jack Sprat and his wife figuratively—or literally if we prefer—"lick the platter clean"; in *simile* form, a snail is "like a little Kyloe cow."

As for *tone,* humor with delight is more prevalent than any other. There is laughter in

Barber, barber, shave a pig.
How many hairs will make a wig?
Four and twenty, that's enough.
Give the barber a pinch of snuff.

And there is seriousness in

> Ding Dong Dell, Pussy's in the well!
> Who put her in? Little Johnny Green.
> Who pulled her out? Little Johnny Stout.
> What a naughty boy was that
> To try to drown poor pussy cat
> Who never did him any harm
> But killed the mice in his father's barn.

There is verbal *irony* in

> A dillar, a dollar,
> A ten o'clock scholar,
> What makes you come so soon?
> You used to come at ten o'clock,
> And now you come at noon.

Wonder at romance and possible adventure are awakened in the melodious "Bobby Shafto's gone to sea," or in "I saw a ship a-sailing."

Emotional intensity may be more commonly thought of as a quality of fine lyric poetry, but there is also intensity in children's play and the rhymes that accompany this play. Children chant a teasing rhyme, "Tattle-tale, tattle-tale, hanging on a dog's tail!" Carried along by rhythms and sounds, children sing out variations on names, like

> Sally-bum-balley, tee-alley-go-falley,
> tee-legged, tie-legged, toe-legged Sally.

Or in the universal taunts of childhood, they adapt verses to their playmates' names:

> Janie's mad and I'm glad,
> And I know how to please her.
> A bottle of wine to make her shine,
> A bottle of ink to make her stink,
> And all the boys to tease her.

Caught up in what Robert Frost calls the catchiness of rhythm and rhyme, children recite and improvise.

In the nursery or folk rhymes, children also find the excitement of riddles. They ask each other rhythmic or rhyming questions like

> What can go up the chimney down,
> But can't go down the chimney up?

and are surprised that "umbrella" is the answer. And children never forget the involved question, a foretaste of poetry's intriguing nature,

> As I was going to St. Ives,
> I met a man with seven wives.
> Each wife had seven sacks;
> In each sack were seven cats;
> Each cat had seven kits.
> How many were going to St. Ives?

In addition to the rhymes we commonly call Mother Goose, children are made ready for poetry by many other folk rhymes that may have general similarities and local geographical variations. Children from many parts of the country know the ball-bouncing rhyme, "When Buster Brown was one/He learned to suck his thumb." Some children, perhaps from a particular section of a particular state, seem to share common variations of similar rhymes, like the jump-rope verses with the refrain

> Here comes the doctor,
>   Here comes the nurse,
> Here comes the lady
>   With the alligator purse.

Other rhymes seem to appear by some magic, known at first only to an inside group on a particular playground. If the rhymes are catchy enough, they are soon carried across the country by a child who moves away, or by a visitor who returns to a home town. It seems likely that those who have jumped rope to this rhyme will not forget it:

> Fudge, fudge,
> Call the judge.
> Mama's got a baby.
> Ain't no girl,
> Ain't no boy,
> Just a plain old baby.
> Wrap it up in tissue paper.
> Put it on the elevator.
> First floor, miss!
> Second floor, miss!
> Third floor, miss!
> Fourth floor—
> Kick it out the door.[1]

NONSENSE

Nursery rhymes and sidewalk jingles merge with nonsense; there is no line of demarcation, and both prepare the child for poetry. When the cow jumps over the moon, that's nonsense. Of all the animals that Adam named, the least likely moon-jumper is the stodgy cow. Nonsense plays upon our delight in the illogical and the incongruous, upon our pleasure in words cleverly used or misused, upon some secret yearning to see the immutable laws overturned. The best nonsense can do all of these things. Edward Strachey wrote in 1894 in his introduction to Edward Lear's *Nonsense Omnibus* that nonsense is not "a mere putting forward of incongruities and absurdities, but the bringing out of a new and deeper harmony of life in and through its contradictions." Strachey called nonsense the "true work of the imagination, a child of genius, and its writing one of the Fine Arts."

Children thrive on nonsense. They make up and invert words, or make illogical comparisons; one child tells another "It's cold as a bumblebee out!" and both children roll on the floor in glee. They repeat nonsense words in series, just for the pleasure of tasting and hearing their sounds: "Eenie-beenie-pepsi-deenie"; "Hogan-Bogan-Mogan was her name." Like nursery rhymes, nonsense leads to poetry. Nonsense relies upon rhythm, sound patterns, figurativeness, compactness, and emotional intensity—the intensity of laughter that may be repeated, stored in the memory, then shared again and again.

Rhythm and Sound

The *limerick* form, first popularized by Edward Lear in the nineteenth century, is the most traditionally structured nonsense verse. It clearly shows how important to nonsense are rhythm and sound:

> There was an Old Lady named Crockett
> Who put a new plug in a socket;
>   But her hands were so wet
>   She flew up like a jet
> And came roaring back down like a rocket!

Suitable to the tone—light-hearted laughter—the rhythm is quick, with the syllables more frequently unaccented than accented. The sounds are short, with happy rather than serious overtones.

Compactness and Surprise

Much of the humor in nonsense verse comes from surprising names, events, or words. Laura E. Richards had a gift for nonsense. "The Owl and the Eel and the Warming Pan" is made up of perfectly assorted incongruities, since more unlikely characters and events are hard to assemble:

> The owl and the eel and the warming-pan,
> They went to call on the soap-fat man.
> The soap-fat man he was not within:
> He'd gone for a ride on his rolling-pin.
> So they all came back by the way of the town
> And turned the meeting-house upside down.

The light-hearted treatment of disaster or the slightly macabre are often subjects for nonsense; its verses often comment on current fads, as well, as does X.J. Kennedy in "A Choosy Wolf."

> "Why don't you eat me, wolf," I asked.
> "It wouldn't be much fun to.
> Besides, I'm into natural foods
> That nothing has been done to."

In the rhythm and rhyme of nonsense, ordinary creatures become extraordinary, as this anonymous verse notes.

> What a wonderful bird the frog are—
> When he stand he sit almost;
> When he hop, he fly almost.
> He ain't got no sense hardly;
> He ain't got no tail hardly either.
> When he sit, he sit on what he ain't got almost.

Perhaps Lewis Carroll wrote the most compact and intense nonsense, so witty that not a word is wasted, not a sound is out of place. "The White Rabbit's Verses" from *Alice in Wonderland,* for example, uses over forty pronouns, and yet has only five nouns which the multitude of pronouns might refer to. The twenty-four lines are written in such logical word order—subject, verb, complement—that they thoroughly convince us of their truth. And yet, when we finish the six verses, we have no idea what we are now convinced of. Carroll's most admired nonsense is "Jabberwocky," a mystifying tale of valor.

" 'Twas brillig, and the slithy toves
Did gyre and gimble in the wabe;
All mimsy were the borogoves,
And the mome raths outgrabe.

"Beware the Jabberwock, my son!
The jaws that bite, the claws that catch!
Beware the Jubjub bird, and shun
The fruminous Bandersnatch!"

He took his vorpal sword in hand:
Long time the manxome foe he sought—
So rested he by the Tumtum tree,
And stood awhile in thought.

And as in uffish thought he stood,
The Jabberwock, with eyes of flame,
Came whiffling through the tulgey wood;
And burbled as it came!

One, two! One, two! And through and through
The vorpal blade went snicker-snack!
He left it dead, and with its head
He went galumphing back.

"And hast thou slain the Jabberwock?
Come to my arms, my beamish boy!
O frabjous day! Callooh! Callay!"
He chortled in his joy.

" 'Twas brillig, and the slithy toves
Did gyre and gimble in the wabe;
All mimsy were the borogoves,
And the mome raths outgrabe."

Perhaps the best-known popularizer of nonsense verse in the past decades has been Ogden Nash, many of whose verses are known by adult and child alike. Nash's nonsense employs rhythm and made-up words. For compactness, one could not improve on

Dentists' anterooms
Give me tanterooms.

POETRY

We move from nursery rhymes and nonsense to poetry with a feeling, perhaps, that now the discussion will become difficult to follow. Something about the idea of getting meaning beyond amusement from brief groups of words in short lines, each line or phrase usually beginning at the left margin, seems to frighten many readers. Strange to say, we can read along easily in paragraphed pages, but if the same words are placed in stanza form, and if the meaning is not quickly apparent, we are lost.

The difference between poetry and prose is not as great as it may seem. Much of what we encounter in poetry we have already met in rhymes or in prose. Flow or cadence in prose may become more regular in poetry and be called rhythm, or meter. Sound patterns in prose, like alliteration and onomatopoeia, exist in poetry to even greater degree. Connotative meaning in prose acquires heightened significance in poetry. Figurative language that compares unlike things exists in prose, but occurs more frequently in poetry. What seems to take us by surprise and to make us feel that the two forms are totally different lies elsewhere.

The principal difference between prose and poetry is *compactness.* A single word in a poem says far more than a single word in prose; the connotations and images hint, imply, and suggest other meanings. In a sense, the poet distills meaning in brief and vivid phrases. Economy and suggestion evoke our response.

The characteristics of poetry that set it apart from prose are essentially *rhythm, sound patterns, figurativeness, compactness,* and *emotional intensity.* The last two qualities are to a large extent the results of effective use of rhythm, sound patterns, and figurative language to produce compressed expression in words. This compactness in turn results in emotional intensity, a particular quality of poetry.

Analysis of rhythm in such metrical patterns as anapestic or iambic, or of such line patterns as dimeter or tetrameter seem irrelevant to our discussion of rhythm in poetry for children. We focus here not on naming the forms of meter, but on the use of rhythm.

One question seems in order. What is the difference between poetry for adults and poetry for children? Once again, we say that the difference is not in kind, but in degree. We may arbitrarily divide poetry for adults by theme and subject—love or nature lyrics, death or war lyrics, for example. Adults are also concerned about the passage of time, the inevitability of death, and the changing of relationships. Just as the interests of adults are the subjects of their poetry, the concerns of childhood are the subjects of children's poetry. Since much of childhood is spent in play, or in wonder at what is common and yet not commonplace, in marveling at what surrounds children in their constantly unfolding world, these are the subjects of children's poetry.

Some poetry appeals to both children and adults, and it seems impossible and unnecessary to designate it as poetry for either group. However, in discussing rhyme and poetry for children, we *can* be somewhat more concise, although no less arbitrary. Nursery or Mother Goose rhymes are the rhythmic verses of early childhood; they can also be said to include riddles, chants, and tongue-twisters. As the inventive rhymes focus more on the incongruous and the surprising or unexpected, they become more nonsensical, and we tend to call them nonsense rather than nursery rhymes. Where the division comes, anyone or no one can say. When nonsense seems masterfully created, we may find ourselves calling it poetry, and yet where poetry and nonsense begin and end—again, anyone and no one can say. What does seem important is that we appreciate the particular qualities of language form that are distinctively poetic. In our discussion of the arbitrary categories—nursery rhymes, nonsense, and poetry—we are focusing in varying degrees upon these qualities. The essential point remains that poetry is poetry, and that poetry for children differs from poetry for adults in degree, but not in kind. Subject matter may differ, but our standards remain the same.

Many have tried to define poetry, and most have found such definitions difficult. A. E. Housman sardonically calls poetry a secretion, "whether a natural secretion, like turpentine in the fir, or a morbid secretion like the pearl in the oyster." Robert Frost calls it simply "a performance in words." Most definitions of poetry, however, return to at least one central idea derived from the Greek origin of the word. A poet is a maker, and poetry is *made;* every word counts.

Unlike the word "created," which implies inspiration and mystery, the term "made" suggests materials and effort. If poetry is made, it does not emerge perfect from the writer's pen. Like anything that is made, poetry follows a pattern of development; conception, effort, technical discipline, and refining and polishing, before the maker is pleased with the thing made. Most likely the poem is written and rewritten; words are crossed out, substituted for, perhaps replaced with earlier words, rewritten, crossed out, substituted for—until the maker-poet feels the poem is finally right. Of course, effort alone does not make a poem, any more than it makes good fiction. Skill, patience, and the critical judgment of the disciplined mind are a more likely combination.

First, let us note that there is a difference between poetry and the *verse* we may sometimes call poetry. Some critics maintain that while poetry is an end in itself, verse has a specific purpose. T. S. Eliot, for example, who seems almost to dismiss verse as "a superior amusement," describes poetry by contrasting it to verse. He says that while feeling and imaginative power are found in real poetry, verse is merely a matter of structure, formal metrical order, and rhyme pattern. Its structure, furthermore, may seem more important than its meaning. Proverbial wisdom occurs in verses as simple as "A stitch in time/Saves nine." The purpose of other verses is to sell diet drinks and chewing gum; still others convey traditional sentiments. We know what greeting card verse is, and, perhaps without knowing why, have a feeling that it is not poetry. Some of such verse is humorous, some sentimental, and some so incongruous that it may provoke a condescending smile: "To love a father is no fad/When he's a father like my dad."

Verses can be pleasant and entertaining; they can remind us of sentiments and ideas with which we agree, but often their expression is trite and awkward, with rigid metrical structure, ordinary images, obvious rhymes, or phrases twisted to produce rhyme. They are not poetry as T. S. Eliot has described it—the distilled and imaginative expression of feeling. Notice, for example, the pointlessness of "I Keep Three Wishes Ready," a verse with a regular rhythm that takes over the meaning. Prose would say more clearly and with far more brevity the idea expressed in sixteen lines filled with empty, throwaway words.

> I keep three wishes ready,
> Lest I should chance to meet,
> Any day a fairy
> Coming down the street.
>
> I'd hate to have to stammer,
> Or have to think them out,
> For it's very hard to think things up
> When a fairy is about.
>
> And I'd hate to lose my wishes,
> For fairies fly away,
> And perhaps I'd never have a chance
> On any other day.
>
> So I keep three wishes ready,
> Lest I should chance to meet,
> Any day a fairy
> Coming down the street.

We have a tendency to see the name of a poet, like Alfred Noyes or John Ciardi, and assume that everything that person writes is fine poetry. That is not the case. Both Noyes and Ciardi, as well as many, many other poets, have written verse—some clever and some pedestrian. We assume, too, that since Robert Louis Stevenson's *A Child's Garden of Verses* has been around so long, it is all poetry. Or that A. A. Milne who delights us with his Winnie-the-Pooh tales is writing poetry in *When We Were Very Young.* Verse is verse. The line may sometimes be difficult to distinguish, but the difference between verse and poetry lies in intensification of feeling and in distillation of language, not in regular end rhymes and predictable figures of speech. Available to children are large quantities of both verse and poetry. With exposure, children grow in awareness of the pleasure that artful poetry can bring. Greater experience with imaginative poetry can lead children to an awareness and appreciation of Walter de la Mare's "rarest of the best."

We sometimes simplify the classification of poetry and say that it is of two kinds: **narrative** or story poetry, and **lyric** or song poetry. Lasting pleasure from narrative poetry has been found in the old **folk ballads,** stories told in vivid and concrete language. For example, "John Henry," like other ballads that were originally sung, flows with singing cadence.

Other poems are lyrics or song-like poems, which use words and sounds and rhythms to express emotional response to some brief moment of experience. Such a poem is by Langston Hughes:

> How thin and sharp is the moon tonight!
> How thin and sharp and ghostly white
> Is the slim curved crook of the moon tonight!

Some adult poems are a pleasure to both children and adults; conversely most children's poems can be enjoyed by adults. However, the intense experience of lyric poetry is often given more clearly to children in some kind of story form.

Rhythm

Look now at the characteristics of poetry, several of which are known to children through rhymes and nonsense. The recurrence of stress is called **rhythm.** In our discussion of rhythm in prose, we mention cadence or flow, but when rhythm is set into a more regular pattern as it is in verse or poetry, we speak of **meter.** The poet uses rhythm to enhance the feeling that the poet's words express. In choosing the rhythm for a poem, whether it be unvarying metrical form or more freely flowing lines, the poet makes several commonsense choices. When we are happy, we speak quickly; when we are sad, or serious, or matter-of-fact, our words come more slowly. The poet in the same way uses a quickly moving line with many unaccented syllables and short vowels to express light-heartedness in lines that move as quickly as those of the limerick. When the poet is expressing serious thoughts, the rhythm moves more slowly with longer vowels and a higher proportion of accented syllables. Within the line, rhythm may also vary as the poet wishes to stress an idea or a single word. And within the poem the rhythm slows or quickens to vary the mood or shift the tone.

The best poetry uses rhythm to add meaning to words. Look, for example, at David McCord's "The Pickety Fence":

The pickety fence
The pickety fence
Give it a lick it's
The pickety fence
Give it a lick it's
A clickety fence
Give it a lick it's
A lickety fence
Give it a lick
Give it a lick
Give it a lick
With a rickety stick
Pickety
Pickety
Pickety
Pick

The overwhelming impulse and the noisy delight of running a stick along a picket fence are clearly expressed in words; we have a new and even an emotional experience of a picket fence. Here meter is not only helpful but essential. Like the happy stick-clicker, the poem clicks along with a clickety-lickety-pickety sound that duplicates perfectly the tuneful rhythm of a stick on pickets, and the joy of spontaneous play.

Similarly, Robert Louis Stevenson reproduces the arc of pendulum movement by using regular and lilting rhythm in his poem "The Swing":

How do you like to go up in the swing,
    Up in the air so blue.
Oh, I do think it the pleasantest thing
    Ever a child can do!

Up in the air and over the wall,
    Till I can see so wide,
Rivers and trees and cattle and all
    Over the countryside—

Till I look down on the garden green,
    Down on the roof so brown—
Up in the air I go flying again,
    Up in the air and down!

But notice, by contrast, the rhythm of "Falling Snow." The words fall into a regular pattern of beats, a strong accent on every second syllable and a far cry from the gentle and noiseless falling of actual snow. Notice the regular, heavy beat of the lines, far different from the soft drifting of flakes that accumulate so slowly. The hard, rhythmic beat defies the meaning rather than enhances it.

> See the pretty snowflakes /˘/˘/˘
>   Falling from the sky;   /˘/˘/
> On the walk and housetop/˘/˘/˘
>   Soft and thick they lie. /˘/˘/

Here regular meter seems more important to the writer than the experience of snow; rhythm in this verse exists for itself. A marching rhythm cannot describe falling snow.

As Eve Merriam says about "Inside a Poem," rhythm is important:

> It doesn't always have to rhyme,   ˘/˘/˘/˘/
> but there's the repeat of a beat, somewhere ˘/˘˘/˘˘/˘/
> an inner chime that makes you want to   ˘/˘/˘/˘/˘
> tap your feet or swerve in a curve;   /˘/˘/˘˘/
> a lilt, a leap, a lightning split:—   ˘/˘/˘/˘/

The quick, changeable beat contributes to meaning, saying that poetry is joyful discovery of meaning, assisted by rhythm. Here the first line is a serious statement about rhyme, and Merriam's rhythm enforces the factual meaning of the line by regularity and uniformity. The first line has four accented syllables, as do all the others. The second line has the same number of accented syllables, but the line's rhythm picks up speed with the use of two additional unaccented syllables, a ratio of six light to four heavier syllables. The more unaccented syllables, the more quickly the line runs, and the more lightness the meaning acquires. Line three also has four accented syllables, but it includes five unaccented ones; in line four the final anapestic foot (˘˘/) also adds to the lightness and the unexpected quality of the rhythm. Again in line five, there are four accented syllables, but this time the internal punctuation interrupts the rhythm. The scansion looks the same as that of the first line (˘/˘/˘/˘/), but the commas cause us to stop and start, stop and start. The surprise we feel as we pause for the two final *t*'s of "lilt" and "split" and the final *p* of "leap," when added to the short vowels and the plosive consonants, are all part of what Merriam is saying about rhythm: rhythm need not be absolutely regular, but it does suit meaning. The idea of the poem—that while a poem need not rhyme, its rhythm suits its meaning—is clear. The poem demonstrates its own point by skillful use of rhythm, but note too that while we are told that a poem need not rhyme, Merriam uses rhyme, but in unexpected places. The sound of "rhyme" reappears in "chime" a bit later; "repeat of a beat" and "swerve in a curve" are not the regular and predictable rhymes occurring in end positions, but rhymes nonetheless. Merriam uses rhyme as she uses rhythm—not as an end in itself as the versifier does—but as a means to enforce meaning.

Sound Patterns

In "Lost," Carl Sandburg uses musical devices and sound patterns that are exceptionally helpful as they add to meaning. The poet personifies the fogbound boat as a lost child, and the harbor as a mother:

> Desolate and lone
> All night on the lake
> Where fog trails and mist creeps,
> The whistle of a boat
> Calls and cries unendingly,
> Like some lost child
> In tears and trouble
> Hunting the harbor's breast
> And the harbor's eyes.

The long sounds of the words "calls and cries" are not the only desolate ones, since every line echoes the feeling of desolation. The long vowels in "lone," "all," "long," "fog," "trails," and "creeps" give added duration to the words. Sandburg calls the vessel a "boat," its long *o* adding to the loneliness far more than would the word "ship" with its short *i* sound. Consonants are largely liquid *l*'s and *r*'s or nasal *m*'s, *n*'s, and *ng*'s held together with sibilant *s*'s. The long vowel duration, and the consonants that further pull and stretch the words, called phonetic intensives, create the slow groping of the fogbound ship. The sounds of the two lines dealing with "mother," the protective harbor, are quite different. Because vowels are short and decisive, and the words are spoken more swiftly, the effect of the lines is reassuring.

As for rhythm, stressed syllables in "Lost" are far more frequent than unstressed syllables, and the effect is a slowly moving poem —movement like a fogbound boat. Sound devices combined with imagery and figurativeness have created a visible and audible scene. The short poem has given us a fresh picture, and its sound has strengthened both the meaning and the impact.

In the same way the phonetic sounds of the words in "Days" by Karle Wilson Baker help to reinforce meaning. Notice how slowly the vowel and consonant sounds of the first four lines move, telling us of dull, depressing days; then notice how swiftly fly the sounds of the second four lines, telling us of exciting, glorious days:

> Some days my thoughts are just cocoons—
>   all cold, and dull and blind,
> They hang from dripping branches in the grey
>   woods of my mind;
> And other days they drift and shine—such free
>   and flying things!
> I find the gold-dust in my hair left by
>   their brushing wings.

Figurativeness

As we noted in our discussion of style, figurative language is a means by which a writer says one thing in terms of another, and by which the writer makes comparisons. It is this quality of which Christopher Fry speaks when he says that poetry "has the virtue of being able to say twice as much as prose in half the time, and the drawback, if you do not . . . give it your full attention, of seeming to say half as much in twice the time."

When a poem makes either implied or explicit comparisons, the images called up may acquire connotative meaning, or may be seen in a fresh way. For example, Dorothy Aldis in "On a Snowy Day" describes a fencepost topped by the little white cylinder of snow; the personified posts wear metaphorical marshmallow hats. The shapes are aptly compared, and the metaphor and image are not only vivid, but also connotatively pleasant.

A less successful poem may make use of familiar objects for comparisons, forgetting that some qualities of the two things being compared may cloud rather than clarify the metaphor. Take the elephant cement-mixer comparison in Patricia Hubbell's "Concrete Mixers":

> The drivers are washing the concrete mixers;
> Like elephant tenders they hose them down.
> Tough grey-skinned monsters standing ponderous,
> Elephant-bellied and elephant-nosed,
> Standing in muck up to their wheel-caps,
> Like rows of elephants, tail to trunk.

Their drivers perch on their backs like mahouts,
Sending the sprays of water up.
They rid the trunk-like trough of concrete,
Direct the spray to the bulging sides,
Turn and start the monsters moving.
      Concrete mixers
      Move like elephants
      Bellow like elephants,
      Spray like elephants,
Concrete mixers are urban elephants,
Their trunks are raising a city.

A cement mixer is bulky, dusty, and gray, and thus far, it is an elephant. But can we picture an elephant without its most intriguing asset—that convenient, slender, and sinuous trunk? A stolid cement-mixer-elephant, since it would have to be content with a mere smear nose that neither sprays nor spanks, is hard to see as an elephant.

The moon is a favorite object for poets' contemplation; its changes are mysterious to us all, and particularly to the child. Emily Dickinson's poem which notes the moon's changes begins with a figurative picture of the crescent moon:

The moon was but a chin of gold
   A night or two ago—
And now she turns her perfect face
   Upon the world below—

Her forehead is of amplest blond;
   Her cheeks like beryl hewn—
Her eye unto the summer dew
   The likest I have known.

If the crescent moon is "but a chin of gold," then the full moon must be a "perfect face," with forehead, cheeks, and eyes. The metaphor is perfectly suited to the changing shape of the moon.

Vachel Lindsay in his figurative description of the phases of the moon begins with the full moon:

The Moon's the North Wind's cooky.
He bites it day by day,
Until there's but a rim of scraps
That crumble all away.

The South Wind is a baker.
He kneads clouds in his den,
And bakes a crisp new moon that . . . greedy
North . . . Wind . . . eats . . . again!

A cookie, rich in connotative meaning particularly for children, begins as whole and round, and ends in crumbs. But soon another cookie-moon appears to be eaten, and to continue the process.

Like the jigsaw puzzle already put together, the poem with obvious figurative comparisons—the moon is a golden ball—denies the reader the excitement of a personal search and discovery. When the figurative comparisons are ineptly chosen, they confuse meaning rather than reveal it. In "Night," by Patricia Hubbell, this is the case:

Night is a purple pumpkin,
Laced with a silver web,
And the moon a golden spider,
Wandering through the strands.
At dawn the purple pumpkin,
Rolling slowly around,
Leans against the star-web,
Moving the spider down.
The silver web slides slowly,
Slowly across the sky,
And the spider moon creeps slowly,
Slowly by.
The twinkling stars cease spinning
Their skeins of silver gray,
The spider moon
Crawls down the strands
And night turns into day.

Night itself is compared to a pumpkin that is purple. Can we, in our wildest imaginings, picture a pumpkin that is not orange? Somewhere, sometime, there may be green pumpkins, but every one we recall seeing is orange. Carved, perhaps, or caved-in, or baked in a pie—but orange. The moon is further compared to a gold-colored spider. Was there ever a spider without eight legs? That's the horror of the spider. The moon is golden and round; a spider is neither. The poet adds to the eight-legged moon a crawling movement, and now not only is the glow of the mysterious sphere gone, but the marvel of its imperceptible climb and descent as well. The inept and confusing metaphor has obscured the night, not illumined it.

The poet's use of metaphors may delay our discovery of meaning. However, at the same time, these comparisons make the puzzle more intriguing and the discovery more exciting. Look, for example, at the completely compatible figurative devices that John Updike uses in his poem "October," each one a reference to either autumn weather or to Halloween.

The month is amber,
    Gold, and brown.
Blue ghosts of smoke
    Float through the town.

Great V's of geese
    Honk overhead,
And maples turn
    A fiery red.

Frost bites the lawn.
    The stars are slits
In a black cat's eye
    Before she spits.

At last, small witches,
    Goblins, hags,
And pirates armed
    With paper bags,

Their costumes hinged
    On safety pins,
Go haunt a night
    Of pumpkin grins.

Sometimes we may be puzzled by the figurative language in a poem; the more complex the poem, the more puzzling the metaphors may be. The simplest way to check the meaning and suitability of comparisons is by means of simple "this = that" equations. The similes and metaphors in Elizabeth Coatsworth's "Tracks in the Snow" form a series of figurative equations:

Out of the dark
To the sill of the door   snow = floor.
Lay the snow in a long
Unruffled floor,
And the candlelight fell
Narrow and thin,
A carpet unrolled   candlelight streak = carpet
For the cat to walk in

Slowly, smoothly,
Black as the night,   night black = cat black
With paws unseen,
White upon white,
Like a queen who walks   queen's bearing = cat's grace
Down a corridor,
The black cat paced   light streak = corridor
The cold smooth floor,
And left behind her
Bead upon bead   tracks = beads
The track of small feet
Like dark fernseed.   tracks = fernseed

"A cat walks out the door into the snow" is a summary statement of the twenty lines, but surely the experience of these words is not the same as the experience of the poem. The rightness of Coatsworth's figurative comparisons has made a fresh experience from what might have been an ordinary one.[2]

Imagery further stretches our perceptions to see details and figurative comparisons otherwise only vaguely noted. Cats are sleek and fat, plump and thin, make unpleasant screeching noises as well as pleasant humming ones. But look at how Rosalie Moore tells us these facts in her poem "Catalog":

Cats sleep fat and walk thin.
Cats, when they sleep, slump;
When they wake, pull in—
And where the plump's been
There's skin.
Cats walk thin.

Cats wait in a lump,
Jump in a streak.
Cats, when they jump, are sleek
As a grape slipping its skin—
They have technique.
Oh, cats don't creak.
They sneak.

Cats sleep fat.
They spread comfort beneath them
Like a good mat,
As if they picked the place

And then sat.
You walk around one
As if he were the City Hall
After that.

The value of such images is clear when we look at verse which
minimizes sensory appeal. As Herbert Read says, "Poetry is not made
up of words like pride and pity, or love and beauty. . . . The poet
distrusts such words and always tries to use words that have a suggestion of outline and shape, and represent things seen as clear and precise
as crystal."[3] Although Stevenson, for example, in his poem "The
Swing" successfully duplicates the rhythm of the swing, his terms are
not sensory. "Rivers," "trees," "cattle," "countryside," and "pleasantest
thing" make little appeal to our senses. Although the roof is brown, we
do not see truly vivid sights. We do not smell, hear, taste, or touch them,
and both reader and poem are the poorer for lack of sensory appeals.

Whispers, on the other hand, are a very common part of life,
and might be vaguely described. But whispers are exciting, bringing
secrets for cherishing, then for sharing, and perhaps for embellishing.
Once whispers were merely audible, but never again, because "Whispers" by Myra Cohn Livingston captures other sensory qualities. Notice, too, the pleasant connotations of the many sensory appeals:

Whispers
    tickle through your ear
    telling things you like to hear.

Whispers
    are as soft as skin
    letting little words curl in.

Whispers
    come so they can blow
    secrets others never know.

Whispers will never be the same, because not only do we hear them,
but we feel whispers when they "tickle," "blow," and are "soft as skin";
we see them as the "words curl in." Because of the connotative meanings of the words, we delight in whispers, feeling their tender softness
and seeing their spiral curl headed for listening ears.

The best chosen words for a poem add by *connotations* new dimensions of meaning to words we have always known. However, sometimes the connotations of words are distracting rather than helpful in
uncovering the meaning of the poem. This is the case in "Feeding the
Fairies," where fairies are compared to hens and roosters:

> Fairies, fairies, come and be fed,
>   Come and be fed like hens and cocks;
> Hither and thither with delicate tread,
>   Flutter around me in fairy flocks.

First, the title deceives us. Instead of finding ourselves in a quiet grove or a magic circle where we might hope and expect to find fairies, we are taken to the barnyard where clucking, pecking chickens live their unmagical lives. Next the chickens' "flutter" and "delicate tread" (an incongruous phrase because *delicate* connotes the opposite of *tread*) have connotations incompatible with the fragile appearance and delicate movement of fairies. The connotations are wrong for this comparison.

Compactness

Poetry exists for itself, an end in itself. It has no mission nor message beyond discovery, beyond the emotion and thought of the reader as he or she explores the lines. A poem is best said in few and artfully chosen words; it follows that if we change a word, we change the poem. Nothing can be altered, for example, in Ogden Nash's compact poem "The Eel":

> I don't mind eels
> Except at meals
> And the way they feels.

Nash's purpose is not to instruct or to inform us about eels, but through his words to make us experience them. Change a single word and we change the experience. "I don't like to touch or to eat eels," is no substitute for Nash's three-line poem. It is already so compact that it can bear no paraphrase nor summary; it says twice as much in half the time.

Poems are brief and condensed. The poet must make the best possible use of each word, often choosing one term to convey many meanings, or relying on connotation to extend our awareness of the experience. The unknown Anglo-Saxon poet of the eighth century who wrote "Frost Shall Freeze" has condensed meaning into a seven-line stanza, but it is not merely the absence of extra words like vague adjectives or unnecessary conjunctions that makes the poem compact. In such phrases as "ice shall bridge,/Shall roof the waters," the words call up pictures in our minds as we see figurative sights and comparisons:

Frost shall freeze; fire melt wood;
Earth shall blossom; ice shall bridge
And roof the waters, wondrously lock
Earth's budding growth. One shall unbind
The fetters of frost, Almighty God.
Winter shall pass, fair weather return,
Sun-hot summer and restless sea.

Emily Dickinson compresses the experience of reading a book into a poem of eight lines. To make her poem compact she relies upon three figurative comparisons, each one expanded in meaning by its richness in connotations:

There is no frigate like a book
    To take us lands away,
Nor any courser like a page
    Of prancing poetry—
This traverse may the poorest take
    Without oppress of toll—
How frugal is the chariot
    That bears the human soul!

Dickinson does not say that a book is like a mere boat, or even a sailboat; she calls up romance by using the term "frigate." Frigates are sailing vessels used by explorers seeking new lands, by pirates pursuing treasure and adventure, by merchants carrying silks and spices from the Orient to farflung shores. A book is like a "courser," not a mere horse. "Courser" connotes knights charging off on missions fraught with danger and the promise of rescue. No car nor wagon could have the mystery of a "chariot," a fragile royal cart flying along behind the hoofs of a thoroughbred. Other words as well, like "prancing," "frugal," and "toll," are rich in connotative meaning. Specific terms with rich meanings expand the ideas in the compact comparisons. By means of these connotations, the total experience of a book becomes adventure, wealth, discovery, suspense, intrigue, danger, romance, and a multitude of other possibilities. This poem, like that which Eve Merriam describes in "How to Eat a Poem," has nothing unnecessary, nothing to throw away—not a seed nor a pit, a stem, a core, nor a rind.

Emotional Intensity

Like fiction at its best, poetry at its best lets us enjoy an old experience with new insight, or understand one that we have never met. However, unlike fiction, the poet condenses the experience. Poetry attempts to capture the reader where he or she is, and to involve the reader briefly but intensely.

The successful poem is an intense emotional experience. "There Is No Frigate" is an experience of a book. It is not a description of a book, nor of the feelings a child might have while reading a book. By its richly connotative words and its varied sensory images, the poem becomes an intense emotional experience. The same can be said of McCord's "Pickety Fence." The poem is not a prosy description of a fence nor the sounds a child might hear when drawing a stick along a picket fence. Because of its sounds and rhythms, the poem is an emotional experience of a picket fence. The poem has used the devices of poetry—rhythm, sound, compactness—to give us insight into the experience.

We have noted how rhythm, sound, and figurative language contribute to compactness, and compactness to emotional intensity. Langston Hughes's poem "Dream Deferred" has emotional intensity, intensity created particularly by his skillful use of unusual figurative comparisons and sensory appeals:

> What happens to a dream deferred?
> Does it dry up
>   like a raisin in the sun?
>
> Or fester like a sore—
> And then run?
> Does it stink like rotten meat?
> Or crust and sugar over—
> like a syrupy sweet?
>
> Maybe it just sags
> like a heavy load.
>
> *Or does it explode?*

From the poem we have an intense emotional experience of frustration. A festering sore, stinking meat—these are ugly images that cause us to experience the emotions that accompany frustration. The images connote neglect, usefulness turned to decay. What was a simple sore is now painfully infected; what was edible meat is now stinking uselessness.

Negative Qualities in Poetry

The negatives of literature, *didacticism, sentimentality,* and *condescension,* make their appearances in poetry, too, but only in poor poetry. These qualities are often expressed in words with distracting connotations, in trite comparisons, commonplace imagery, repetitive and unvaried beat, or in sound unsuited to meaning and tone. Kipling's didactic verse "If" is representative of the preaching verse adults often hear in the so-called inspirational speech. But children are even more often subjected to verses with preaching purpose, and Abbie Farwell Brown's "A Music Box" is one. The first stanza sets up a metaphor; the two that follow preach a sermon:

> I am a little Music Box
> Wound up and made to go,
> And play my little living-tune
> The best way that I know.
>
> If I am naughty, cross, or rude
> The music will go wrong,
> My little works be tangled up,
> And spoil the pretty song.
>
> I must be very sweet and good
> And happy all the day,
> And then the little Music Box
> In tune will always play.

Intrigued with the metaphor, we are fooled into thinking that "A Music Box" will be a pleasurable experience; then we learn that our sins spoil the song. By the final stanza—"I must be very sweet and good"—we are thoroughly disenchanted, disappointed that what began by intriguing us ends by instructing us to be happy models of perfection.

As for sentimentality and condescension, a poem that speaks to a worm about pain, assuming its pain to be comparable to the pain a person might feel if jumped on by a giant, that poem surely condescends to readers as it tries to rouse our emotions beyond justification:

> No, little worm, you need not slip
> Into your hole, with such a skip;
> Drawing the gravel as you glide
> On to your smooth and slimy side.
> . . .
> For my part, I could never bear
> Your tender flesh to hack and tear,
> Forgetting that poor worms endure
> As much as I should, to be sure,
> If any giant would come and jump
> On to my back, and kill me plump,
> Or run my heart through with a scythe,
> And think it fun to see me writhe![4]

It is not the subject of the poem that is inappropriate for poetry; it is the sentimental tone. Notice, by contrast, the quality of wonder in Elizabeth Madox Roberts's poem "The Worm," in which the poet duplicates a childhood experience, relying almost exclusively upon imagery to draw us into experiencing the children's wondering intentness. As the children dig with broken shell, tin, and spade, they find a small clod with a worm inside:

> We watched him pucker up himself
> And stretch himself to walk away.
> He tried to go inside the dirt,
> But Dickie made him wait and stay.

The children marvel at the sheen of the soft, wet skin, and they forget to dig their wells. They wonder if the worm knows it is a worm:

> And while we tried to find it out,
> He puckered in a little wad,
> And then he stretched himself again
> And went back home inside the clod.

Digging up a worm and looking at it intently can be an experience for poetry, an experience so compact that even adults become children once again during their involvement in twenty-four lines. In Roberts's poem there is neither sentimentality nor condescension.

The best poetry is made with care and artistry. Sometimes, in fact, poetry is found in paragraph form; the writer has chosen each word for its imagery and connotative power, asking of the reader concentration and imagination to discover meaning. On the other hand, prose or prosaic writing is sometimes put into the form usually reserved for poetry—irregular lines and stanza arrangement. But by failing to use words rich in connotative meaning, by failing to make figurative comparisons or to use rhythm to enhance meaning, the writer has written prose. Line or stanza arrangement has not made poetry out of prose. The best prose and the best poetry are both written with care and skill. The difference lies primarily in the compactness and the intensity of the expression. Figurative devices, rhythmic flow, and sound patterns occur in prose. There is then no line to be drawn between prose and poetry; the difference is simply in degree. As rhythm becomes more regular, imagery more vivid, and statements more compact, emotions become more intense. The reader feels the increased intensity and becomes aware of the expression as poetry.

SUMMARY

Rhymes and sidewalk jingles are many children's first experience with literature, and surely their first introduction to poetry. The rhymes not only may provide an easy and loving bridge between the parents' childhoods and the new generation, but their simple stylistic devices of rhythm, sound, and comparison, their colorful characters involved in elementary tensions, and their occasional themes about the lives of human beings are sufficient reasons for including them as literature for the youngest child. They may or may not influence children's understanding, but the pleasure they give is undeniable.

The nursery and nonsense rhymes of childhood contain on different levels many of the elements of literature—of poetry and its style. Rhymes give pleasure through story and sounds. Nonsense delights us by its inventiveness, its unexpected turns and surprises. With its rapid rhythms and unexpected rhymes, and its topsy-turvy, no-sense way of looking at the logic of life, nonsense provides children with a great deal of joy—whether the joy is awakened by a patterned limerick, a gem of concentrated wit, or by children's own creations. Nonsense, too, is a way into poetry.

Poetry stands as an experience in itself. Rhythm, sound, and connotation expand meaning; imagery heightens our sensory awareness, and apt figurative comparisons tempt our imaginations. A distilled representation of an experience, poetry at its best permits the reader to participate, but without the burden of didacticism or sentimentality.

Since the whole range from rhyme to nonsense to imaginative poetry is available to children, it seems only fair to introduce them to it all. Led easily from simple rhymes and nonsense to poetry, children, as Herbert Reed says, deserve to be enticed and invited, wheedled and persuaded by poetic art. The experience of the best efforts of skillful poets is enlarging; it gives pleasure and promotes understanding. To keep that pleasure forever, let children memorize as they choose.

Reading and Evaluating

1 Find six editions of the Mother Goose nursery rhymes and compare them for completeness and for attractiveness in format. Which edition focuses on the most familiar rhymes? In the familiar rhymes can you see any pattern that might have made them more familiar—like musical qualities, vivid images, and stories. Which rhymes might give the child some understanding beyond the pure pleasure of sounds and stories? Among the familiar rhymes, are there any you disapprove of? Why?

2 *Find a volume of nonsense verse from folk tradition, like* A Rocket in My Pocket *by Carl Withers. Do you see variations that you can expect from folk literature? What accounts for the popularity of folk rhymes with children?*

3 *Collect from your friends their jump-rope, ball-bouncing, and counting-out rhymes. What devices of style have they in common? How do you account for their popularity?*

4 *Find a volume of literary nonsense like* What a Wonderful Bird the Frog Are, *edited by Myra Cohn Livingston, or one by Laura E. Richards, Edward Lear, Ogden Nash, or another writer. Why are the rhymes often so brief? What is the effect on the reader when the verses are long? What are the common sources of laughter? What patterns of structure are used?*

5 *Find a volume of poems by a single poet whose poetry is open to children, like David McCord, Eve Merriam, Aileen Fisher, Harry Behn, or another writer. Have any of these poets become old-fashioned in their tone? Describe each poet in terms of use of imagery, rhythm, figurative language, sound patterns, and use of connotative words. Which poets seem to appeal to older readers? younger readers? Which poets have compressed meaning and feeling to produce emotional intensity? Give examples.*

6 *Find a large anthology of poetry for children. Select two poems for superior use of connotative language, for imagery, for figurative language, sound patterns, and emotional intensity. Check dates of publication of your choices. What conclusion can you reach about aging and agelessness in poetry?*

NOTES

[1]Francelia Butler in her study of jump-rope rhymes around the world seems to have discovered more brutality and violence in rhymes from America than in those from other countries. (See "Over the Garden Wall/I Let the Baby Fall: The Poetry of Rope-Skipping." *Children's Literature,* Vol. 3, Storrs, Conn.: Journal of the Modern Language Association and The Children's Literature Association, 1974.

[2]You might try a series of figurative equations on Joyce Kilmer's "Trees"; try drawing a picture of the woman that a tree is like.

[3]"What Is Poetry? An Afterthought" in *This Way, Delight,* New York, Pantheon, 1956, p. 140.

[4]Ann Taylor (1782–1866) published verses during a period when instruction was the only excuse for poetry to be published for children. *Original Poems for Infant Minds,* written by Ann, Jane, and their brother Isaac, was published in 1804.

Books Cited In This Chapter*

Arbuthnot, May Hill, and Shelton L. Root, Jr. *Time for Poetry.* 3rd ed., Glenview, Ill.: Scott, 1968.

Baker, Karle Wilson. *Blue Smoke.* New Haven: Yale Univ. Press, 1919.

Carroll, Lewis. *Alice's Adventures in Wonderland.* New York: Macmillan, 1963.

———. *Through the Looking Glass.* New York: Macmillan, 1963.

Coatsworth, Elizabeth. *Away Goes Sally.* New York: Macmillan, 1934.

Dickinson, Emily. *The Complete Poems of Emily Dickinson.* Boston: Little, 1960.

Frost, Frances, *Pool in the Meadow.* Boston: Houghton, n.d.

Hughes, Langston. *Selected Poems of Langston Hughes.* New York: Knopf, 1926.

———. *The Panther and the Lash.* New York: Knopf, 1967.

Kennedy, X. J. *The Phantom Ice Cream Man: More Nonsense Verse.* New York: Atheneum, 1979.

Lindsay, Vachel. *The Congo and Other Poems.* New York: Macmillan, 1914.

Livingston, Myra Cohn, ed. *What a Wonderful Bird the Frog Are.* New York: Harcourt, 1973.

———. *Whispers and Other Poems.* New York: Harcourt, 1958.

McCord, David. *Far and Few.* Boston: Little, 1952.

Merriam, Eve. *Inside a Poem.* New York: Atheneum, 1962.

Nash, Ogden. *The Face Is Familiar.* Garden City, N.Y.: Garden City, 1941.

———. *Family Reunion.* Boston: Little, 1950.

Richards, Laura E. *Tirra Lirra: Rhymes Old and New.* Boston: Little, 1955.

Roberts, Elizabeth Madox. *Under the Tree.* New York: Viking, 1930.

Sandburg, Carl. *Chicago Poems.* New York: Holt, 1916.

Stevenson, Robert Louis. *A Child's Garden of Verses.* New York: Watts, 1966. (first published 1885)

Untermeyer, Louis. *Golden Treasury of Poetry.* New York: Western, 1959.

Updike, John. *A Child's Calendar.* New York: Knopf, 1965.

*Because of their very nature, anthologies and collections of poetry are not always consistent in their quality. Therefore, the list here is a list of books cited in the chapter, but not necessarily a list of recommended books.

Nonfiction

Adults range widely in their reading interests, from the financial page of the daily newspaper to a favorite comic strip, and on to particular curiosities, whether they be genealogy or strip mining. In between, there run floods of enthusiasm for "everything *that* writer ever wrote" to "everything I see about organic gardening." And yet we are continually surprised at the diversity in children's taste or at their sudden enthusiasms for horses or baseball players. People are alike, and often we find that the interesting adult with a multitude of curiosities is the grown child whose reading may have begun with an omnivorous—and simultaneous—devouring of animal fantasy and atomic fission.

What does interest a child in nonfiction? Of course, older children may go in search of information, but small children frequently find fiction and nonfiction shelved in the same section of their libraries. In search of another good book "like the one last week about the ducklings in the park," they encounter another good book—but this time it is about the color wheel and how one color merges with another to form tones and shades and tints and other colors. Both books may be equally fascinating. At other times children who have moved away from the picture book section may happen upon a shelf where there are numbers on the backs of the books, instead of just the initial *E*. And there, wonder of wonders, are all kinds of books about how animals really live, and eat, and raise their babies, and fight to survive. From this discovery, children may take off on a nonfiction binge. In all of this meandering there seems to be a thread that holds one book or group of books to another—curiosity.

The line between fiction and nonfiction is a fine one in books for children. In a great many story books, there is much information about the world, animals, people, history, nature. After all, we learn about spinnerets and the parts of the spider's legs in *Charlotte's Web*. But when we discuss nonfiction, we are really less interested in how suspense is built and more interested in how facts are presented, less interested in character and more in discovery of the relationship and application of concepts to the natural world. Sometimes the writer tells the story of the life of an individual. Sometimes the writer uses a chronological arrangement of some kind, a narrative, that makes the nonfiction resemble fiction. Sometimes the writer speaks of "you" and "we" to make the explanation personal or like a story. However, the fact remains that the functions of fiction and poetry are pleasure and understanding, while the purpose of nonfiction is the discovery of factual or conceptual information and truth. That the two purposes mingle in one book is of course possible, but we do look at the two somewhat differently.

In the pages that follow we shall notice that the nonfiction writer is concerned with *facts first of all.* But in addition to facts, the writer tries to show the reader that these facts add up to or lead into a *concept,* just as the facts about chemical composition inside the egg lead us to the concept of how the yolk becomes an embryo and then a chick. Affecting our acceptance of fact and concept is *tone,* the writer's attitude toward the subject and the readers. We shall be concerned with all three.

NONFICTION DEFINED

Anyone who has spent time with a child knows that children have enormous curiosity. They are filled with questions that lead to more questions, which when answered lead to still other questions. Many of these questions can be answered by the right nonfiction book, whether it is a book about a single topic like trees, an explanation of a concept like energy, a biography of a person like Amelia Earhart, or a book that awakens awareness to an issue like overpopulation. As Margery Fisher says in *Matters of Fact,* [1] an information book evokes many responses:

> A child uses information books to assemble what he knows, what he feels, what he sees, as well as to collect new facts. His reaction to something as ordinary as a loaf [of bread] may be, at one time or another, one of wonder, excitement, interest, aesthetic pleasure, physical satisfaction, curiosity.

When adults seek answers, they may turn to encyclopedias; a solid page of factual information does not frighten nor confuse them. Their experience helps them to sift out the specific items that they need from the mass of information; they can extract the essential from the nonessential, the clear from the too complex. With the help of a book, the child to whom the world is new and perhaps confusing may also recognize order in what she or he already sees or knows. This recognition of order and this assembling and sorting help to organize and stabilize the multitude of surrounding facts. The curious child moves from order to comparison, and on to new understanding of concept. To satisfy such needs, the child must have books that combine individuality with clarity in a combination of words that give color and significance to the subject, and make it clear.

The limited experience of the child poses specific problems for the nonfiction writer. First the writer must satisfy curiosity without squelching a sense of wonder; yet the writer must avoid suggesting miracles. "Wonder" connotes curiosity and interest, while "miracle" connotes mystery and the unknowable. The successful writer of nonfiction opens a door to discovery, but does not suggest that any of the facts outside are miraculous or beyond ultimate comprehension. There are facts as yet unknown, and principles as yet undiscovered, it is true, but if the child is to be led to discovery, he or she must feel that the search will be rewarding, and will not merely dead-end at unknowable mystery.

Adults usually choose their nonfiction for utilitarian purposes; they need to know. However, to a child, for whom everything in the opening world is astonishing, wonder is more often the motivation. Curiosity is the force that leads to discovery of all kinds. It led, for example, to the discovery of electricity; the unexplained needed explanation.

In *How Did We Find Out About Electricity,* Isaac Asimov begins his explanation with a narrative situation very similar to the reader's search for answers. Something piques the boy's curiosity as it does the reader's. Asimov takes us back 2500 years ago, to the village of Magnesia on the coast of Turkey, where a shepherd boy used an iron-tipped stick to help him climb. As the iron stuck to a stone, the boy was mystified, but he could find nothing sticky on either surface. The odd rock came to the attention of a wise man named Thales, who was a person we would call a scientist; Thales experimented with the stone and discovered that it attracted only iron. Asimov's account follows a pattern very similar to that which our curiosity follows as it is provoked by the unusual; we notice, we experiment, we seek to discover what we can, and when we need help we go to authority.

While Asimov stimulates wonder in one way, Jean George stimulates wonder in another. Without giving human traits to animals, she makes the hermit crab so distinctive and so unusual that we are curious about it and its problems of changing shells, a very dangerous necessity for the crab:

> First he unhooked the muscle at the spiral end of his old shell. Then he pulled himself out and stood vulnerable, so naked that even a windblown grain of sand could kill him. His exposed belly was so delicate that a nodding grass blade could

cut him in half. . . . He slashed his tail through the air and stuck it into the new shell. Backing carefully, he reached his tail down and around until he felt the last coil of the shell. Then he hooked onto it with a grip so strong that few could pull him out. When at last he had a firm hold, he contracted all his muscles and slammed himself deep into the shell.

The meticulous description of the crab's vulnerability and actions during the move sets us wondering at the complexity and variety of nature. What other exciting secrets may lie ahead in *Spring Comes to the Ocean*?

In the opening paragraphs of *The Sea Around Us,* Rachel Carson, who is writing for more mature readers, rouses wonder by means of surprise. First Carson reminds us that we cannot really know how the oceans were formed, since there were no people there to see and to report:

> Beginnings are apt to be shadowy, and so it is with the beginnings of that great mother of life, the sea. Many people have debated how and when the earth got its ocean, and it is not surprising that their explanations do not always agree. For the plain and inescapable truth is that no one was there to see, and in the absence of eyewitness accounts, there is bound to be a certain disagreement. . . .

Then Carson surprises us by saying that it is possible, just the same, to find out what may have happened aeons ago. In her opening pages, Carson anticipates her explanation about the origins of the oceans that can be discovered in the evidence of ancient rocks:

> [I]t must be a story pieced together from many sources and containing whole chapters the details of which we can only imagine. The story is founded on the testimony of the earth's most ancient rocks which were young when the earth was young. . . .

Carson goes on to suggest the range of estimated age for rocks found on the earth—2.3 billion to 2.5 billion years, an astonishing figure for us who find a month or a year a long time. As we follow Carson's speculations about the earth changing from a ball of whirling gases to a molten mass, and then to patterns of layered materials, our wonder is aroused, and we are led into Carson's hypothesis about the origins of the oceans.

As for biography, we often turn to the lives of significant people because we wish to discover more about what it was like to be alive and aware in a period of history we have just discovered. Or we may become curious about the "what if" of being a frontier hero—"What if I had been one?" Or a winning sportsman, or a worker in the slums. We may be wondering how people become writers or architects. Or we may have discovered that once people didn't even know about bacteria, and we wish to know about that discovery and its relationship to disease. Curiosity, wonder, the possibility of discovery—any of a number of related motives may lead us to read about the lives of individuals.

The function of the nonfiction book for children as for adults is to give this desired information. If the book is to stimulate the child to reach for more, it must be written with strict attention not only to factual accuracy, but also to tone and style that attract and lead to discovery.[2] The successful nonfiction book manages to supply information and yet make the reader sense that discovery is open-ended. There is more to be known, and finding out is exciting. Because the attitude of wonder is stimulated, we assimilate the facts and come to understand concept.

INFORMATIONAL BOOKS

Organization and Scope

Common sense tells us that facts cannot be dumped upon a reader all at one time; in that situation we would have to make order out of masses of information, a task for an authority, not for an inquirer. The writer of nonfiction must select the key ideas, put them in the simplest forms, relate them to facts already known or to concepts already understood, and from this point begin to clarify. Breaking down the ideas into component parts that can be easily understood, the writer arranges them in coherent sequences from simplest to most complex, from familiar to unfamiliar, or from early development to later development, for example.

Since this task is not as easy as it sounds, not all writers are successful in finding the natural order. Some writers—like some teachers we may know—have a difficult time communicating concepts to those without backgrounds comparable to their own. These writers may have the understanding, but lack the capacity to recall what it was like when they were uninformed and needed elementary and orderly explanations.

In an example of simple and coherent ordering of facts, R. J. Lefkowitz leads children from raindrops—which they all know—to the ocean—which they may not know. In *Water for Today and Tomorrow,* he writes,

When it rains, some of the water goes into the ground. But the earth can't soak up all of the water. Water runs along the ground in tiny rivers, called *rivulets.*

Many rivulets running along the ground come together to make a brook. Then the brook bubbles along until it becomes part of a big stream. Water from many brooks may empty into the stream.

From all over, streams rush across the land toward a meetingplace. They end their journey at a mighty river. The river winds along, taking all the water to the ocean.

The scope of this book is clearly not to tell all that is known about water. The simple vocabulary makes clear the point about how water flows, but without dealing with confluence and estuaries; the book is written for a young reader. Another book, perhaps even one by the same writer, may explain in more depth and complexity the water flow, as well as explain water tables, water pollution, and water treatment. The scope of books depends to a large extent upon the interest and maturity of the reader.

The successful writer of informational books begins the explanation of an unfamiliar concept at the child's level. Mary Lou Clark, for example, manages to introduce us to her subject in *You and Relativity* by beginning where we are, on familiar ground. She suggests that if several persons all want to go to the same place, the third floor of a building, they will not all go up. One, who is on the sixth floor, will have to go down; another on the first floor will have to go up. And she introduces the concept of relativity by saying that *'relative* to the sixth floor, the third floor is down, but *relative* to the first floor, the third is up." Then Clark introduces us to the term "frame of reference," which we must understand before we can go on. Clark prepares us for more complicated ideas; we are on our way to discovery when we begin with this simple and ordinary concept of movement from floor to floor in a building. Order in the explanation of these concepts is from the known to the unknown. Organization has been determined in large part by the amount of information the reader is expected to have.

Narrative Form for Younger Readers

In nonfiction for the younger child, the writer often weaves information into a narrative. Robert McCloskey in his picture book *Time of Wonder* demonstrates that a slight unifying narrative can convey information about the New England shore. The island has a very old rock at the point, a rock that was hot as fire when it was new to a new world, and as cold as ice when the weight of the glacier ground into it. The seal sniffs, while the fishhawks and eider ducks listen and watch. The colors of the ferns change from green to yellow and brown. The robins have flown, and the swallows have left their boathouse nest, but their places are taken by birds that rest in migration as they fly south. Gulls and crows fuss and feud, and hummingbirds find the late petunias. Trees that have fallen during the storm leave jagged holes where their roots have been, and we understand the wind's power. A snow-white heap of shells left long ago by the Indians crumbles at a touch, and we realize that once the Indians lived where we are standing, before the white man came. We have moved down the beach, discovered a bit about geology, seen the effect of the storm on the trees, then sensed the aging agelessness of the Maine seacoast. These facts have been tied together by the slight narrative.

Although Jeanne Bendick does not use a continuous narrative to hold together her book *Why Can't I?* she does use children to wonder about the things they see. From a series of comparisons, we discover why we can't do several things such as breathe under water like a fish, or walk on the ceiling like a fly. On the bottom of each of the fly's six feet is a pad of stiff and sticky hairs. As the fly is walking on a smooth surface, these pads flatten and make the fly stick. Able to hold more than just the fly's weight, they keep him on the ceiling. She points out:

> The bottoms of *your* feet are smooth and slippery. You can make them a *little* sticky by wearing sneakers. But you're still too heavy to walk up a wall or across the ceiling.

The relating of the facts to the reader, the "I" of the title and the "you" of the text, makes these facts personal, interesting, and remarkable. Comparisons make the facts understandable, and each comparison has some narrative quality. The young reader is involved in this explanatory situation by the simplest of narrative elements.

Sometimes, however, because the writer is intent upon narrative suspense, he or she may not make the facts clear. In *How People Live in the Big City,* for example, we wander through the city and we learn that some people are living in very tall buildings with walls of glass. We read that such buildings sometimes are called glass houses, but we do not discover that they are far more often called apartment houses until the term is used later. We learn that riding on the stairs that move is like "floating up, up, up," but not that these stairs are called an escalator. Sometimes writers seem to fear words of more than two syllables will not be understood by children. But children's vocabularies are filled with big words: *hamburger* has three, after all, and *refrigerator* five.

Sometimes, for the sake of the narrative, information is completely lost, or is so distorted that it is untrue. *When the Root Children Wake*

Up, for example, is a misleading fairy tale, explaining the coming of spring:

distortion —

> Wide awake at last, in their root house, the root chil-
> dren work busily on their new Spring dresses. Each chooses the
> color she loves best—violet, yellow, blue, white, orange or red
> —and with needle, thread and thimble, sews happily till her
> work is done.

> the root boys. . . . wake up the sleeping insects—the beetles,
> grasshoppers, lady-bugs. . . . They sponge them and brush them
> and paint their shells with bright Spring colors . . .

Personification is not the only cause for distortion here; the writer in her eagerness to interest the reader in an account of the changes brought by spring has replaced facts with fantasy.

Robert McClung is far more successful at weaving facts of nature into narrative form. In a factually accurate narrative called *Possum,* McClung faces the reality of the possum's life. We follow a family of nine babies and discover that they are easy prey; one is caught by a fox, another by a great horned owl, a third by a rattlesnake, another by a giant snapping turtle, and a fifth is run over as it crosses the road. These are the facts of life in the possums' world: nine babies, four survivors. Within the narrative form, *Possum* remains factually accurate. A more ambitious purpose unifies McClung's *Samson, Last of the California Grizzlies.* In this vivid narrative account, Samson, to satisfy the frontiersmen's craving for excitement, is pitted against Diablo the bull:

> The crowd roared as the two great beasts tangled again.
> Samson crouched low trying to seize the bull's head in his huge
> paws, while Diablo thrust his horns downward in a deadly
> twisting sweep. As Samson rolled sideways to parry the blow,
> the tip of one of the bull's horns caught in a link of the chain
> that held the bear. There was a sudden loud snap as the chain
> broke, and Samson rolled free.

Here is a verifiable narrative of action on the frontier; there is sympathy for the two struggling animals forced to fight till death, but there is no sentimental distortion.

Style

How the writer uses language is style. In nonfiction, as in fiction or poetry, style is an integral part of meaning, and not merely decoration or embellishment added to explanations and descriptions. Style is part of all written matter. Some writers of nonfiction neglect artistry in language as a means of making their subjects interesting, while others are keenly aware of their responsibility to use language effectively.

⌈Simplicity need not be either triteness or banality. Comparisons are one means of making concepts clear to the reader, and some writers use comparisons simply and effectively.⌉Irving Adler in *The Story of Light* uses a reference to the familiar Aladdin story. Aladdin rubbed a lamp to summon the Jinni. We flick a switch to summon light. Adler goes on to remind us of how difficult it is to get rid of light; it streams in through windows and drapes, or through keyholes. Light cannot be held by force; although we try to grab it, it slides through our fingers. But if we learn about its tricks, we can put to work the energy of light. Referring next to a common experience, bumping into things in the dark, Adler then compares light to a messenger:

> If only the chair could have sent you a message across space, warning you of its presence! Fortunately for you, it can *when there is light in the room,* for the light serves as everybody's messenger. It travels from the table to you and tells you that the table is there.

⌈Frequent comparisons are particularly helpful in the explanations of complex ideas or startling facts.⌉In one picture book for small children, for example, we read the factual statement that the temperature on the sun's surface is close to 10,000 degrees Fahrenheit, and that the temperatures at the sun's center may be close to 32,000 degrees. But we have no frame of reference for these facts. Referring to familiar temperatures like our body heat of around 98°, or water that boils and steam that scalds at 212° would make such high temperatures with so many zeroes even more startling and somewhat more comprehensible.

⌈Some writers simplify their texts by relying upon the simplest sentence structure—subject, verb, complement. Such writers risk losing the interest of children who may weary of the monotonous rhythm created by repeated word patterns.⌉Children, after all, do talk in compound and complex sentences; they are more able to read complex sentence forms than some writers of nonfiction assume. *The First Book of New Zealand* is filled with generalizations that suggest that all New Zealanders are alike—an unjust and inaccurate statement. But the style of the book is often monotonous and repetitious as well. We are lulled into boredom and disbelief by its declarative sentences, the drumbeat of omniscient authority:

> The New Zealanders of today are law-abiding, practical, and conscientious people. They dislike extremes of any kind. They usually own their own homes. The houses are sur-

rounded by flower gardens, for New Zealanders like to plant
and grow things. . . .

Maori women practice as doctors and dental assistants;
they teach school where both the Maoris and *pakehas* are stu-
dents. They also work as news commentators on the radio.
Maori girls are extremely clever. . . .

Under the illusion that they are making their meaning more
accessible, other writers simplify their language by breaking up compound sentences into halting and choppy fragments:

How did the glacier do it?
A glacier works just like a plow. But instead of one
blade, it has a thousand. For every rock frozen into its bottom
acts like a plowshare.

By contrast, notice the clear and vivid description in *Gorilla
Gorilla.* In this book we have facts, but they are given to us in sentences
of varying length, with words and phrases in varying orders.

facts made interesting

The hoots grew louder and faster, faster and faster still.
Suddenly the huge leader thrust himself to his short legs. He
tore up great clumps of bush and vine, tossed them with a
furious heave high into the air, and began to thump his massive
chest like a frenzied drummer. The drumming boomed and
leapt into the leafy jungle, across the high meadows and jutting
cliffs of the rain forest—an increasing chorus of beats. The
hoots melted into a blurred growl.

Variety in sentence length and construction gives interest to this passage. Further interest in what Carol Fenner wants us to know about
gorillas is created by the use of imagery. We hear the drumming and
thumping of the huge gorilla and we see his actions. As the leader is
compared in a simile to a "frenzied drummer," the drumming booms
and leaps. We see the "leafy jungle" and the "jutting cliffs," and hear
the "blurred growl." These words are chosen to convey precise meaning
by creating sight and sound images. The result of Fenner's style is that
we learn the facts of the gorilla's hooting, and of his feats of strength.
But by seeing and hearing him in his natural habitat, we also discover
something about the concept explored in the book: captivity influences
gorilla behavior.

Any impression that all dress in early America was extremely simple, sensible, and drab is contradicted in *Colonial Living* in
Edwin Tunis's word pictures of the Dutch apparel. Relying upon

imagery for clarity, Tunis vividly describes the New Netherlanders' dress:

> In an age of ballooning britches, a Dutchman's out-swelled all others. His hat was a big plumed hat, not too well suited to his stocky build. Shoe buckles seem to have been popular. . . . the prosperous among the Dutch clung to the starched ruff. . . .
> Ruffs were a great nuisance and a great expense. They had to be laundered by experts. . . . The starched flutes . . . were arranged on "setting sticks" and fixed into shape with hot metal "poking sticks." Even then it was necessary to wear a wire "under-propper" to hold a ruff up.

Detailed imagery may also serve to make action clear. In vigorous language, Robert Leckie shows and explains the process of loading the Revolutionary War guns in *The World Turned Upside Down*. Notice Leckie's use of action verbs in differing forms as the British soldier bit the

> cartridge open . . . sprinkled a little powder on the pan of his piece. Then, placing the musket butt-downward, he poured the rest of the powder down the barrel. Next, he pushed in the ball. Crumpling the paper into a wad, he crammed that in afterward. Finally, seizing his rifle rod, he rammed all—powder, ball, and paper—down tight inside the barrel.
> To fire the musket, he placed the butt against his shoulder and pulled the trigger. This released a cock which struck its flint against a piece of steel to send a shower of sparks into the pan. When the powder here ignited, it flashed through a touch-hole into the bottom of the barrel and exploded the charge which propelled the bullet down the barrel.

A child reading such a description sees that readying the Brown Bess for action was a slow and complicated process; the child may understand that the war play of "rat-a-tat-tat" doesn't apply to the battles of the American Revolution.

Images and figurative comparisons not only contribute to an interesting style, but they are also the means by which the writer clarifies meaning. To create visual pictures filled with comparisons, Jean George uses color imagery and figurative language. In *The Moon of the Monarch Butterfly*, she expresses wonder at the beauty of the monarch by comparing wings to stained-glass windows and antennae to knotted wands:

Before sundown she came to rest on a wisteria vine that entwined the porch of a small white house in the country. Clinging to a purple flower, she closed her wings above her back, as butterflies do. Her wing tops were burnt orange, their undersides yellow. Black veins spread through them like lead in a stained-glass window and their edges seemed as if the night and day had been knitted together into sparkles of white and black. Her antennas were like wands, slender, with knots on the ends for sensing the flowers, the winds, and other monarch butterflies.

Scientific details and various kinds of eating equipment are made surprisingly clear and easy to understand when Millicent Selsam makes vivid figurative comparisons. In *How the Animals Eat,* the chapter on dinner in the water has several sub-headings and captions, each an image suggesting a comparison. Sea Soup or plankton is a tiny animal that drifts together with tiny plants. In some animals Sea Strainers or gill rakers work as built-in strainers holding the sea soup back for the fish to swallow as water passes out through mouth and gills. A Sea Sword is the upper jaw of the fish grown out into a bony, sharp point; it stabs a hole in a big fish and kills it. A Flexible Snout is a trunk-like tube that can poke around among the stones in the mud on the bottom of the sea, picking up little sea animals as the hose of a vacuum cleaner sucks up dirt. And Thousands of Oars are little hairs on the soft, moist body of an oyster, moving together to sweep water in from the outside. Each of the metaphors compares in words the unfamiliar manner of eating to something already known to the child. Each verbal comparison becomes vivid and clear. Style, in such cases, can serve as the agent for stimulating wonder and for starting the child's exploration of a subject.

The writer of nonfiction relies upon illustration somewhat differently from the writer of fiction. There is no need for characterization, for example; only occasionally does text evoke mood. In nonfiction, illustration helps to clarify. Sometimes the book makes use of photographs, but often photographs can be less valuable than drawings or diagrams, since they sometimes seem to oversimplify, catching only the external appearances of objects or concepts. Although illustrations are necessary to nonfiction, the writer who cannot achieve corresponding effects of clarity with the use of words is depriving the child of a discovery that words can tell just as pictures can. Discovery through words gives the child an opportunity for greater growth. Continuous reliance upon illustration for clarity does not expose children to new words nor develop in them the habit of using words to express themselves. Books, like television, then, make little contribution to growth in language skills if illustration is relied upon too heavily.

Tone

Tone is an important part of nonfiction, just as it is of fiction. Many children involve themselves more easily in a nonfiction account if they feel that a real person is conveying the facts to them. Writers may become persons in their own accounts by using the pronouns "we" and "you." To satisfy further this need for person in the communication, the writer also adopts a particular attitude toward the facts and the readers.

Sometimes the writer of books about nature, science, processes, or other facts names the book—*The Wonderful World of*—and we are startled to discover that our city sewer system is wonderful. Although the word *wonder* is overworked, there are a great many subjects about which it is perfectly reasonable to wonder. But when the writer uses the title *The Mystery of Chlorophyll,* he or she adopts a tone of surprise and intrigue. Science and the natural world are not miraculous, because as man discovers more about them, their opening mysteries continue to provoke wonder—but they become less mysterious. If books of fact are to stimulate the minds of children to further exploration, the writer's tone or attitude might better say, "Remarkable as all this is, we can know it. If we investigate it, we are amazed and enlightened."

Writers of nonfiction, like those of fiction, sometimes fall into a tone of condescension, oversimplifying, thinking of the readers as dear little things, or guarding their ears from the whole truth. Although this condescension may occur in a purely factual account, it seems to appear more frequently in facts tied together with a slight narrative.

History, and particularly remote history, is sometimes narrated in a pattern of condescension. In discussing *The Land and People of Iceland,* Erick Berry describes the Vikings, using the accounts in the Sagas recorded in about 1000 A.D. Berry makes these warriors' lives ridiculous. In violent and purposeless battle, they cut off each others' heads, and at nightfall their heads

> were miraculously restored, so that they might all sit down together and feast and drink all night. To resume fighting again next morning. Presumably their morning-after headaches also disappeared by magic.

Berry, however, does go on to explain the Vikings' early governmental bodies whose purpose was to settle disputes; "man-made words sought to wipe man-made violence from the land." The effort at humor seems out of place in a chapter that seriously traces Icelandic history from piracy to democracy.

When Edwin Tunis writes of the American Indian in *Indians,* he manages to treat objectively a subject that is often the victim of intellectual snobbery—superstition. Because of the matter-of-fact tone of the account, we accept the Indians' fears:

> There was no Indian who was even reasonably free from superstition: it covered everything in the world. When every animal and every tree, and every stream and every natural phenomenon was possessed of a spirit, probably malevolent, it took a lot of finger-crossing and wood-knocking to ward off evil. The Indian was afraid of everything. . . . of killing snakes and wolves. . . . of witchcraft and of the owls he associated with it . . . superstition . . . pervaded all Indian living.

Tone also affects our acceptance of our austere Plymouth forebears who become less forbidding and more human when we read Samuel Eliot Morison's account of *The Old Colony of "New Plymouth.* [Explicit facts and details tinged with humor show us that these were ordinary people with unexpected problems and surprising solutions:]

> Crows and blackbirds appear to have been more enterprising here than elsewhere, or else the Easthamites were poor shots: for the town voted in 1667 that every householder must kill at least three crows or twelve blackbirds per annum. This order was repeated annually, and toward the close of the century was reinforced by another, that each bachelor in town must kill at least six blackbirds or three crows per annum, and would not be allowed to marry until he had done his whack for the year!

In books about animals, condescension often takes the form of *anthropomorphism,* an attitude that suggests a lack of interesting qualities in the animals themselves and a need to jazz up their lives by making them more nearly human. When pets are given human qualities, we are not surprised, but it seems unacceptable and highly unscientific to attribute human qualities to prehistoric beasts. In one book about dinosaurs, a brontosaurus is called "terribly dumb"; the tylosaurus, described as clever, fierce, and cruel, seems vicious rather than—more accurately— carnivorous. In *Here Come the Wild Dogs,* which is about the life of a fox family, the father fox thinks to himself,

> What a fine morning for racing with the dogs!
> Excitement!
> Adventure!
> And yes, even danger!

As we follow the race in which the fox outwits the dogs, we hear the victorious fox say, "What fun!" While these may be reasonable emotions for people, the child reading that the fox has such thoughts and feelings is misled about reality. The child may even be led to believe that foxes relish the danger and adventure of being hunted. Animal stories are great favorites with children; it is important that when the child expects a factual report, a factual report is given. Any narrative should be kept within the realm of real possibility. The wild animals of McClung's *Shag, Last of the Plains Buffalo* do not play hide and seek with danger. Their lives are filled with serious battles—with pioneers, blizzards, mountain lions, wolves, and hunger. Although the reality of natural struggle includes terms usually used to describe human behavior, such as "lonely and afraid," "leaping in terror," and "wanting to get away," the book shows far more convincingly than the fox book how an animal responds physically to its natural enemies.

The writer of *Ookie, the Walrus Who Liked People* goes a step further than the writer of the fox book; he regards the walrus as almost totally human.[3] We read that she wasn't much interested in the penguin pool; she didn't think they'd be the sort of creatures that would be fun to play with; the seals, however, were the playmates she liked when she was lonely. The huge and yet sleekly graceful walrus becomes cute and coy, like the cartooned characters of a Disney animation. Wonder and curiosity do not urge us to discover more about walruses; the account stops discovery short by making the walrus neither human nor animal.

While accounts of the animal world are particularly subject to the condescension of anthropomorphism, some writers show great respect for their animal objects. Jean George is one of these authors. The reader, while absorbing detailed information about the gray wolves, acquires at the same time an admiration for their grace and intelligence. In *The Moon of the Gray Wolves,* we watch the wolf as he watches the caribou herd, and looks for prey:

> The black wolf waited until the main herd passed around the bend of the Toklat. Then, studying the forest and tundra for laggers, he tightened his muscles and sprang into a trot. His narrowly spaced wolf-shoulders gave him the stride of a horse rather than that of a dog, and in the manner of all wolves he glided along the ridge like a thoroughbred. Stiff, long guardhairs grew beyond his fuzzy underfur and fended off ice and snow. They glistened like glass as he swept back to his pack.

We further discover that the wolf is an essential predator, since by "harvesting" the weak and the old, the wolf keeps the caribou herd healthy, and their numbers balanced with the available food supply.

Here George's tone is objective and yet respectful, suitable for her description.

Phyllis Borea is even more factual in tone in her account of *Seymour, a Gibbon.* In order to make the descriptions clear to the reader, Borea often compares the monkeys' actions to those of people, but she carefully avoids lapsing into personification:

> Gibbons . . . live in family groups—father, mother, one or two youngsters, and sometimes a very old gibbon, perhaps a grandfather or mother. . . . only gibbons enjoy this close way of living rather like our own. The family wakes at dawn after a night together in their sleeping tree, because, also like us, the higher primates sleep at night and are up and about during the day.

Although Borea compares gibbon families to human families, the two are said to be "perhaps" similar, but never the same. And since Borea cannot know the reasons for the gibbons' morning cries, she only speculates:

> For an hour or more after waking, they greet the dawn and their neighbors with cries that have been called songs and set down on paper like music. . . . their morning songs may be a way of letting other gibbon families know these particular trees are lived in. The songs may also be just for the fun of it, the way some ASPCA Junior Members sing in the shower of a morning.

Herbert S. Zim is another writer intent upon giving the reader the facts and the facts alone. He makes few human comparisons; he gives only verifiable information. In *Monkeys,* Zim uses a completely objective and matter-of-fact tone:

> Records kept at zoos show that monkeys have a fairly long life span compared to other mammals. A mandrill has been known to live 27 years, a macaque up to 29, and a baboon to 45. But these may be special cases, and wild monkeys, on an average, may not live much over 10 or 12 years.

Didacticism

When a writer chooses a controversial topic such as drugs or narcotics as a subject for a children's book, he or she is probably impelled by a desire to persuade the readers, or to influence their thinking about the dangers of narcotics or of smoking. As a result, writers who are concerned about children and the future of the world may have a difficult time separating their facts from their propaganda. The writer, however, has as a first obligation the presentation of generalizations supported by factual information. Experiments, statistics, descriptions of studies, and references to authorities should be the meat of the book. If the facts are carefully arranged, the evidence gathers and builds to prove the point. Preachment is unnecessary.

If, on the other hand, the book lacks sufficient evidence and relies upon generalizations that the writer knows to be true but has not bothered to support with evidence for the reader's examination, the book then raises questions that have not been answered. How do we know? Who says so? When did that happen? If these questions are left unanswered by the data, the reader says "That's just opinion; it's never proved." If the writer realizes that all the data martialed are insufficient proof, he or she then may support one side with firmly stated opinion, but the effect on the reader's mind is a quick write-off: "Propaganda. Pure propaganda." Doubt and distrust result.

While some concepts have been well-researched and a variety of experiments has led to the same conclusions—smoking endangers the smoker's health—others are still in the process of being tested and proved. Scientists conduct experiments, note results, and draw hypotheses; they then test these hypotheses in an effort to reach a conclusion. But many of these series of experiments are still in hypothetical stages, insufficiently proved. It is most often these hypotheses that turn into propaganda for unproved theories.

The writer of nonfiction has a responsibility to use and to foster the scientific attitude. It is the writer's obligation when dealing with theory not fully proven to make us aware that there are theories and counter-theories on the subject. Perhaps—if society is lucky—the child-readers will be so intrigued by the puzzlement of scientists that they themselves will wish to find the solution some day.

Careful lest the reader confuse theory with truth, A. H. Drummond, Jr., in *The Population Puzzle,* describes a series of experiments concerning the relationship of overcrowding and rats. He says that the rats die off, but then he carefully asks, "Will human population die off from overcrowding?"

> After reading about Calhoun's experiment, you may want to agree. Be careful, however. It is dangerous to leap to conclusions when animal and human behavior are compared. Let's look at some additional experimental work.

Again, after accounts of related experiments, we read,

Do these results apply to people? Again, we must be cautious and look for more evidence before drawing any conclusions. Suppose, though, that something similar does happen to people.

And, finally,

Thus, we see that even among primates . . . overcrowding seems to bring about stresses that lead to abnormal and antisocial behavior⌐The temptation is great to conclude that these findings apply also to human populations. Unfortunately, we should not do this for the evidence is not as yet conclusive.⌐

In a similarly objective fashion, Robert J. Lowenherz in *Population* asks,

Was Malthus right? Some experts assure us that modern science will find ways to feed our growing world population. Other experts warn us that famine is just around the corner. This disagreement over population and food continues.

Lowenherz does not preach that family planning is essential to avoid destructive world overpopulation; he notes arguments against family planning given by people from all over the world: my children are my old age security; God sends children and it is a sin to prevent their birth; if we grow few in numbers, we grow weak; an illiterate population will never understand. But Lowenherz's purpose is clear from the beginning when he states that the world is overpopulated, and then goes on to build a case for limiting families. The question he finally leaves open is how it is to be done, but he first presents facts about hunger, demography, and space and water sharing.

Adults often seek opinion books because they wish to know a particular expert's opinion or attitude toward a subject. The child, however, not knowing that the facts surrounding a social problem can be interpreted through the individual perspectives of various kinds of experts, approaches a book expecting to find facts and objectivity. The child will then be less likely to detect bias. It seems reasonable to say that children's books that inform should not be propaganda. Freedom to draw our own conclusions from the facts is a precious right. If a writer has a bias, we should expect it to be stated openly at some point.

Children can't distinguish between opinion & fact — dangerous

BIOGRAPHY

In our discussion of nonfiction books for children we have noted that each of them includes three essentials: facts, a concept that facts relate to, and an attitude toward the subject and the reader. ***Biography***, the history of the life of an individual, has similar essentials. First of all, the facts are expected to be accurate, up-to-date, and authentic as they depict the person and the period of his or her life. The objective biographer must include or omit the events and details as they suit the interests and age level for which the biography is intended. As for concept, we assume that the subject of the biography is worth reading about, just as it is worth the writer's time spent in research and writing. A subject for biography has done something or been something, discovered or demonstrated something that makes her or his life significant—more significant, say, than your life or your sister's or brother's. As for attitude, we assume that the attitude of the writer is interested and enthusiastic. If the writer finds the subject worth writing about, she or he finds the subject worth writing about with the skill we call style. The skillful biographer uses words imaginatively, even in the simplest biographies, for younger readers.

Within our definition of biography—biography is the history of the life of an individual—are two terms, and each presents a separate obligation for the writer. The first term, *history,* implies facts, and biography, like other nonfiction, should be factually accurate. Information about the life of the subject comes from such sources as letters, journals, diaries, court records, newspaper accounts, recorded conversations, and interviews, wherever feasible. Although not all biographies for children include a bibliography, it is a useful addition. A quick glance at the foreword or acknowledgments may also tell something about the writer's research, and perhaps suggest other readings to the curious child. A closer look at the text itself will reveal dates, quotations, places, and names as they fit into the narrative. But again the numbers of such details depend upon the age of the intended readers. Such data make the book seem factually authentic, and we are then ready to take other information on faith.

The term *history* implies another obligation on the part of the writer; history when properly written is objectively reported. The historian neither shows personal bias nor assumes omniscience about thoughts and feelings of historical figures. The conscientious biographer, despite interest and enthusiasm for the subject, is bound by similar limitations; he or she does not get into the mind of the subject, but limits the information to verifiable matters and to emotions, fantasies, or thoughts the subject has spoken or recorded. Partiality yields to fact and objectivity. (Invention in biography for children is discussed later.)

By definition, a biography is about an individual, and here lies a second problem. Children who become interested in the lives of presidents, for example, often have difficulty sorting out the life of one president from the life of another, because aside from living in differing historical periods, presidents in children's biographies seem to become stereotypes of all that is good. Their differences are slight; Washington is honest, Lincoln kind, Wilson scholarly, Theodore Roosevelt nonconforming but commanding. Servants to society like Jane Addams, Clara Barton, or Florence Nightingale are unselfishly devoted to helping others; freed slaves like Amos Fortune may be cardboard figures of self-denial. The process of writing biography, like that of writing informational books, is a process of constant decision-making: what to select and what to omit. The biographer wishes to show the individual as a believable human being, complete with such flaws as occasional self-interest, irritability, or faulty judgment. Although there is a trend toward showing the less admirable traits in the character of the subject, we still usually ignore socially disapproved behavior. Poor biography, however, often ignores completely any negative qualities and presents only the good. The result is sometimes a book colored by an approving tone that may be disproportionate to the subject's achievements or character and in any case is unrealistic.

Susan Heimann in *Christopher Columbus* gives him credit for his achievements; nonetheless, she does show him as a believable human being. Columbus, in writing about the Indians in the newly discovered land, says of them that

> "they ought to be good servants and of good skill . . . they would easily be made Christians, because it seems that they belonged to no religion."

Heimann goes on to say that Columbus has revealed in these words that while the first motive for the voyage—bringing religion to the natives —is still important, it now seems to come second to "using" these people as skillful servants. Since children often read biography because of curiosity about a hero to emulate, it seems important that the subject of the biography not be so unreal, or so saintly, that the reader feel emulation is impossible. The subject when honestly described is real enough to encourage the reader to similar efforts and achievements.

We hear the terms "biographical fiction" and "fictional biography," and it is difficult to tell the difference. To put it simply, in the first term the noun or more important word is *fiction,* and in the second the more important word is *biography.* It is not the two terms that matter, however; it is the author's focus. In both cases, the writer is inventing; the difference is a matter of degree.

The problem for the writer of biography for children lies to a great extent in his answers to two basic questions: How much fact shall I include? How much narrative may I invent to make it interesting? If we draw a continuum or a line extending from pure fiction at one end to pure fact at the other, perhaps we can place biography for the younger child nearer the fictional end of the line; she or he enjoys fewer facts and more story.

F. N. Monjo, for example, uses some of the facts of Lincoln's life, but he uses a fictional storytelling device: Tad is the first-person narrator in *Me and Willie and Pa.* Tad tells, among other things, of crawling into Pa's bed when he was lonely after his brother Willie's death. The book uses historical facts, but the child's interest is held by the fictional narrative.

Biography for the older child might fall closer to the factual end of the line; the older child can absorb more facts and requires less story. Too much factual detail makes the page dense with the capital letters of places, people, and events, and the appearance is that of an encyclopedia. The response to such a biography may be "This is more than I really want to know." And yet, too much invention prompts the response, "What can I really believe?" Carl Sandburg in writing about his biography of Lincoln stated that he did not invent dialogue or incident to prove a point; he adhered to fact. And yet Sandburg's work, from which *Abe Lincoln Grows Up* is drawn, is unsurpassed as a definitive biography of Lincoln, both for accuracy and interest. It is possible to stick to the facts and to write an interesting book. But if the writer does invent, these inventions should be historically true to the times, and not merely possible, but probable.

People who live active lives are naturally and easily made interesting for children; when adventure is part of the subject's life, the narrative pulls the reader along. Such is the case in the lives of explorers like Magellan, frontiersmen like Daniel Boone, generals like Sam Houston, or sports figures like Billie Jean King. Biographies of philosophers, poets, or musicians who lived quietly with little drama or action in their lives are more difficult to make interesting, especially for younger readers. The obligation remains, however, for the biographer to focus upon the nature of the person as well as upon the exciting events of his or her life. Where the subject's achievement is less filled with action or adventure, the writer faces the necessity to hold interest in the subject and yet to keep invented action to a minimum. This dual responsibility is not easy to fulfill, and invention is sometimes the biographer's compromise.

The reader ought also to expect of biography suitable tone and appropriate style. In five different accounts of Columbus's landing in what he thought to be the Indies, five biographers refer to the Indians and explorers in different ways. One account seems to call undue attention to the Indians' nakedness, and by using quiet verbs and exotic descriptions creates a romantic, fairytale tone. Notice the effect of "scarlet" instead of red, for example:

> Columbus and his men saw a new beautiful world.
> Here were brown men with no clothes at all. Their bodies were painted red and other bright colors. . . . They came to the ships in canoes, or swimming, with gifts of cotton and parrots and food. They were pleased to take gifts of bells and beads and scarlet caps. They were a gentle and friendly people.
> And on the island there were palm trees and trees so tall they seemed to reach the sky. . . . the twelfth day of October . . . as green and beautiful as the trees of Spain in the month of May.

Although sentence structure is repetitious and dull, another account, by focusing on visual detail regarding the Indians themselves, seems more factual. The Indians

> who had been hiding behind trees and rocks came up to the white men. They came in the friendliest manner. These natives were light brown in color, and rather tall. They had straight, coarse, black hair, and large eyes. They stroked the Spaniards' clothes and their beards.

A third biographer seems to condescend because he places quotation marks around "talk" and "told," as he describes in minimal terms the sign language used by both the Indians and the explorers:

> Columbus finally managed to "talk" to the Indians by making signs with his hands. The Indians made signs too. They "told" Columbus he was welcome. . . .

A fourth account by its tone of wonder makes the Indians seem like children and the explorers seem, even to the reader, to be like gods. All Columbus saw

> were naked, red-skinned savages. They threw themselves to the ground and worshiped Columbus and his bearded men. The natives had never seen white men or sails before. They thought that gods had descended from the heavens on white-winged birds. They led the white gods to their homes. . . .

And a fifth writer, Heimann, wins our belief by narrating facts in a convincingly objective tone:

> Curiosity quickly overcame fear on the part of the people of the island, and soon they came out to meet these strange men from another world. These "very handsome people" were Tainos, . . . called their island Guanahani, and because Columbus thought it was part of the Indies, he called them Indians. He described them as gentle and helpful in every way. They wore no clothes, and many of the men painted their bodies.

The writer's tone reflects his or her attitude toward subject and readers, and we are influenced by that tone. We are made to see the subject as being trivial, or exotic, or as possessing value and dignity. These biographies contrast not only in age level, but also in tone.

The biographer, facing the necessity to arouse and hold the reader's interest, may be tempted to create sympathy for the subject and to make a tearjerker out of early trials. One biographer in writing of the young composer Beethoven has made from some factual information a sentimental story of Beethoven's being victimized by a tyrannical teacher. He says, "Poor Ludwig!" and describes Ludwig's day as long, hard, and wearying. Ludwig stumbles off to bed, but is shaken awake in the middle of the night and called a lazy rascal. Then he is made to stay awake and write music. Ludwig's unreasonable teacher stands over him, thunders at Ludwig's drowsiness, forces the exhausted boy back to work, then goes to bed leaving the weary boy struggling with fatigue as he finishes the writing. Here again it is not the facts we question so much as the tone.

Paderewski the pianist might have been treated with equal sentimentality as he goes off to the Warsaw Conservatory. However, Charlotte Kellogg in *Paderewski* is unsentimental:

> But he was not learning what he needed most to know: the science of piano playing—such things as correct fingering and pedaling. More than discouraging was his first experience in a piano class. "Not hands for playing," the teacher declared. "That thumb, that third finger, too short." He gave Ignace a trial, then told him to leave, to take up some other instrument.

Didacticism

Concept is needed in biography as it is in other literature; our preoccupation with fact must not blind us to idea. The title *Invincible Louisa* suggests a concept behind the biography; the same can be said for *Carry*

On, Mr. Bowditch, or *Up From Slavery.* Other biographies, while they may not indicate the unifying idea in their titles, do have implicit within them a concept—the reasons for the writer's having chosen these people as subjects. Sometimes the reason is that this leader unified his or her country, this scientist persisted until research bore fruit, this athlete overcame difficulties, or this composer was an innovator. Any of these reasons for writing the biography can unify the account to make it a coherent whole.

However, having a reason to choose a subject for biography does not give the writer license to preach. Intent upon making a point about the worthiness of the subject, the writer may lapse into didacticism. Writing of Louisa May Alcott's early life, Cornelia Meigs insists that we recognize the idealism behind Bronson Alcott's efforts to form the perfect social community. Such insistence intervenes between the readers and Louisa, the real subject; it shakes a finger at the readers to make them accept Meigs's views.

preaching   We must remember, however, that Bronson and his friends, wise in some ways, mistaken in others, had the courage to find out, by the only possible means, where they were right and where they were wrong. There is only one method of testing a system of living; that is by living it.

Louisa saw Concord soldiers march away to the Civil War, and such a picture is relevant to the biography. But here, too, Meigs intervenes:

> There is no experience in the world that can ever match that of seeing soldiers go away, of seeing the gaiety and the excitement and of knowing the black and hopeless tragedy which is behind it all. There is little that is so terrible as seeing strong, wholesome young men, every one of them beautiful in the flush of their high patriotism, as watching them go and knowing that they are surely to die.

By contrast, there is information coupled with vitality in *Carry On, Mr. Bowditch.* Jean Lee Latham tells of Nathaniel Bowditch's discovery of a new and simpler way to make lunar calculations at sea. Without preaching, she manages simultaneously to explain the process, record the action, and reproduce the excitement of discovery.

> Tonight ought to be a good one for a lunar. The moon was due to pass over a star that was bright enough to see in spite of its nearness to the moon. . . . Just when the moon neared the bright star, a cloud got in the way. Nat shrugged and sighed.

There ought to be a better way to work a lunar! He studied the glittering heavens. Was there another star bright enough to-night—that the moon would pass over? Of course not. He knew that. That one . . . the moon would pass below it . . . that one . . . the moon would pass above it . . . that one. . . .

The idea hit Nat so suddenly that he gasped. He raced below and for the second time that night crashed into Prince's cabin without knocking.

A unifying concept and accurate details about manners, costumes, or the appearance of city streets are not enough. Like all nonfiction, biography, too, should arouse the reader's curiosity to want to know more about the time period, the movements in history, or the subject's life or achievements. If biography is to open the world to children, it should stimulate them as they finish the book to believe not "Now I know all about this person, this period, this vocation," but "I wonder what else I can find out—" The biography will then have served, in Fisher's words, not as a stopper but as a starter.

SUMMARY

The purpose of nonfiction is to help the reader toward knowledge—knowledge as contrasted to merely information or fact. It is natural then that techniques will be subordinated to this end. Within each nonfiction book we expect to find fact, concept, and attitude. Curiosity or wonder, the motivation for children seeking out nonfiction, is stimulated by the quality of what they read, tempting them to wish to discover more about worthy people, foreign lands, far-off times, scientific concepts, natural elements and animals, or ways of solving society's problems. Since the order in which facts and concepts are presented influences how well we understand, a narrative structure is often used for younger children's books. There are other equally effective means of explanation, and moving from the known to the unknown is the most effective.

Biography is obliged by its definition to be factually accurate in depicting a unique individual whose life has unusual value; the biographer faces the necessity to keep the account interesting but truthful. Tone influences nonfiction just as it does fiction. Condescension looks down upon its subject; anthropomorphism fantasizes about it; sentimentality distorts it; and propaganda invalidates it. The best choice of tone always enlivens the subject.

Style, though it must be clear, need not be banal or trite; imagery, figurative language, and varied sentence structure make the writing lively and stimulating. The best nonfiction can prompt a reader's response: I want to know more!

Reading and Evaluating

1 *Examine three nonfiction books intended for the same level of age or reading maturity and that explore similar topics (e.g., cities, frontier life, Puritan days). Which have narrative order? Which begin with the known and move to the unknown? Is the progress of the explanation clear? Are there other methods of development? Are there unexplained gaps? Is too much information given at one time, without giving the reader opportunity for assimilation or comparisons? Explain your answers.*

2 *Examine three nonfiction books for differing age or reading maturity levels that explore the same concept. Does the book stimulate wonder? What is the tone? Identify any passages you feel are condescending. Is the book so packed with closely related information that the reader feels he or she will never understand? Is it a starter book, one that leads the child to explore? Or is it a stopper, one that makes the child think that is all there is to know on the subject? Explain.*

3 *Examine three books of natural history for their objective reporting. Does the book make the animal interesting without personifying it? Does it attribute to animals traits that are observable by actions? Does it suggest that animals are interesting in themselves? Or does it suggest that animals are interesting only if they are made human?*

4 *Compare three biographies of the same person, checking them for evidence of the writer's research. Is any one of them too packed with information, reading more like an encyclopedia than like an interesting personal history? Is the biographer's point of view objective? Give evidence. Or does the biographer, like the writer of fiction, assume omniscience about how the subject feels and thinks? Give evidence.*

5 *What evidence of stylistic artistry do you find in any of these nonfiction books? Are there figurative comparisons and imagery to make appearances and actions clear and interesting? Is sentence structure varied, or does it move haltingly? If the book is historical, does it convince the reader that these were real people rather than stereotypes of a historical period? How? What devices of style are used, and how are they effective?*

NOTES

[1]Throughout this chapter I am grateful to Margery Fisher for many of my ideas. Her book *Matters of Fact* (Brockhampton, 1973) is an excellent discussion of what should be expected of nonfiction books for children.

[2]Fisher contrasts two terms: A starter makes the child "want to pursue it further. A stopper can be quickly skimmed and will be as quickly forgotten because it gives the deadly impression of being self-contained and yet incomplete." (p. 23).

[3]William Bridges's book is classified as nonfiction.

[4]I am grateful for the discussion of biography found in *Children and Books* (Glenview, Ill., Scott, Foresman, 1981).

Recommended Books Cited in this Chapter

Adler, Irving. *The Story of Light.* Irvington-on-Hudson: Harvey House, 1971.

Asimov, Isaac. *How Did We Find Out About Electricity?* New York: Walker, 1973.

———. *Inside the Atom.* London: Abelard, 1966.

Bendick, Jeanne. *Why Can't I?* New York: McGraw, 1969.

Borea, Phyllis and Raimondo. *Seymour, a Gibbon.* New York: Atheneum, 1973.

Carson, Rachel. *The Sea Around Us.* New York: Oxford University Press, 1961.

Clark, Mary Lou. *You and Relativity.* Chicago: Children's, 1965.

Drummond, G. H., Jr. *The Population Puzzle.* Reading, Mass.: Addison, 1973.

Fenner, Carol. *Gorilla Gorilla.* New York: Random, 1973.

George, Jean. *The Moon of the Gray Wolves.* New York: Crowell, 1969.

———. *The Moon of the Monarch Butterfly.* New York: Crowell, 1968.

———. *Spring Comes to the Ocean.* New York: Crowell, 1966.

Graham, Alberta Powell. *Christopher Columbus, Discoverer.* New York: Abingdon, 1950.

Heimann, Susan. *Christopher Columbus.* New York: Watts, 1973.

Kellogg, Charlotte. *Paderewski.* New York: Viking, 1956.

Latham, Jean Lee. *Carry On, Mr. Bowditch.* Boston: Houghton, 1955.

Leckie, Robert. *The World Turned Upside Down.* New York: Putnam, 1973.

Lefkowitz, R. J. *Water for Today and Tomorrow.* New York: Parents Magazine, 1973.

Lowenherz, Robert J. *Population.* Mankato: Creative Education, 1970.

McCloskey, Robert. *Time of Wonder.* New York: Viking, 1957.

McClung, Robert. *Possum.* New York: Morrow, 1963.

———. *Shag, Last of the Plains Buffalo.* New York: Morrow, 1963.

———. *Samson, Last of the California Grizzlies.* New York: Morrow, 1973.

Meigs, Cornelia. *Invincible Louisa.* Boston: Little, 1961.

Monjo, F. N. *Me and Willie and Pa.* New York: Simon, 1973.

Morison, Samuel Eliot. *The Old Colony of "New Plymouth."* New York: Knopf, 1956.

Sandberg, Carl. *Abe Lincoln Grows Up.* New York: Harbrace, 1931.

Selsam, Millicent. *How the Animals Eat.* Eau Claire, Wis.: E. N. Hale, (n.d.).

Tunis, Edwin. *Colonial Living.* New York: World, 1957.

———. *Indians.* New York: World, 1959.

Zim, Herbert S. *Monkeys.* New York: Morrow, 1955.

Glossary

Allegory: a literary work in which characters and actions represent abstractions

Alliteration: repetition of initial consonant sound

Allusion: indirect reference to something or someone outside the literary work

Antagonist: force in conflict with protagonist; usually designated as self, another person, society, nature

Anthropomorphism: the giving of human qualities to nonhuman animals or objects

Assonance: repetition of vowel sound in phrase

Backdrop setting: generalized or relatively unimportant setting

Cadence: rhythmic flow in prose

Character: human being, real or personified animal, personified object taking a role in literature

Character development: filling out a variety of character traits to provide the complexity of a human being

Chronology: order dictated by passing of time

Classic: literary work that lives to be read and reread

Cliché: overused term which has lost meaning

Cliffhanger: unresolved suspense that concludes a chapter

Climax: action that precipitates resolution of conflict

Closed ending: conclusion leaving no plot questions unanswered

Coincidence: chance concurrence of events

Complication: early action; part of rising action

Conflict: struggle between protagonist and opposing force

Connotation: associative or emotional meaning of a word

Consonance: repetition of consonant sound in phrase

Denotation: explicit or dictionary meaning

Denouement: final or closing action following climax

Diction: choice of words or wording

Didacticism: in literature, an instructive or moralistic lesson often at the expense of entertainment

Dramatic or objective point of view: third-person narration in which actions and speeches are recorded without interpretation

Dynamic character: one who changes in the course of the story

Echo: words repeated in familiar pattern

Epic: long narrative poem about a heroic figure whose actions reveal the values of the culture

Episodic plot: plot with independent, short story-like chapters linked by characters or theme more than by action

Explicit theme: theme stated clearly in the story

Exposition: presentation of essential information needed for understanding of the action

Fable: very brief story, usually with animal characters, that states a didactic theme or moral

Falling action: final or closing action following climax; denouement

Fantasy: story about a non-existent or unreal world in which action may depend upon magic or the supernatural

Figurative language: devices making comparisons, saying one thing in terms of another

First-person point of view: "I" in narration in which a person's experiences, thoughts, and feelings are told by himself/herself

Flashback: return to event that occurred before present scene; retrospect

Flat character: one that is little developed

Foil: a character whose contrasting traits point up those of a central character

Folk ballad: narrative poem passed down by word of mouth; often about a hero

Folk rhyme: rhymes passed down by word of mouth

Folk tale: story passed down by word of mouth

Foreshadowing: hints of what is to come

Hyperbole: exaggeration or overstatement

Imagery: verbal appeals to the senses

Implicit theme: theme implied from the story's context

Inevitability: sense that it had to happen; in literature a sense that the outcome was necessary and inescapable

Integral setting: essential and specific setting which influences character, plot, and theme

Legend: a traditional narrative of a people, often with some basis in historical truth

Limerick: five-line humorous verse with traditional rhythm and rhyme pattern

Limited omniscient point of view: third-person narration in which story is seen through the mind(s) of one or few characters

Lyric poem: song-like poem, compact expression of feeling

Metaphor: implied comparison
Meter: somewhat regular rhythm pattern of stressed and unstressed syllables in a line of poetry
Motif: recurring element in literary work, often found in traditional literature
Myth: story originating in folk beliefs and showing supernatural forces operating

Narrative order: sequence in which events are recounted
Narrative poem: poem that tells a story

Objective or dramatic point of view: third-person narration in which actions and speeches are recorded without interpretation
Omniscient point of view: an all-knowing writer tells the story in third person
Onomatopoeia: words that sound like their meanings, such as *meow, moo*
Open ending: final outcome of conflict unknown

Parody: imitation of known form for comic effect
Personification: giving human traits to nonhuman beings or objects
Plot: sequence of events involving character in conflict
Poetry: distilled and imaginative expression of feeling
Point of view: the mind(s) through which the reader sees the story
Primary theme: major underlying and unifying truth of a story
Progressive plot: plot with central climax
Protagonist: central character in the conflict

Realism: story based upon the possible, though not necessarily probable
Resolution: falling action following climax
Rhyme: repetition of identical or similar stressed sound or sounds
Rhythm: recurring flow of strong and weak beats
Rising action: exposition and complications that lead to the climax
Round character: a fully developed or three-dimensional character

Science fiction: story that relies upon invention or extension of nature's laws, not upon the supernatural or magical
Secondary theme: less important or minor theme of a story
Sensationalism: focus upon the thrilling or startling
Sentiment: emotion or feeling
Sentimentality: overuse of sentiment, false arousal of feelings
Setting: the time and place in which the action occurs

Simile: stated comparison, usually using *like* or *as*

Static character: one who does not change in the course of the story

Stereotype: character possessing expected traits of a group rather than being an individual

Stock character: flat character with very little development found in numerous stories

Style: mode of expression

Suspense: state of uncertainty that keeps reader reading

Symbol: person, object, situation, or action operating on two levels of meaning—literal and figurative or suggestive

Theme: statement giving the underlying truth about people, society, or the human condition, either explicitly or implicitly

Tone: writer's attitude toward his or her subject and readers

Touchstone: example of excellence referred to for comparison

Understatement: reverse exaggeration or playing down

Verse: here used to denote rhyming metrical structure with less emotional intensity than poetry

Appendix:
Children's Book Awards

THE NEWBERY MEDAL

Named in honor of John Newbery (1713–1767), the first English publisher of children's books, this medal has been given annually (since 1922) by the American Library Association's Children's Services Division. The recipient is recognized as author of the most significant book in children's literature published in the United States in the preceding year. The award is limited to citizens or residents of the United States.

1922   *The Story of Mankind* by Hendrik Willem van Loon, Liveright
Honor Books: *The Great Quest* by Charles Hawes, Little; *Cedric the Forester* by Bernard Marshall, Appleton; *The Old Tobacco Shop* by William Bowen, Macmillan; *The Golden Fleece and the Heroes Who Lived Before Achilles* by Padraic Colum, Macmillan; *Windy Hill* by Cornelia Meigs, Macmillan

1923   *The Voyages of Doctor Dolittle* by Hugh Lofting, Lippincott
Honor Books: No record

1924   *The Dark Frigate* by Charles Hawes, Atlantic/Little
Honor Books: No record

1925   *Tales from Silver Lands* by Charles Finger, Doubleday
Honor Books: *Nicholas* by Anne Carroll Moore, Putnam; *Dream Coach* by Anne Parrish, Macmillan

1926   *Shen of the Sea* by Arthur Bowie Chrisman, Dutton
Honor Book: *Voyagers* by Padraic Colum, Macmillan

1927   *Smoky, The Cowhorse* by Will James, Scribner's
Honor Books: No record

1928   *Gayneck, The Story of a Pigeon* by Dhan Gopal Mukerji, Dutton
Honor Books: *The Wonder Smith and His Son* by Ella Young, Longmans; *Downright Dencey* by Caroline Snedeker, Doubleday

1929   *The Trumpeter of Krakow* by Eric P. Kelly, Macmillan
Honor Books: *Pigtail of Ah Lee Ben Loo* by John Bennett, Longmans; *Millions of Cats* by Wanda Gág, Coward; *The Boy Who Was* by Grace Hallock, Dutton; *Clearing Weather* by Cornelia Meigs, Little; *Runaway Papoose* by Grace Moon, Doubleday; *Tod of the Fens* by Elinor Whitney, Macmillan

1930   *Hitty, Her First Hundred Years* by Rachel Field, Macmillan
Honor Books: *Daughter of the Seine* by Jeanette Eaton, Harper; *Pran of Albania* by Elizabeth Miller, Doubleday; *Jumping-Off Place* by Marian Hurd McNeely, Longmans; *Tangle-Coated Horse and Other Tales* by Ella Young, Longmans; *Vaino* by Julia Davis Adams, Dutton; *Little Blacknose* by Hildegarde Swift, Harcourt

1931   *The Cat Who Went to Heaven* by Elizabeth Coatsworth, Macmillan
        Honor Books: *Floating Island* by Anne Parrish, Harper; *The Dark Star of
        Itza* by Alida Malkus, Harcourt; *Queer Person* by Ralph Hubbard,
        Doubleday; *Mountains Are Free* by Julia Davis Adams, Dutton; *Spice
        and the Devil's Cave* by Agnes Hewes, Knopf; *Meggy Macintosh* by
        Elizabeth Janet Gray, Doubleday; *Garram the Hunter* by Herbert Best,
        Doubleday; *Ood-Le-Uk the Wanderer* by Alice Lide and Margaret
        Johansen, Little

1932   *Waterless Mountain* by Laura Adams Armer, Longmans
        Honor Books: *The Fairy Circus* by Dorothy P. Lathrop, Macmillan;
        Calico Bush by Rachel Field, Macmillan; *Boy of the South Seas* by Eunice
        Tietjens, Coward; *Out of the Flame* by Eloise Lownsbery, Longmans;
        Jane's Island by Marjorie Allee, Houghton; *Truce of the Wolf and Other
        Tales of Old Italy* by Mary Gould Davis, Harcourt

1933   *Young Fu of the Upper Yangtze* by Elizabeth Foreman Lewis, Winston
        Honor Books: *Swift Rivers* by Cornelia Meigs, Little; *The Railroad to
        Freedom* by Hildegarde Swift, Harcourt; *Children of the Soil* by Nora
        Burglon, Doubleday

1934   *Invincible Louisa* by Cornelia Meigs, Little
        Honor Books: *The Forgotten Daughter* by Caroline Snedeker, Doubleday;
        Swords of Steel by Elsie Singmaster, Houghton; *ABC Bunny* by Wanda
        Gág, Coward; *Winged Girl of Knossos* by Erik Berry, Appleton; *New Land*
        by Sarah Schmidt, McBride; *Big Tree of Bunlahy* by Padraic Colum,
        Macmillan; *Glory of the Seas* by Agnes Hewes, Knopf; *Apprentice of
        Florence* by Anne Kyle, Houghton

1935   *Dobry* by Monica Shannon, Viking
        Honor Books: *Pageant of Chinese History* by Elizabeth Seeger, Longmans;
        Davy Crockett by Constance Rourke, Harcourt; *Day on Skates* by Hilda
        Van Stockum, Harper

1936   *Caddie Woodlawn* by Carol Brink, Macmillan
        Honor Books: *Honk, The Moose* by Phil Stong, Dodd; *The Good Master*
        by Kate Seredy, Viking; *Young Walter Scott* by Elizabeth Janet Gray,
        Viking; *All Sail Set* by Armstrong Sperry, Winston

1937   *Roller Skates* by Ruth Sawyer, Viking
        Honor Books: *Phebe Fairchild: Her Book* by Lois Lenski, Stokes; *Whistler's
        Van* by Idwal Jones, Viking; *Golden Basket* by Ludwig Bemelmans,
        Viking; *Winterbound* by Margery Bianco, Viking; *Audubon* by
        Constance Rourke, Harcourt; *The Codfish Musket* by Agnes Hewes,
        Doubleday

1938   *The White Stag* by Kate Seredy, Viking
        Honor Books: *Pecos Bill* by James Cloyd Bowman, Little; *Bright Island*
        by Mabel Robinson, Random; *On the Banks of Plum Creek* by Laura
        Ingalls Wilder, Harper

1939   *Thimble Summer* by Elizabeth Enright, Rinehart
        Honor Books: *Nino* by Valenti Angelo, Viking; *Mr. Popper's Penguins*
        by Richard and Florence Atwater, Little; *"Hello the Boat!"* by Phyllis
        Crawford, Holt; *Leader by Destiny: George Washington, Man and Patriot* by
        Jeanette Eaton, Harcourt; *Penn* by Elizabeth Janet Gray, Viking

1940 *Daniel Boone* by James Daugherty, Viking
Honor Books: *The Singing Tree* by Kate Seredy, Viking; *Runner of the Mountain Tops* by Mabel Robinson, Random; *By the Shores of Silver Lake* by Laura Ingalls Wilder, Harper; *Boy with a Pack* by Stephen W. Meader, Harcourt

1941 *Call It Courage* by Armstrong Sperry, Macmillan
Honor Books: *Blue Willow* by Doris Gates, Viking; *Young Mac of Fort Vancouver* by Mary Jane Carr, T. Crowell; *The Long Winter* by Laura Ingalls Wilder, Harper; *Nansen* by Anna Gertrude Hall, Viking

1942 *The Matchlock Gun* by Walter D. Edmonds, Dodd
Honor Books: *Little Town on the Prairie* by Laura Ingalls Wilder, Harper; *George Washington's World* by Genevieve Foster, Scribner's; *Indian Captive: The Story of Mary Jemison* by Lois Lenski, Lippincott; *Down Ryton Water* by Eva Roe Gaggin, Viking

1943 *Adam of the Road* by Elizabeth Janet Gray, Viking
Honor Books: *The Middle Moffat* by Eleanor Estes, Harcourt; *Have You Seen Tom Thumb?* by Mabel Leigh Hunt, Lippincott

1944 *Johnny Tremain* by Esther Forbes, Houghton
Honor Books: *These Happy Golden Years* by Laura Ingalls Wilder, Harper; *Fog Magic* by Julia Sauer, Viking; *Rufus M.* by Eleanor Estes, Harcourt; *Mountain Born* by Elizabeth Yates, Coward

1945 *Rabbit Hill* by Robert Lawson, Viking
Honor Books: *The Hundred Dresses* by Eleanor Estes, Harcourt; *The Silver Pencil* by Alice Dalgliesh, Scribner's; *Abraham Lincoln's World* by Genevieve Foster, Scribner's; *Lone Journey: The Life of Roger Williams* by Jeanette Eaton, Harcourt

1946 *Strawberry Girl* by Lois Lenski, Lippincott
Honor Books: *Justin Morgan Had a Horse* by Marguerite Henry, Rand; *The Moved-Outers* by Florence Crannell Means, Houghton; *Bhimsa, The Dancing Bear* by Christine Weston, Scribner's; *New Found World* by Katherine Shippen, Viking

1947 *Miss Hickory* by Carolyn Sherwin Bailey, Viking
Honor Books: *Wonderful Year* by Nancy Barnes, Messner; *Big Tree* by Mary and Conrad Buff, Viking; *The Heavenly Tenants* by William Maxwell, Harper; *The Avion My Uncle Flew* by Cyrus Fisher, Appleton; *The Hidden Treasure of Glaston* by Eleanore Jewett, Viking

1948 *The Twenty-one Balloons* by William Pène du Bois, Viking
Honor Books: *Pancakes-Paris* by Claire Huchet Bishop, Viking; *Li Lun, Lad of Courage* by Carolyn Treffinger, Abingdon; *The Quaint and Curious Quest of Johnny Longfoot* by Catherine Besterman, Bobbs; *The Cow-Tail Switch, and Other West African Stories* by Harold Courlander, Holt; *Misty of Chincoteague* by Marguerite Henry, Rand

1949 *King of the Wind* by Marguerite Henry, Rand
Honor Books: *Seabird* by Holling C. Holling, Houghton; *Daughter of the Mountains* by Louise Rankin, Viking; *My Father's Dragon* by Ruth S. Gannett, Random; *Story of the Negro* by Arna Bontemps, Knopf

1950 *The Door in the Wall* by Marguerite de Angeli, Doubleday
Honor Books: *Tree of Freedom* by Rebecca Caudill, Viking; *The Blue Cat*

of Castle Town by Catherine Coblentz, Longmans; *Kildee House* by
Rutherford Montgomery, Doubleday; *George Washington* by Genevieve
Foster, Scribner's; *Song of the Pines* by Walter and Marion Havighurst,
Winston

1951 *Amos Fortune, Free Man* by Elizabeth Yates, Aladdin
Honor Books: *Better Known as Johnny Appleseed* by Mabel Leigh Hunt,
Lippincott; *Gandhi, Fighter Without a Sword* by Jeanette Eaton, Morrow;
Abraham Lincoln, Friend of the People by Clara Ingram Judson, Follett; *The
Story of Appleby Capple* by Anne Parrish, Harper

1952 *Ginger Pye* by Eleanor Estes, Harcourt
Honor Books: *Americans Before Columbus* by Elizabeth Baity, Viking;
Minn of the Mississippi by Holling C. Holling, Houghton; *The Defender*
by Nicholas Kalashnikoff, Scribner's; *The Light at Tern Rock* by Julia
Sauer, Viking; *The Apple and the Arrow* by Mary and Conrad Buff,
Houghton

1953 *Secret of the Andes* by Ann Nolan Clark, Viking
Honor Books: *Charlotte's Web* by E. B. White, Harper; *Moccasin Trail*
by Eloise McGraw, Coward; *Red Sails to Capri* by Ann Weil, Viking;
The Bears on Hemlock Mountain by Alice Dalgliesh, Scribner's; *Birthdays
of Freedom,* Vol. 1 by Genevieve Foster, Scribner's

1954 *. . . and now Miguel* by Joseph Krumgold, T. Crowell
Honor Books: *All Alone* by Claire Huchet Bishop, Viking; *Shadrach* by
Meindert DeJong, Harper; *Hurry Home Candy* by Meindert DeJong,
Harper; *Theodore Roosevelt, Fighting Patriot* by Clara Ingram Judson,
Follett; *Magic Maize* by Mary and Conrad Buff, Houghton

1955 *The Wheel on the School* by Meindert DeJong, Harper
Honor Books: *The Courage of Sarah Noble* by Alice Dalgliesh, Scribner's;
Banner in the Sky by James Ullman, Lippincott

1956 *Carry on, Mr. Bowditch* by Jean Lee Latham, Houghton
Honor Books: *The Secret River* by Marjorie Kinnan Rawlings,
Scribner's; *The Golden Name Day* by Jennie Lindquist, Harper; *Men,
Microscopes, and Living Things* by Katherine Shippen, Viking

1957 *Miracles on Maple Hill* by Virginia Sorensen, Harcourt
Honor Books: *Old Yeller* by Fred Gipson, Harper; *The House of Sixty
Fathers* by Meindert DeJong, Harper; *Mr. Justice Holmes* by Clara
Ingram Judson, Follett; *The Corn Grows Ripe* by Dorothy Rhoads,
Viking; *Black Fox of Lorne* by Marguerite de Angeli,
Doubleday

1958 *Rifles for Watie* by Harold Keith, T. Crowell
Honor Books: *The Horsecatcher* by Mari Sandoz, Westminster;
Gone-Away Lake by Elizabeth Enright, Harcourt; *The Great Wheel* by
Robert Lawson, Viking; *Tom Paine, Freedom's Apostle* by Leo Gurko, T.
Crowell

1959 *The Witch of Blackbird Pond* by Elizabeth George Speare, Houghton
Honor Books: *The Family Under the Bridge* by Natalie S. Carlson,
Harper; *Along Came a Dog* by Meindert DeJong, Harper; *Chucaro: Wild
Pony of the Pampa* by Francis Kalnay, Harcourt; *The Perilous Road* by
William O. Steele, Harcourt

1960   *Onion John* by Joseph Krumgold, T. Crowell
Honor Books: *My Side of the Mountain* by Jean George, Dutton; *America Is Born* by Gerald W. Johnson, Morrow; *The Gammage Cup* by Carol Kendall, Harcourt

1961   *Island of the Blue Dolphins* by Scott O'Dell, Houghton
Honor Books: *America Moves Forward* by Gerald W. Johnson, Morrow; *Old Ramon* by Jack Schaefer, Houghton; *The Cricket in Times Square* by George Selden, Farrar

1962   *The Bronze Bow* by Elizabeth George Speare, Houghton
Honor Books: *Frontier Living* by Edwin Tunis, World; *The Golden Goblet* by Eloise McGraw, Coward; *Belling the Tiger* by Mary Stolz, Harper

1963   *A Wrinkle in Time* by Madeleine L'Engle, Farrar
Honor Books: *Thistle and Thyme* by Sorche Nic Leodhas, Holt; *Men of Athens* by Olivia Coolidge, Houghton

1964   *It's Like This, Cat* by Emily Cheney Neville, Harper
Honor Books: *Rascal* by Sterling North, Dutton; *The Loner* by Ester Wier, McKay

1965   *Shadow of a Bull* by Maia Wojciechowska, Atheneum
Honor Book: *Across Five Aprils* by Irene Hunt, Follett

1966   *I, Juan de Pareja* by Elizabeth Borten de Trevino, Farrar
Honor Books: *The Black Cauldron* by Lloyd Alexander, Holt; *The Animal Family* by Randall Jarrell, Pantheon; *The Noonday Friends* by Mary Stolz, Harper

1967   *Up a Road Slowly* by Irene Hunt, Follett
Honor Books: *The King's Fifth* by Scott O'Dell, Houghton; *Zlateh the Goat and Other Stories* by Isaac Bashevis Singer, Harper; *The Jazz Man* by Mary H. Weik, Atheneum

1968   *From the Mixed-Up Files of Mrs. Basil E. Frankweiler* by E. L. Konigsburg, Atheneum
Honor Books: *Jennifer, Hecate, Macbeth, William McKinley, and Me, Elizabeth* by E. L. Konigsburg, Atheneum; *The Black Pearl* by Scott O'Dell, Houghton; *The Fearsome Inn* by Isaac Bashevis Singer, Scribner's; *The Egypt Game* by Zilpha Keatley Snyder, Atheneum

1969   *The High King* by Lloyd Alexander, Holt
Honor Books: *To Be a Slave* by Julius Lester, Dial; *When Shlemiel Went to Warsaw and Other Stories* by Isaac Bashevis Singer, Farrar

1970   *Sounder* by William H. Armstrong, Harper
Honor Books: *Our Eddie* by Sulamith Ish-Kishor, Pantheon; *The Many Ways of Seeing: An Introduction to the Pleasures of Art* by Janet Gaylord Moore, World; *Journey Outside* by Mary Q. Steele, Viking

1971   *Summer of the Swans* by Betsy Byars, Viking
Honor Books: *Kneeknock Rise* by Natalie Babbitt, Farrar; *Enchantress from the Stars* by Sylvia Louise Engdahl, Atheneum; *Sing Down the Moon* by Scott O'Dell, Houghton

1972   *Mrs. Frisby and the Rats of NIMH* by Robert C. O'Brien, Atheneum
Honor Books: *Incident at Hawk's Hill* by Allan W. Eckert, Little; *The Planet of Junior Brown* by Virginia Hamilton, Macmillan; *The Tombs of Atuan* by Ursula K. Le Guin, Atheneum; *Annie and the Old One* by

Miska Miles, Atlantic/Little; *The Headless Cupid* by Zilpha Keatley Snyder, Atheneum

1973 *Julie of the Wolves* by Jean George, Harper
Honor Books: *Frog and Toad Together* by Arnold Lobel, Harper; *The Upstairs Room* by Johanna Reiss, Crowell; *The Witches of Worm* by Zilpha Keatley Snyder, Atheneum

1974 *The Slave Dancer* by Paula Fox, Bradbury
Honor Book: *The Dark Is Rising* by Susan Cooper, Atheneum/McElderry

1975 *M. C. Higgins, the Great* by Virginia Hamilton, Macmillan
Honor Books: *Figgs & Phantoms* by Ellen Raskin, Dutton; *My Brother Sam Is Dead* by James Lincoln Collier & Christopher Collier, Four Winds; *The Perilous Gard* by Elizabeth Marie Pope, Houghton; *Philip Hall Likes Me, I Reckon Maybe* by Bette Greene, Dial

1976 *The Grey King* by Susan Cooper, Atheneum/McElderry
Honor Books: *The Hundred Penny Box* by Sharon Bell Mathis, Viking; *Dragonwings* by Lawrence Yep, Harper

1977 *Roll of Thunder, Hear My Cry* by Mildred D. Taylor, Dial
Honor Books: *Abel's Island* by William Steig, Farrar; *A String in the Harp* by Nancy Bond, Atheneum/McElderry

1978 *Bridge to Terabithia* by Katherine Paterson, Crowell
Honor Books: *Anpao: An American Indian Odyssey* by Jamake Highwater, Lippincott; *Ramona and Her Father* by Beverly Cleary, Morrow

1979 *The Westing Game* by Ellen Raskin, Dutton
Honor Book: *The Great Gilly Hopkins* by Katherine Paterson, Crowell

1980 *A Gathering of Days: A New England Girl's Journal, 1830–32* by Joan Blos, Scribner's
Honor Book: *The Road from Home: The Story of an Armenian Girl* by David Kherdian, Greenwillow

1981 *Jacob Have I Loved* by Katherine Paterson, Crowell
Honor Books: *The Fledgling* by Jane Langton, Harper; *A Ring of Endless Light* by Madeleine L'Engle, Farrar

THE CALDECOTT MEDAL

Since 1938, the Children's Services Division of the American Library Association has awarded the Caldecott Medal to the illustrator of the most outstanding picture book published in the United States in the preceding year. The recipient must be a citizen or resident of the United States. The medal is named in tribute to the well-loved English illustrator Randolph Caldecott (1846–1886).

1938 *Animals of the Bible* by Helen Dean Fish, ill. by Dorothy P. Lathrop, Lippincott
Honor Books: *Seven Simeons* written and ill. by Boris Artzybasheff,

Viking; *Four and Twenty Blackbirds* by Helen Dean Fish, ill. by Robert Lawson, Stokes

1939   *Mei Li* written and ill. by Thomas Handforth, Doubleday
Honor Books: *The Forest Pool* written and ill. by Laura Adams Armer, Longmans; *Wee Gillis* by Munro Leaf, ill. by Robert Lawson, Viking; *Snow White and the Seven Dwarfs* written and ill. by Wanda Gág, Coward; *Barkis* written and ill. by Clare Newberry, Harper; *Andy and the Lion* written and ill. by James Daugherty, Viking

1940   *Abraham Lincoln* written and ill. by Ingri and Edgar Parin d'Aulaire, Doubleday
Honor Books: *Cock-A-Doodle Doo* . . . written and ill. by Berta and Elmer Hader, Macmillan; *Madeline* written and ill. by Ludwig Bemelmans, Viking; *The Ageless Story,* ill. by Lauren Ford, Dodd

1941   *They Were Strong and Good* written and ill. by Robert Lawson, Viking
Honor Book: *April's Kittens* written and ill. by Clare Newberry, Harper

1942   *Make Way for Ducklings* written and ill. by Robert McCloskey, Viking
Honor Books: *An American ABC* written and ill. by Maud and Miska Petersham, Macmillan; *In My Mother's House* by Ann Nolan Clark, ill. by Velino Herrera, Viking; *Paddle-to-the-Sea* written and ill. by Holling C. Holling, Houghton; *Nothing at All* written and ill. by Wanda Gág, Coward

1943   *The Little House* written and ill. by Virginia Lee Burton, Houghton
Honor Books: *Dash and Dart* written and ill. by Mary and Conrad Buff, Viking; *Marshmallow* written and ill. by Clare Newberry, Harper

1944   *Many Moons* by James Thurber, ill. by Louis Slobodkin, Harcourt
Honor Books: *Small Rain: Verses from the Bible* selected by Jessie Orton Jones, ill. by Elizabeth Orton Jones. Viking; *Pierre Pigeon* by Lee Kingman, ill. by Arnold E. Bare, Houghton; *The Mighty Hunter* written and ill. by Berta and Elmer Hader, Macmillan; *A Child's Good Night Book* by Margaret Wise Brown, ill. by Jean Charlot, W. R. Scott; *Good Luck Horse* by Chih-Yi Chan, ill. by Plao Chan, Whittlesey

1945   *Prayer for a Child* by Rachel Field, ill. by Elizabeth Orton Jones, Macmillan
Honor Books: *Mother Goose* ill. by Tasha Tudor, Walck; *In the Forest* written and ill. by Marie Hall Ets, Viking; *Yonie Wondernose* written and ill. by Marguerite de Angeli, Doubleday; *The Christmas Anna Angel* by Ruth Sawyer, ill. by Kate Seredy, Viking

1946   *The Rooster Crows* . . . (traditional Mother Goose) ill. by Maud and Miska Petersham, Macmillan
Honor Books: *Little Lost Lamb* by Golden MacDonald, ill. by Leonard Weisgard, Doubleday; *Sing Mother Goose* by Opal Wheeler, ill. by Marjorie Torrey, Dutton; *My Mother Is the Most Beautiful Woman in the World* by Becky Reyher, ill. by Ruth Gannett, Lothrop; *You Can Write Chinese* written and ill. by Kurt Wiese, Viking

1947   *The Little Island* by Golden MacDonald, ill. by Leonard Weisgard, Doubleday
Honor Books: *Rain Drop Splash* by Alvin Tresselt, ill. by Leonard

Weisgard, Lothrop; *Boats on the River* by Marjorie Flack, ill. by Jay Hyde Barnum, Viking; *Timothy Turtle* by Al Graham, ill. by Tony Palazzo, Viking; *Pedro, the Angel of Olvera Street* written and ill. by Leo Politi, Scribner's; *Sing in Praise: A Collection of the Best Loved Hymns* by Opal Wheeler, ill. by Marjorie Torrey, Dutton

1948   *White Snow, Bright Snow* by Alvin Tresselt, ill. by Roger Duvoisin, Lothrop
Honor Books: *Stone Soup* written and ill. by Marcia Brown, Scribner's; *McElligot's Pool* written and ill. by Dr. Seuss, Random; *Bambino the Clown* written and ill. by George Schreiber, Viking; *Roger and the Fox* by Lavinia Davis, ill. by Hildegard Woodward, Doubleday; *Song of Robin Hood* ed. by Anne Malcolmson, ill. by Virginia Lee Burton, Houghton

1949   *The Big Snow* written and ill. by Berta and Elmer Hader, Macmillan
Honor Books: *Blueberries for Sal* written and ill. by Robert McCloskey, Viking; *All Around the Town* by Phyllis McGinley, ill. by Helen Stone, Lippincott; *Juanita* written and ill. by Leo Politi, Scribner's; *Fish in the Air* written and ill. by Kurt Wiese, Viking

1950   *Song of the Swallows* written and ill. by Leo Politi, Scribner's
Honor Books: *America's Ethan Allen* by Stewart Holbrook, ill. by Lynd Ward, Houghton; *The Wild Birthday Cake* by Lavinia Davis, ill. by Hildegard Woodward, Doubleday; *The Happy Day* by Ruth Krauss, ill. by Marc Simont, Harper; *Bartholomew and the Oobleck* written and ill. by Dr. Seuss, Random; *Henry Fisherman* written and ill. by Marcia Brown, Scribner's

1951   *The Egg Tree* written and ill. by Katherine Milhous, Scribner's
Honor Books: *Dick Whittington and His Cat* written and ill. by Marcia Brown, Scribner's; *The Two Reds* by Will, ill. by Nicolas, Harcourt; *If I Ran the Zoo* written and ill. by Dr. Seuss, Random; *The Most Wonderful Doll in the World* by Phyllis McGinley, ill. by Helen Stone, Lippincott; *T-Bone, the Baby Sitter* written and ill. by Clare Newberry, Harper

1952   *Finders Keepers* by Will, ill. by Nicolas, Harcourt
Honor Books: *Mr. T. W. Anthony Woo* written and ill. by Marie Hall Ets, Viking; *Skipper John's Cook* written and ill. by Marcia Brown, Scribner's; *All Falling Down* by Gene Zion, ill. by Margaret Bloy Graham, Harper; *Bear Party* written and ill. by William Pène du Bois, Viking; *Feather Mountain* written and ill. by Elizabeth Olds, Houghton

1953   *The Biggest Bear* written and ill. by Lynd Ward, Houghton
Honor Books: *Puss in Boots* by Charles Perrault, ill. and tr. by Marcia Brown, Scribner's; *One Morning in Maine* written and ill. by Robert McCloskey, Viking; *Ape in a Cape* written and ill. by Fritz Eichenberg, Harcourt; *The Storm Book* by Charlotte Zolotow, ill. by Margaret Bloy Graham, Harper; *Five Little Monkeys* written and ill. by Juliet Kepes, Houghton

1954   *Madeline's Rescue* written and ill. by Ludwig Bemelmans, Viking
Honor Books: *Journey Cake, Ho!* by Ruth Sawyer, ill. by Robert McCloskey, Viking; *When Will the World Be Mine?* by Miriam Schlein, ill. by Jean Charlot, W. R. Scott; *The Steadfast Tin Soldier* by Hans

Christian Andersen, ill. by Marcia Brown, Scribner's; *A Very Special House* by Ruth Krauss, ill. by Maurice Sendak, Harper; *Green Eyes* written and ill. by A. Birnbaum, Capitol

1955 *Cinderella, or the Little Glass Slipper* by Charles Perrault, tr. and ill. by Marcia Brown, Scribner's
Honor Books: *Book of Nursery and Mother Goose Rhymes,* ill. by Marguerite de Angeli, Doubleday; *Wheel on the Chimney* by Margaret Wise Brown, ill. by Tibor Gergely, Lippincott; *The Thanksgiving Story* by Alice Dalgliesh, ill. by Helen Sewell, Scribner's

1956 *Frog Went A-Courtin'* ed. by John Langstaff, ill. by Feodor Rojankovsky, Harcourt
Honor Books: *Play with Me* written and ill. by Marie Hall Ets, Viking; *Crow Boy* written and ill. by Taro Yashima, Viking

1957 *A Tree Is Nice* by Janice May Udry, ill. by Marc Simont, Harper
Honor Books: *Mr. Penny's Race Horse* written and ill. by Marie Hall Ets, Viking; *1 Is One* written and ill. by Tasha Tudor, Walck; *Anatole* by Eve Titus, ill. by Paul Galdone, McGraw; *Gillespie and the Guards* by Benjamin Elkin, ill. by James Daugherty, Viking; *Lion* written and ill. by William Pène du Bois, Viking

1958 *Time of Wonder* written and ill. by Robert McCloskey, Viking
Honor Books: *Fly High, Fly Low* written and ill. by Don Freeman, Viking; *Anatole and the Cat* by Eve Titus, ill. by Paul Galdone, McGraw

1959 *Chanticleer and the Fox* adapted from Chaucer and ill. by Barbara Cooney, T. Crowell
Honor Books: *The House That Jack Built* written and ill. by Antonio Frasconi, Harcourt; *What Do You Say, Dear?* by Sesyle Joslin, ill. by Maurice Sendak, W. R. Scott; *Umbrella* written and ill. by Taro Yashima, Viking

1960 *Nine Days to Christmas* by Marie Hall Ets and Aurora Labastida, ill. by Marie Hall Ets, Viking
Honor Books: *Houses from the Sea* by Alice E. Goudey, ill. by Adrienne Adams, Scribner's; *The Moon Jumpers* by Janice May Udry, ill. by Maurice Sendak, Harper

1961 *Baboushka and the Three Kings* by Ruth Robbins, ill. by Nicolas Sidjakov, Parnassus
Honor Book: *Inch by Inch* written and ill. by Leo Lionni, Obolensky

1962 *Once a Mouse . . .* written and ill. by Marcia Brown, Scribner's
Honor Books: *The Fox Went Out on a Chilly Night* written and ill. by Peter Spier, Doubleday; *Little Bear's Visit* by Else Holmelund Minarik, ill. by Maurice Sendak, Harper; *The Day We Saw the Sun Come Up* by Alice E. Goudey, ill. by Adrienne Adams, Scribner's

1963 *The Snowy Day* written and ill. by Ezra Jack Keats, Viking
Honor Books: *The Sun Is a Golden Earring* by Natalia M. Belting, ill. by Bernarda Bryson, Holt; *Mr. Rabbit and the Lovely Present* by Charlotte Zolotow, ill. by Maurice Sendak, Harper

1964 *Where the Wild Things Are* written and ill. by Maurice Sendak, Harper
Honor Books: *Swimmy* written and ill. by Leo Lionni, Pantheon; *All in*

the Morning Early by Sorche Nic Leodhas, ill. by Evaline Ness, Holt;
Mother Goose and Nursery Rhymes ill. by Philip Reed, Atheneum

1965   *May I Bring a Friend?* by Beatrice Schenk de Regniers, ill. by Beni
Montresor, Atheneum
Honor Books: *Rain Makes Applesauce* by Julian Scheer, ill. by Marvin
Bileck, Holiday; *The Wave* by Margaret Hodges, ill. by Blair Lent,
Houghton; *A Pocketful of Cricket* by Rebecca Caudill, ill. by Evaline
Ness, Holt

1966   *Always Room for One More* by Sorche Nic Leodhas, ill. by Nonny
Hogrogian, Holt
Honor Books: *Hide and Seek Fog* by Alvin Tresselt, ill. by Roger
Duvoisin, Lothrop; *Just Me* written and ill. by Marie Hall Ets, Viking;
Tom Tit Tot written and ill. by Evaline Ness, Scribner's

1967   *Sam, Bangs & Moonshine* written and ill. by Evaline Ness, Holt
Honor Book: *One Wide River to Cross* by Barbara Emberley, ill. by Ed
Emberley, Prentice

1968   *Drummer Hoff* by Barbara Emberley, ill. by Ed Emberley, Prentice
Honor Books: *Frederick* written and ill. by Leo Lionni, Pantheon;
Seashore Story written and ill. by Taro Yashima, Viking; *The Emperor and
the Kite* by Jane Yolen, ill. by Ed Young, World

1969   *The Fool of the World and the Flying Ship* by Arthur Ransome, ill. by Uri
Shulevitz, Farrar
Honor Book: *Why the Sun and the Moon Live in the Sky* by Elphinstone
Dayrell, ill. by Blair Lent, Houghton

1970   *Sylvester and the Magic Pebble* written and ill. by William Steig,
Windmill
Honor Books: *Goggles!* written and ill. by Ezra Jack Keats, Macmillan;
Alexander and the Wind-Up Mouse written and ill. by Leo Lionni,
Pantheon; *Pop Corn & Ma Goodness* by Edna Mitchell Preston, ill. by
Robert Andrew Parker, Viking; *Thy Friend, Obadiah* written and ill. by
Brinton Turkle, Viking; *The Judge* by Harve Zemach, ill. by Margot
Zemach, Farrar

1971   *A Story—A Story* written and ill. by Gail E. Haley, Atheneum
Honor Books: *The Angry Moon* by William Sleator, ill. by Blair Lent,
Atlantic/Little; *Frog and Toad Are Friends* written and ill. by Arnold
Lobel, Harper; *In the Night Kitchen* written and ill. by Maurice Sendak,
Harper

1972   *One Fine Day* written and ill. by Nonny Hogrogian, Macmillan
Honor Books: *If All the Seas Were One Sea* written and ill. by Janina
Domanska, Macmillan; *Moja Means One: Swahili Counting Book* by
Muriel Feelings, ill. by Tom Feelings, Dial; *Hildilid's Night* by Cheli
Duran Ryan, ill. by Arnold Lobel, Macmillan

1973   *The Funny Little Woman* retold by Arlene Mosel, ill. by Blair Lent,
Dutton
Honor Books: *Anansi the Spider* adapted and ill. by Gerald
McDermott, Holt; *Hosie's Alphabet* by Hosea, Tobias and Lisa Baskin,

ill. by Leonard Baskin, Viking; *Snow-White and the Seven Dwarfs*
translated by Randall Jarrell, ill. by Nancy Ekholm Burkert, Farrar;
When Clay Sings by Byrd Baylor, ill. by Tom Bahti,
Scribner's

1974 *Duffy and the Devil* by Harve Zemach, ill. by Margot Zemach, Farrar
Honor Books: *Three Jovial Huntsmen* written and ill. by Susan Jeffers,
Bradbury; *Cathedral: The Story of Its Construction* written and ill. by
David Macaulay, Houghton

1975 *Arrow to the Sun* adapted and ill. by Gerald McDermott, Viking
Honor Book: *Jambo Means Hello* by Muriel Feelings, ill. by Tom
Feelings, Dial

1976 *Why Mosquitoes Buzz in People's Ears* retold by Verna Aardema, ill. by
Leo and Diane Dillon, Dial
Honor Books: *The Desert Is Theirs* by Byrd Baylor, ill. by Peter Parnall,
Scribner's; *Strega Nona* retold and ill. by Tomie de Paola, Prentice

1977 *Ashanti to Zulu: African Traditions* by Margaret Musgrove, ill. by Leo
and Diane Dillon, Dial
Honor Books: *The Amazing Bone* written and ill. by William Steig,
Farrar; *The Contest* retold & ill. by Nonny Hogrogian, Greenwillow;
Fish for Supper written and ill. by M. B. Goffstein, Dial; *The Golem*
written and ill. by Beverly Brodsky McDermott, Lippincott; *Hawk,
I'm Your Brother* by Byrd Baylor, ill. by Peter Parnall, Scribner's

1978 *Noah's Ark* ill. by Peter Spier, Doubleday
Honor Books: *Castle* written and ill. by David Macaulay, Houghton;
It Could Always Be Worse retold & ill. by Margot Zemach, Farrar

1979 *The Girl Who Loved Wild Horses* written and ill. by Paul Goble,
Bradbury
Honor Books: *Freight Train* written and ill. by Donald Crews,
Greenwillow; *The Way to Start a Day* by Byrd Baylor, ill. by Peter
Parnall, Scribner's

1980 *Ox-Cart Man* by Donald Hall, ill. by Barbara Cooney, Viking
Honor Books: *Ben's Trumpet* written and ill. by Rachel Isadora,
Greenwillow; *The Garden of Abdul Gasazi* written and ill. by Chris Van
Allsburg, Houghton

1981 *Fables* written and ill. by Arnold Lobel, Harper
Honor Books: *The Grey Lady and the Strawberry Snatcher,* ill. by Molly
Bangs; *Truck* ill. by Donald Crews, Greenwillow; *Mice Twice,* written
and ill. by Joseph Low, Atheneum; *The Brementown Musicians,* ill. by
Ilse Plume, Doubleday

THE LAURA INGALLS WILDER AWARD

This award was first given in 1954, and since 1960 has been presented every
five years by the Association for Library Services. The award recognizes an

author or illustrator whose works, published in the United States, have made a major contribution to children's literature.

1954   Laura Ingalls Wilder
1960   Clara Ingram Judson
1965   Ruth Sawyer
1970   E. B. White
1975   Beverly Cleary
1980   Theodor Geisel (Dr. Seuss)

THE NATIONAL BOOK AWARD

Since 1969, the National Book Award for Children's Literature has been given annually to the American author of the most significant juvenile book published in the United States during the previous year.

1969   *Journey from Peppermint Street* by Meindert DeJong, Harper
1970   *A Day of Pleasure: Stories of a Boy Growing Up in Warsaw* by Isaac Bashevis Singer, Farrar
1971   *The Marvelous Misadventures of Sebastian* by Lloyd Alexander, Dutton
1972   *The Slightly Irregular Fire Engine* by Donald Barthelme, Farrar
1973   *The Farthest Shore* by Ursula K. Le Guin, Atheneum
1974   *The Court of the Stone Children* by Eleanor Cameron, Dutton
1975   *M. C. Higgins, The Great* by Virginia Hamilton, Macmillan
1976   *Bert Breen's Barn* by Walter D. Edmonds, Little
1977   *The Master Puppeteer* by Katherine Paterson, Crowell
1978   *The View from the Oak* by Judith and Herbert Kohl, Scribner's
1979   *The Great Gilly Hopkins* by Katherine Paterson, Crowell
1980   *A Gathering of Days: A New England Girl's Journal, 1830–1832,* Joan Blos, Scribner's

NATIONAL COUNCIL OF TEACHERS OF ENGLISH AWARD FOR EXCELLENCE IN POETRY FOR CHILDREN

This annual (since 1977) award is presented by the National Council of Teachers of English to a living American poet whose works have made a substantial contribution to children's literature.

1977   David McCord
1978   Aileen Fisher
1979   Karla Kuskin
1980   Myra Cohn Livingston
1981   Eve Merriam

THE CARNEGIE MEDAL

The British Library Association gives this medal each year to the author of a distinguished children's book written in English and first published in the United Kingdom. The award was established in 1937.

1936 *Pigeon Post* by Arthur Ransome, Cape
1937 *The Family from One End Street* by Eve Garnett, Muller
1938 *The Circus Is Coming* by Noel Streatfeild, Dent
1939 *Radium Woman* by Eleanor Doorly, Heinemann
1940 *Visitors from London* by Kitty Barne, Dent
1941 *We Couldn't Leave Dinah* by Mary Treadgold, Penguin
1942 *The Little Grey Men,* by B. B., Eyre & Spottiswoode
1943 No Award
1944 *The Wind on the Moon* by Eric Linklater, Macmillan
1945 No Award
1946 *The Little White Horse* by Elizabeth Goudge, Brockhampton Press
1947 *Collected Stories for Children* by Walter de la Mare, Faber
1948 *Sea Change* by Richard Armstrong, Dent
1949 *The Story of Your Home* by Agnes Allen, Transatlantic
1950 *The Lark on the Wing* by Elfrida Vipont Foulds, Oxford
1951 *The Wool-Pack* by Cynthia Harnett, Methuen
1952 *The Borrowers* by Mary Norton, Dent
1953 *A Valley Grows Up* by Edward Osmond, Oxford
1954 *Knight Crusader* by Ronald Welch, Oxford
1955 *The Little Bookroom* by Eleanor Farjeon, Oxford
1956 *The Last Battle* by C. S. Lewis, Bodley Head
1957 *A Grass Rope* by William Mayne, Oxford
1958 *Tom's Midnight Garden* by Philippa Pearce, Oxford
1959 *The Lantern Bearers* by Rosemary Sutcliff, Oxford
1960 *The Making of Man* by I. W. Cornwall, Phoenix
1961 *A Stranger at Green Knowe* by Lucy Boston, Faber
1962 *The Twelve and the Genii* by Pauline Clarke, Faber
1963 *Time of Trial* by Hester Burton, Oxford
1964 *Nordy Banks* by Sheena Porter, Oxford
1965 *The Grange at High Force* by Philip Turner, Oxford
1966 No Award
1967 *The Owl Service* by Alan Garner, Collins
1968 *The Moon in the Cloud* by Rosemary Harris, Faber
1969 *The Edge of the Cloud* by K. M. Peyton, Oxford
1970 *The God Beneath the Sea* by Leon Garfield and Edward Blishen, Kestrel
1971 *Josh* by Ivan Southall, Angus & Robertson
1972 *Watership Down* by Richard Adams, Rex Collings
1973 *The Ghost of Thomas Kempe* by Penelope Lively, Heinemann
1974 *The Stronghold* by Mollie Hunter, Hamilton
1975 *The Machine-Gunners* by Robert Westall, Macmillan
1976 *Thunder and Lightnings* by Jan Mark, Kestrel

1977   *The Turbulent Term of Tyke Tiler* by Gene Kemp, Faber
1978   *The Exeter Blitz* by David Rees, Hamish Hamilton
1979   *Tulku* by Peter Dickinson, Dutton

THE KATE GREENAWAY MEDAL

The Kate Greenaway Medal, given annually by the British Library
Association, recognizes the outstanding illustration of a children's book first
published in the United Kingdom in the preceding year.

1956   *Tim All Alone* written and ill. by Edward Ardizzone, Oxford
1957   *Mrs. Easter and the Storks* written and ill. by V. H. Drummond,
        Faber
1958   No Award
1959   *Kashtanka and a Bundle of Ballads* written and ill. by William Stobbs,
        Oxford
1960   *Old Winkle and the Seagulls* by Elizabeth Rose, ill. by Gerald Rose,
        Faber
1961   *Mrs. Cockle's Cat* by Philippa Pearce, ill. by Antony Maitland,
        Kestrel
1962   *Brian Wildsmith's ABC* written and ill. by Brian Wildsmith, Oxford
1963   *Borka* written and ill. by John Burningham, Cape
1964   *Shakespeare's Theatre* written and ill. by C. W. Hodges, Oxford
1965   *Three Poor Tailors* written and ill. by Victor Ambrus, Hamilton
1966   *Mother Goose Treasury* written and ill. by Raymond Briggs,
        Hamilton
1967   *Charlie, Charlotte & the Golden Canary* written and ill. by Charles
        Keeping, Oxford
1968   *Dictionary of Chivalry* by Grant Uden, ill. by Pauline Baynes, Kestrel
1969   *The Quangle-Wangle's Hat* by Edward Lear, ill. by Helen Oxenbury,
        Heinemann; *Dragon of an Ordinary Family* by Margaret May Mahy, ill.
        by Helen Oxenbury, Heinemann
1970   *Mr. Gumpy's Outing* written and ill. by John Burningham, Cape
1971   *The Kingdom Under the Sea* written and ill. by Jan Pienkowski, Cape
1972   *The Woodcutter's Duck* written and ill. by Krystyna Turska,
        Hamilton
1973   *Father Christmas* written and ill. by Raymond Briggs, Hamilton
1974   *The Wind Blew* written and ill. by Pat Hutchins, Bodley Head
1975   *Horses in Battle* written and ill. by Victor Ambrus, Oxford; *Mishka*
        written and ill. by Victor Ambrus, Oxford
1976   *The Post Office Cat* written and ill. by Gail E. Haley, Bodley Head
1977   *Dogger* written and ill. by Shirley Hughes, Bodley Head
1978   *Each Peach Pear Plum* written and ill. by Janet and Allan Ahlberg,
        Kestrel
1979   *Haunted House* written and ill. by Jan Pienkowski, Dutton

THE CANADIAN LIBRARY AWARDS

This award is given each year (since 1947) by the Canadian Library Association to a distinguished children's book authored by a citizen of Canada. A similar medal has been given annually (since 1954) to a significant children's book published in French.

1947 *Starbuck Valley Winter* by Roderick Haig-Brown, Collins
1948 *Kristli's Trees* by Mabel Dunham, Hale
1949 No Award
1950 *Franklin of the Arctic* by Richard S. Lambert, McClelland & Stewart
1951 No Award
1952 *The Sun Horse* by Catherine Anthony Clark, Macmillan of Canada
1953 No Award
1954 No English Award
  Mgr. de Laval by Emile S. J. Gervais, Comité des Fondateurs de l'Eglise Canadienne
1955 No Awards
1956 *Train for Tiger Lily* by Louise Riley, Macmillan of Canada
  No French Award
1957 *Glooskap's Country* by Cyrus Macmillan, Oxford
  No French Award
1958 *Lost in the Barrens* by Farley Mowat, Little
  Le Chevalier du Roi by Béatrice Clément, Les Editions de l'Atelier
1959 *The Dangerous Cove* by John F. Hayes, Copp Clark
  Un Drôle de Petit Cheval by Hélène Flamme, Editions Léméac
1960 *The Golden Phoenix* by Marius Barbeau and Michael Hornyansky, Walck
  L'Eté Enchanté by Paule Daveluy, Les Editions de l'Atelier
1961 *The St. Lawrence* by William Toye, Oxford
  Plantes Vagabondes by Marcelle Gauvreau, Centre de Psychologie et de Pédagogie
1962 No English Award
  Les Iles du Roi Maha Maha II by Claude Aubry, Les Editions du Pélican
1963 *The Incredible Journey* by Sheila Burnford, Little
  Drôle d'Automne by Paule Daveluy, Les Editions du Pélican
1964 *The Whale People* by Roderick Haig-Brown, William Collins of Canada
  Feerie by Cécile Chabot, Librairie Beauchemin Ltée.
1965 *Tales of Nanabozho* by Dorothy Reid, Oxford
  Le Loup de Noël by Claude Aubry, Centre de Psychologie de Montréal
1966 *Tikta'Liktak* by James Houston, Kestrel
  Le Chêne des Tempêtes by Andrée Maillet-Hobden, Fides
  The Double Knights by James McNeal, Walck
  Le Wapiti by Monique Corriveau, Jeunesse
1967 *Raven's Cry* by Christie Harris, McClelland & Stewart
  No French Award

1968   *The White Archer* by James Houston, Kestrel
        Légendes Indiennes du Canada by Claude Mélancon, Editions du Jour
1969   *And Tomorrow the Stars* by Kay Hill, Dodd
        No French Award
1970   *Sally Go Round the Sun* by Edith Fowke, McClelland & Stewart
        Le Merveilleuse Histoire de la Naissance by Lionel Gendron, Les Editions
        de l'Homme
1971   *Cartier Discovers the St. Lawrence* by William Toye, Oxford University
        La Surprise de Dame Chenille by Henriette Major, Centre de Psychologie
        de Montréal
1972   *Mary of Mile 18* by Ann Blades, Tundra
        No French Award
1973   *The Marrow of the World* by Ruth Nichols, Macmillan of Canada
        Le Petit Sapin Qui A Poussé sur une Étoile by Simone Bussières, Presses
        Laurentiennes
1974   *The Miraculous Hind* by Elizabeth Cleaver, Holt of Canada
        No French Award
1975   *Alligator Pie* by Dennis Lee, Macmillan of Canada
        No French Award
1976   *Jacob Two-Two Meets the Hooded Fang* by Mordecai Richler, Knopf
        No French Award
1977   *Mouse Woman and the Vanished Princesses* by Christie Harris, McClelland
        & Stewart
        No French Award
1978   *Garbage Delight* by Dennis Lee, Macmillan
        No French Award
1979   *Hold Fast* by Kevin Major, Clarke, Irwin
        No French Award
1980   *River Runners: A Tale of Hardship and Bravery* by James Houston,
        McClelland & Stewart
        No French Award

Each year since 1971, the Canadian Library Association has given the
Amelia Frances Howard-Gibbon medal for excellence in illustration of a
children's book published in Canada. The recipient must be a citizen or
resident of Canada.

1971   *The Wind Has Wings,* ed. by Mary Alice Downie and Barbara
        Robertson, ill. by Elizabeth Cleaver, Oxford
1972   *A Child in Prison Camp* written and ill. by Shizuye Takashima, Tundra
1973   *Au Dela du Soleil/Beyond the Sun* written and ill. by Jacques de Roussan,
        Tundra
1974   *A Prairie Boy's Winter* written and ill. by William Kurelek, Tundra
1975   *The Sleighs of My Childhood/Les Traineaux de Mon Enfance* written and ill.
        by Carlos Italiano, Tundra
1976   *A Prairie Boy's Summer* written and ill. by William Kurelek, Tundra
1977   *Down by Jim Long's Stage: Rhymes for Children and Young Fish* by Al
        Pittman, ill. by Pam Hall, Breakwater

1978   *The Loon's Necklace* by William Toye, ill. by Elizabeth Cleaver, Oxford
1979   *A Salmon for Simon* by Betty Waterton, ill. by Ann Blades, Douglas & McIntyre
1980   *The Twelve Dancing Princesses* written and ill. by Laszlo Gal, Methuen

THE HANS CHRISTIAN ANDERSEN AWARD

The International Board on Books for Young People awards this honor every two years to a living author whose works have made a substantial and international contribution to children's literature. This award was established in 1956. Since 1966, the Board has also awarded an artist's medal.

1956   Eleanor Farjeon (Great Britain)
1958   Astrid Lindgren (Sweden)
1960   Erich Kästner (Germany)
1962   Meindert DeJong (U.S.A.)
1964   René Guillot (France)
1966   Author: Tove Jansson (Finland)
       Illustrator: Alois Carigiet (Switzerland)
1968   Authors: James Krüss (Germany), Jose Maria Sanchez-Silva (Spain)
       Illustrator: Jiri Trnka (Czechoslovakia)
1970   Author: Gianni Rodari (Italy)
       Illustrator: Maurice Sendak (U.S.A.)
1972   Author: Scott O'Dell (U.S.A.)
       Illustrator: Ib Spang Olsen (Denmark)
1974   Author: Maria Gripe (Sweden)
       Illustrator: Farshid Mesghali (Iran)
1976   Author: Cecil Bødker (Denmark)
       Illustrator: Tatjana Mawrina (U.S.S.R.)
1978   Author: Paula Fox (U.S.A.)
       Illustrator: Svend Otto S. (Denmark)
1980   Author: Bohumil Riha (Czechoslovakia)
       Illustrator: Suekichi Akaba (Japan)

Emily Dickinson. "The Moon was but a Chin of Gold" and "There is No Frigate Like a Book" by Emily Dickinson. Reprinted by permission of the publishers and the Trustees of Amherst College from *The Poems of Emily Dickinson*, edited by Thomas H. Johnson, Cambridge, Mass.: The Belknap Press of the Harvard University Press, Copyright 1951, © 1955, 1979 by the President and Fellows of Harvard College.

Walter D. Edmonds. *Bert Breen's Barn.* Boston: Little, Brown and Company, 1975, pp. 179, 183.

Eleanor Estes. *The Moffats.* New York: Harcourt Brace Jovanovich, Inc., 1941.

Eleanor Farjeon. "Pencil and Paint" by Eleanor Farjeon. Copyright 1926, renewed 1954 by Eleanor Farjeon. Reprinted by permission of J. B. Lippincott Company and Harold Ober Associates Incorporated.

Carol Fenner. Excerpt from *Gorilla Gorilla* by Carol Fenner. Copyright © 1973 by Carol Fenner Williams. Reprinted by permission of Random House, Inc.

Paula Fox. *The Slave Dancer.* Scarsdale, New York: Bradbury Press, 1973, p. 87.

Anne Frank. Excerpts from *Anne Frank: The Diary of a Young Girl* by Anne Frank. Copyright 1952 by Otto H. Frank. Reprinted by permission of Doubleday & Company, Inc. and Vallentine, Mitchell & Co., Ltd., Publishers.

Jean Craighead George. *The Moon of the Grey Wolves.* New York: Thomas Y. Crowell Company, 1969, pp. 10–11.

Jean Craighead George. *Spring Comes to the Ocean.* New York: Thomas Y. Crowell Company, 1965, p. 6.

Jean Craighead George. *The Moon of the Monarch Butterflies.* New York: Thomas Y. Crowell Company, 1968, p. 5.

Alice E. Goudey. Excerpts from *Here Come the Wild Dogs!* by Alice E. Goudey. Copyright © 1958 by Alice E. Goudey. Reprinted by permission of the publisher, Charles Scribner's Sons.

Kenneth Grahame. Excerpts reprinted by permission of Charles Scribner's Sons from *The Wind in the Willows* by Kenneth Grahame. Copyright 1908 Charles Scribner's Sons.

Nikki Grimes. Excerpts from *Something on My Mind*, words by Nikki Grimes. © 1978 by Nikki Grimes. Reprinted with permission of Dial Press.

Susan Heimann. *Christopher Columbus.* New York: Watts, 1973.

Patricia Hubbell. "Night" by Patricia Hubbell. From Patricia Hubbell, *Apple Vendor's Fair.* Copyright © 1963 by Patricia Hubbell (New York: Atheneum, 1963) Reprinted with the permission of Atheneum Publishers.

Patricia Hubbell. "Concrete Mixers" by Patricia Hubbell. From Patricia Hubbell, *8 A.M. Shadows.* Copyright © 1965 by Patricia Hubbell (New York: Atheneum, 1965) Reprinted with the permission of Atheneum Publishers.

Langston Hughes. "Winter Moon" by Langston Hughes. Copyright 1926 by Alfred A. Knopf, Inc. and renewed 1954 by Langston Hughes. Reprinted from *Selected Poems of Langston Hughes*, by Langston Hughes, by permission of Alfred A. Knopf, Inc.

Langston Hughes. "Dream Deferred" by Langston Hughes. Copyright 1951 by Langston Hughes. Reprinted from *The Panther and the Lash: Poems of Our Times*, by permission of Alfred A. Knopf, Inc.

Charles W. Kennedy. "Frost Shall Freeze" from *An Anthology of Old English Poetry*, translated by Charles W. Kennedy. Copyright © 1960 by Oxford University Press, Inc. Reprinted by permission.

X. J. Kennedy. "A Choosy Wolf" by X. J. Kennedy. From X. J. Kennedy, *The Phantom Ice Cream Man: More Nonsense Verse.* Copyright © 1979 by X. J. Kennedy. A Margaret K. McElderry Book. (New York: Atheneum, 1979) Reprinted with the permission of Atheneum Publishers.

R. J. Lefkowitz. Excerpt from *Water for Today and Tomorrow* by R. J. Lefkowitz. Text copyright © 1973 by R. J. Lefkowitz. By permission of Parents' Magazine Press.

Vachel Lindsay. "The Moon's the North Wind's Cooky" by Vachel Lindsay. Reprinted with permission of Macmillan Publishing Co., Inc. from *Collected Poems* by Vachel Lindsay. Copyright 1914 by Macmillan Publishing Co., Inc., renewed 1942 by Elizabeth C. Lindsay.

Myra Cohn Livingston. "Whispers" by Myra Cohn Livingston. Copyright © 1958 by Myra Cohn Livingston from *Whispers and Other Poems*. Reprinted by permission of Marian Reiner for the author.

David McCord. "The Pickety Fence" by David McCord. Copyright 1952 by David McCord. From *Far and Few* by David McCord, by permission of Little, Brown and Co.

Eve Merriam. Excerpt from "Inside a Poem" by Eve Merriam from *It Doesn't Always Have to Rhyme.* Copyright © 1964 by Eve Merriam. Reprinted by permission of the author.

A. A. Milne. Excerpts from *Winnie-the-Pooh* by A. A. Milne. Copyright 1926 by E. P. Dutton & Co.; renewal, 1954, by A. A. Milne. Reprinted by permission of the publishers, E. P. Dutton & Co., Inc.

Rosalie Moore. From "Catalog" by Rosalie Moore. Copyright 1940, © 1978, *The New Yorker Magazine,* Inc. Reprinted by permission.

Ogden Nash. "Obvious Reflection" by Ogden Nash. Copyright 1931 by Ogden Nash. From *The Face Is Familiar* by Ogden Nash, by permission of Little, Brown and Co.

Ogden Nash. "The Eel" by Ogden Nash. Copyright 1942 by Ogden Nash. From *Verses from 1929 On* by Ogden Nash, by permission of Little, Brown and Co.

Mary Norton. *The Borrowers.* New York: Harcourt Brace Jovanovich, Inc., 1952, 1953, pp. 34, 68–69.

Scott O'Dell. *Island of the Blue Dolphins.* Boston: Houghton Mifflin Company, 1960.

Elizabeth Madox Roberts. "The Worm" from *Under the Tree* by Elizabeth Madox Roberts. Copyright 1922 by B. W. Huebsch, Inc., copyright © renewed 1950 by Ivor S. Roberts. Reprinted by permission of The Viking Press, Inc.

Marilyn Sachs. *The Bear's House.* New York: Doubleday & Company, Inc., 1971, p. 37.

Carl Sandburg. "Lost" from *Chicago Poems* by Carl Sandburg, copyright 1916 by Holt, Rinehart and Winston, Inc.; renewed 1944 by Carl Sandburg. Reprinted by permission of Harcourt Brace Jovanovich, Inc.

Ian Serraillier. Excerpts from *Beowulf, The Warrior* by Ian Serraillier, published by Henry Z. Walck, Incorporated, 1961. Reprinted by permission of the publishers.

Edward Tunis. *Colonial Living.* Cleveland and New York: The World Publishing Company, 1957, p. 75.

Edward Tunis. *Indians.* Cleveland and New York: The World Publishing Company, 1959, p. 28.

John Updike. "October" by John Updike. Copyright © 1965 by John Updike and Nancy Burkert. Reprinted from *A Child's Calendar* by John Updike, by permission of Alfred A. Knopf, Inc.

E. B. White. Excerpts from *Charlotte's Web* by E. B. White. Copyright © 1952 by E. B. White. Reprinted by permission of Harper & Row, Publishers, Inc.

Laura Ingalls Wilder. *Little House in the Big Woods.* New York: Harper & Row, Publishers, Inc., p. 85.

Annette Wynne. "I Keep Three Wishes Ready" from *All Through the Year: Three Hundred and Sixty-five New Poems for Holidays and Every Day* by Annette Wynne. Copyright, 1932, © 1960, by Annette Wynne. By permission of J. B. Lippincott, Publishers.

Index